CW01261378

Film, Memory and the Legacy of the Spanish Civil War

Also by Mercedes Maroto Camino

EXPLORING THE EXPLORERS: SPANIARDS IN OCEANIA 1519–1794

PRODUCING THE PACIFIC: MAPS AND NARRATIVES OF SPANISH EXPLORATION (1567–1606)

PRACTISING PLACES: LAZARILLO, SAINT TERESA AND THE EARLY MODERN CITY

THE STAGE AM I: RAPING LUCRECE IN EARLY MODERN ENGLAND

Film, Memory and the Legacy of the Spanish Civil War

Resistance and *Guerrilla* 1936–2010

Mercedes Maroto Camino

palgrave
macmillan

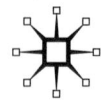

© Mercedes Maroto Camino 2011

All rights reserved. No reproduction, copy or transmission of this publication may be made without written permission.

No portion of this publication may be reproduced, copied or transmitted save with written permission or in accordance with the provisions of the Copyright, Designs and Patents Act 1988, or under the terms of any licence permitting limited copying issued by the Copyright Licensing Agency, Saffron House, 6–10 Kirby Street, London EC1N 8TS.

Any person who does any unauthorized act in relation to this publication may be liable to criminal prosecution and civil claims for damages.

The author has asserted her right to be identified as the author of this work in accordance with the Copyright, Designs and Patents Act 1988.

First published 2011 by
PALGRAVE MACMILLAN

Palgrave Macmillan in the UK is an imprint of Macmillan Publishers Limited, registered in England, company number 785998, of Houndmills, Basingstoke, Hampshire RG21 6XS.

Palgrave Macmillan in the US is a division of St Martin's Press LLC, 175 Fifth Avenue, New York, NY 10010.

Palgrave Macmillan is the global academic imprint of the above companies and has companies and representatives throughout the world.

Palgrave® and Macmillan® are registered trademarks in the United States, the United Kingdom, Europe and other countries.

ISBN 978–0–230–24055–1

This book is printed on paper suitable for recycling and made from fully managed and sustained forest sources. Logging, pulping and manufacturing processes are expected to conform to the environmental regulations of the country of origin.

A catalogue record for this book is available from the British Library.

Library of Congress Cataloging-in-Publication Data
Camino, Mercedes Maroto.
Film, memory and the legacy of the Spanish Civil War : resistance and *guerrilla*, 1936–2010 / Mercedes Maroto Camino.
   p. cm.
Includes bibliographical references and index.
ISBN 978–0–230–24055–1
1. Spain—History—Civil War, 1936–1939—Motion pictures and the war.   2. Spain—History—Civil War, 1936–1939—Influence.   3. Motion pictures—Spain—History—20th century.   I. Title.
DP269.8.M6C37 2011
791.43'65846081—dc23   2011020968

10 9 8 7 6 5 4 3 2 1
20 19 18 17 16 15 14 13 12 11

Printed and bound in Great Britain by
CPI Antony Rowe, Chippenham and Eastbourne

Contents

List of Illustrations vi

Acknowledgements ix

Introduction: The Legacy of the Spanish Civil War and Cinematic Melodrama 1

1 Memory, History and 'Historical Memory' of the Spanish *Maquis* 26

2 Francoism's *Bandoleros* (1954–1964) 43

3 From *Apertura* to Democracy (1970–1980) 74

4 Democratic *Maquis* (1987–2010) 109

5 Documenting 'Historical Memory' (1985–2008) 137

Conclusion 159

Notes 166

Bibliography 198

Index 208

List of Illustrations

2.1 *Dos caminos/Two Paths* (1954). The destiny of Republicans who chose exile is death. © Eos Films   50

2.2 *La ciudad perdida/The Lost City* (1955). Rafael enters Madrid through its Puerta de Hierro. © Pico Films   55

2.3 *La ciudad perdida/The Lost City* (1955). Rafael and María talk in a bar. © Pico Films   57

2.4 *La paz empieza nunca/Peace Never Starts* (1960). López infiltrates a *partida* of *maquis*. © CIFESA   59

2.5 *La paz empieza nunca/Peace Never Starts* (1960). Paula's corpse is held by the policemen. © CIFESA   59

2.6 *El cerco/The Siege* (1955). The raiders of this film *noir* aim their guns at the camera. © Este Films   65

2.7 *Los atracadores/The Raiders* (1962). The three robbers contemplate the murder weapon. © Balcázar Producciones Cinematográficas   66

2.8 *Los atracadores/The Raiders* (1962). The two surviving raiders hear their fate in court. © Balcázar Producciones Cinematográficas   67

2.9 *Carta a una mujer/Letter to a Woman* (1963). El Asturias addresses Flora in the street. © Cine Prodex   69

3.1 *El ladrido/The Barking* (1977). Ramona tries to convince her husband to rob the *maquis*. © Exclusivas Sánchez Ramade, SA   79

3.2 *El ladrido/The Barking* (1977). In a *destape* scene, Luz offers herself to the wounded *maquis*. © Exclusivas Sánchez Ramade, SA   80

3.3 *Casa Manchada/Stained House* (1977). Elvira, the good wife, suffers in silence. © Producciones Hidalgo, SA   83

3.4 *Casa Manchada/Stained House* (1977). The 'new woman' replaces the wife and the lover in Álvaro's affections. © Producciones Hidalgo, SA   83

3.5	*Metralleta Stein/Stein Machinegun* (1975). Mariano kills a policeman in the train's toilet. © CB Films SA	85
3.6	*Pim, pam, pum …¡Fuego!/One, Two, Three … Fire!* (1975). Julio rapes Paca on the floor of the flat. © Producciones José Frade	92
3.7	*Pim, pam, pum … ¡Fuego!/One, Two, Three … Fire!* (1975). Luis and Paca talk about a possible future for them in France. © Producciones José Frade	93
3.8	*Los días del pasado/The Days of the Past* (1978). Juana and Antonio meet surreptitiously. © Impala	98
3.9	*Los días del pasado/The Days of the Past* (1978). Juana travels on the train to take up her appointment as teacher. © Impala	99
3.10	*El corazón del bosque/The Heart of the Forest* (1979). Birds of prey flying over a misty landscape. © Arándano, SA	104
4.1	*Luna de lobos/Wolves' Moon* (1987). Civil Guards arrive to harass the relatives of the men in the mountains. © Brezal PC and J. Sánchez Valdés PC	112
4.2	*Huidos/Runaways* (1993). Of the men at the beginning of the film, only Juan survives. © Producciones Sancho Gracia	114
4.3	Montxo Armendáriz, *Silencio roto/Broken Silence* (2001). Villagers are rounded up after the *maquis* have gone. By permission. © Oria Films SL	118
4.4	Montxo Armendáriz, *Silencio roto/Broken Silence* (2001). View of the mountains which stand in for the *maquis* at several points in the film. By permission. © Oria Films SL	120
4.5	Guillermo del Toro, *El laberinto del fauno/Pan's Labyrinth* (2006). A white flower is used as *memento mori* for Ofelia and the Spanish *maquis*. By permission. © Tele 5	125
4.6	*Caracremada/Burnface* (2010). Solitary landscape as setting for the struggle. © Associació Cultural Passos Llargs/Mallerich Films Paco Poch/Cromosoma	133

4.7 *Caracremada/Burnface* (2010). Last shot of Ramón Vila Capdevila's shoes as his corpse is loaded onto a cart. © Associació Cultural Passos Llargs/Mallerich Films Paco Poch/Cromosoma   133

5.1 *La guerra de Severo/Severo's War* (2008). Contemporary photograph of Severo as respectable teacher 'Don Bernardo'. © Tristana Films   148

5.2 *La guerra de Severo/Severo's War* (2008). Interviewee María Gómez at home. © Tristana Films   149

5.3 *La guerra de Severo/Severo's War* (2008). Still of Severo's house at the time of the documentary. © Tristana Films   150

5.4 *La guerra de Severo/Severo's War* (2008). Old photograph of Severo's house. © Tristana Films   151

Acknowledgements

I am very grateful to the people and institutions that have helped me with this work.

First of all, without the resources and personnel from the Biblioteca Nacional de España and the Filmoteca Nacional, I could not have completed this book. Their help has been truly invaluable, and I am especially grateful to Trinidad del Río and Miguel Soria from the Filmoteca for being so very efficient with films and photographs.

Puy Oria, César Fernández, Ana Izquierdo, Bertha Navarro, Lluís Galter, Marga Gómez, Mario Camus and Manuel Gutiérrez Aragón have kindly given me their time, copies of their material and/or permission to use it, and I am extremely grateful to them. Although every effort has been made to locate the copyright holders of some of the old material used in this book, it has not been always possible to do so or request their permission. All material is, nevertheless, duly accredited and gratefully acknowledged.

Lancaster University granted me sabbatical leave and helped economically with the necessary archival research. The university's 'memory group' and my department have also provided ideas and inspiration. Besides students and colleagues, some anonymous people at conferences have contributed some thoughts, which have been elaborated into segments of this book, and I wish to thank them.

Much of the material about *El laberinto del fauno* and *Silencio roto* that appears here in Chapter 4 was published in my article, 'Blood of an Innocent'. I thank *Studies in Hispanic Cinemas* and Intellect for letting me reuse it here.

I wish to thank also La Gavilla Verde and the Association of Democratic Catalan Lawyers for kindly inviting me to their commemorative events in 2008. Meeting some of the survivors on whose lives and deeds the films studied in my book are based was illuminating, as well as moving.

Among the people who have read this work, I wish to thank Barry Jordan and, especially, Bernard Bentley for his thorough review of Francoist films. Gwyn Fox has been extremely efficient ironing out some of the technical difficulties inherent in editing the manuscript.

Especial thanks are due to Christine Arkinstall, who painstakingly commented on the whole draft, and Dave MacIntyre, who also read the whole manuscript, helped with the Spanish translations and has given much-needed encouragement. I hope he knows how much that has meant. The suggestions provided by Palgrave's anonymous reviewer have been of great help in improving the layout and content, and my editors there have always been extremely helpful and patient with all my queries and delays. Special thanks go to Monica Kendall for her thorough copy-editing and endless patience.

To all these people and many more that I have failed to mention personally, I owe an immense debt. Needless to say, any errors or inconsistencies are solely my responsibility.

Lastly, in every sense of the word, this book is *dedicated* to the memory of all the men and women who defended the Spanish Republic and fought fascism in their own countries and elsewhere.

Introduction: The Legacy of the Spanish Civil War and Cinematic Melodrama

The Spanish Civil War (1936–39) has inspired multiple historical and cultural interpretations. Temporal distance has not acted as a deterrent in the efforts to remember the military uprising against the Republican government elected in 1936 and the subsequent, long-lasting effects of the repression that followed.[1] Instead, the last years of the twentieth century witnessed a resurgence of a phenomenon that has been termed 'historical memory', the most visible outcome of which has been the rise of associations focused on finding the remains of those summarily executed during and after the conflict, as well as the moral and juridical vindication of 'the defeated' ('los vencidos').[2] This 'recovery' has been both the cause and the effect of cultural, social and political events, some of which have legal and moral implications. The ensuing memorializing impulse has also had momentous consequences in the rewriting of history both in the way events are rendered meaningful in the present and how the present inflects or determines our views of the past.

The Spanish processes now grouped under the label 'memory boom' started to gather momentum in the mid-1990s, 20 years after the dictator, Francisco Franco, had died. Soon after Franco's demise, in 1975, the country embarked on a largely peaceful political course aimed at restoring democratic rights, which has come to be known as the *Transición* (Transition). During that time, political prisoners were released, freedom of expression was institutionalized, political parties and unions were legalized, a Constitution was approved and universal suffrage was restored, with the first general election being held in 1977. In fact, it could be said that this Transition marked the end of the Civil War, for the repression that started with the military uprising led by Franco and his acolytes only ended effectively then, as the famous Republican leader Dolores Ibárruri ('La Pasionaria') indicated when Pablo Picasso's painting *Guernica* returned to Spain in 1981. An outspoken supporter of the Republic, Picasso had expressed his wish for *Guernica*, which was made and exhibited in support of the Republic in 1937, to return to Spain once the country had recovered the democratic principles embodied by the Republic. This abstract painting, which became highly symbolic from the time that it was first exhibited, in 1937 Paris, showed in graphic detail the horrors of the bombing of the civilian population of the Basque town of Guernica. It was this raid, undertaken by the German *Luftwaffe* 'Condor Legion' and the Italian fascist *Aviazione Legionaria*, on 26 April 1937, which marked a turning point in the perception of the rebel army of Franco during the Civil War, thanks to the reports of war correspondents such as George Steer of *The Times* (Preston 2008: 308–40). Perhaps even more than the Amnesty Law of 1977 or the Constitution of 1978, the 'return' of Picasso's *Guernica* was thus emblematic for this transitional process, which would be brought to a close when the Spanish Socialist Party (*Partido Socialista Obrero Español*, PSOE) won the general elections of 1982.

The Spanish *Transición* was not sealed by recognition of past crimes, and there was not even the slightest hint of wrongdoing on the part of those in power at the time or thereafter. This is a silence which is still invoked as the 'Spirit of the Transition', normally by right-wing political figures, such as Prime Minister José María Aznar, leader of the Popular Party who served in that role from 1996 until 2004. This 'spirit', it is argued, embodied a collective wish to forgive and forget, enabling Spaniards to move forward instead of addressing or redressing a past of conflict and division within their country. Noticeably, the appeal to this 'spirit' obliterates the fact that, whereas crimes committed on the Republican side, both real and made up, had been publicized, magnified and tried in courts for decades after the Civil War, the disproportionate repression suffered by Republicans during and after the war remains to be acknowledged legally and even morally.[3] It is a 'spirit' that evens out responsibility for the events, which, besides being a historical misinterpretation, obliterates many criminal facts and exonerates those who directed them. *Film, Memory and the Legacy of the Spanish Civil War* will address that historical silence through an investigation of the cinematic representations of the armed resistance that followed the regime's declaration of the war's end.

From its onset as a military coup in 1936, the Franco regime legitimized the deposing of the democratically elected Popular Front that had governed Spain through a conscious effort to render the Spanish Second Republic illegal, with retroactive effects.[4] In order to do so, the regime rehearsed the supposed perils that the Republic and its policies entailed for Catholic, law-abiding citizens, projecting an image of utter social and political lawlessness. To give one example, in what would become the country's 'official history', they magnified and misrepresented actual crimes committed against members of the clergy *after* the coup as *triggers* of the coup. Instead, this violent onslaught against Catholic clergy was, by and large, a direct consequence of the coup, spurred on by the alliance between the oligarchy, the Church and the military before, during and after the Civil War. The sequential inversion of events, however, was rehearsed throughout the duration of Franco's dictatorship, providing moral grounds for the military intervention that led to the Civil War. Publicized at home and abroad as provoking a 'just' war, these crimes were designed to banish the Republic morally and, eventually, judicially. The latter happened when, in February 1939, with the war reaching its final stages, the Franco regime issued the infamous 'Ley de Responsabilidades Políticas' ('Law of Political Responsibilities'), which criminalized the failure to endorse the military rebellion/coup of 1936 with retroactive effect from 1934. This law was addressed

> A las personas, tanto jurídicas como físicas, que desde el primero de octubre de 1934 y antes del 18 de julio de 1936, contribuyeron a crear o gravar la subversión de todo orden de que se hizo víctima a España, y de aquellas otras que, a partir de las segundas de dichas fechas, se hayan opuesto o se opongan al Movimiento con actos concretos o pasividad grande.[5]

Thus, without a hint of irony, Francoism declared illegal any non-opposition to prior governments, implicitly condemning also the coalition of right-wing parties, CEDA, which was in government from 1933 to 1936.[6] This coalition, which had been formed by José María Gil Robles in February 1933, provided six ministers to the right-wing ruler Niceto Alcalá Zamora (1933–36) and was dissolved by Franco in 1937, with most of its members transferring to the Spanish fascist party, Falange.[7]

The legitimizing process of Franco's regime was hammered home initially during the enforced stillness that has come to be known as a Time of Silence, a term especially used to embrace the autarky of the first two decades of the regime (1939–59) and which largely coincided with and benefited from the anti-communism of the Cold War era. Subsequently, the regime buttressed itself by attributing the improved living standards of the 1960s and early 1970s to its policies, using what Paloma Aguilar has called 'performance-based legitimacy' (Aguilar 2002: 102).

The crimes committed against the Spanish civilian population by the Nationalist forces during the Civil War and, especially, throughout its long and protracted aftermath, the *posguerra*, have never been addressed legally on account of the peculiarities of the aforementioned *Transición* to democracy. An Amnesty Law issued in 1977 released political prisoners and closed the legal avenues for any future attempts to redress past injustices, forestalling the possibility of holding to account those responsible for major crimes. The silence with which Francoism started was thus extended to become unofficial policy both during and after the *Transición* in what has (perhaps wrongly) come to be known as *Pacto de Silencio* ('Pact of Silence') or *Pacto del Olvido* ('Pact of Oblivion'). A consequence of this 'pact' is that armed resistance fighters, the Spanish *maquis* of the 1940s and 1950s, were legally considered 'bandits' and common criminals by laws only revoked at the beginning of the twenty-first century, more than 25 years after the dictator's death.

Upon the demise of the dictator in 1975, those in power and various political forces in the opposition held negotiations. Important among the forces opposed to the dictatorship were, at the time, the Spanish Communist Party (*Partido Comunista de España* or PCE) and the Socialist Party (*Partido Socialista Obrero Español* or PSOE).[8] During this time, however, the dictator's diehard adherents, the so-called 'bunker', remained in positions of power in the political and military sphere. In addition to this, there was a sharp increase in the activities of the Basque separatist group, ETA, and other radical groups, as well as an attempted coup in 1981.[9] This rendered the Transition a rather delicate process, which partly accounts for the failure of left-wing political negotiators to impose any sort of 'truth and reconciliation' procedure.

The blanket Amnesty Law of 1977 released left-wing political prisoners and closed the possibility of future prosecution of crimes related to the past regime, thus exempting those in power and complicating issues of justice or social reconciliation. Some of these started to be addressed from the fin-de-siècle onwards, spearheaded by the work of several grassroots organizations and prominent jurists such as Baltasar Garzón, who saw these as 'massive crimes against humanity' that do not expire in international law.[10]

During its transition to a new democratic era, Spain, therefore, straddled a difficult social and political divide, with the right split between those who thought that change was necessary and those seeking the resuscitation of their 'crusade' against 'reds'. In this context, the left contributed to the country's 'reconciliation' by accepting implicitly and explicitly to focus on the future, consolidating an unofficial obliteration of the past in many public forums. This was equally visible in the cultural arena, where avant-garde pop movements in music and the arts became not only officially accepted but were actively promoted as flagships for the process of change, as happened with the Madrid phenomenon that came to be known as *La movida* (c. 1976–85).[11] The 'defeated' in the Spanish Civil War and those who suffered the tyranny that followed it were historically and morally disregarded. The regime, moreover, victimized not just those who supported or defended the Republican Popular Front that had been voted into power in the 1936 elections but many whose association with the war was at best circumstantial, as will be seen throughout this book.

If the repression that followed upon the Civil War embraced all those who had so much as worked for the Republic from 1934 to 1939, including councillors, teachers, cleaners and civil servants, those resisting Francoism actively knew that they would face not just death or torture, but also the economic oppression and endless humiliation of their friends and families. Michael Richards itemizes this repression as follows, alluding to the autocratic 'pact of hunger' that was visited on relatives or friends of resistance fighters, regardless of their attitude towards the struggle:

> In areas where some kind of armed anti-regime *guerrilla* movement was achieved, mainly in rural, mountainous regions, the authorities made the populace in general suffer. The so-called

'*pacto del hambre*', ensuring that the wives of *guerrilleros* had no employment and, therefore, no food to live, was widely enforced by the authorities. The tactic of starving out the 'Reds' was used, subjecting entire villages to martial law and curfew regimes. Any shelter given to the *maquis* was punishable by death. Women, for example, were imprisoned as 'bait' for *guerrilla* fighters on the run. They were particular targets for repression against families, reflecting a gender-specific aspect of Francoist violence. (Richards 1998: 53)[12]

Although the 'vanquished' in the Spanish Civil War did not have their plight addressed in courts after the end of the dictatorship, they were the subject of many books and some films, which contributed to the creation of a literary and cinematic genre in its own right.[13] Both films and books appeared in reasonable quantities very soon after the dictator's death and their production gathered momentum at the onset of the third millennium, following what could be best described as a lull, especially marked during the years that the Socialist Party, PSOE, held power (1982–96).

Even though the number of films bears no comparison to that of books, it is worth mentioning that the number of post-1975 cinematic productions vindicating Spain's fascist past is close to nil. By and large, most fictional and documentary productions coming from democratic Spain have focused either on the vanquished or on the civilian population that did not take a direct part in the struggle, making them visible to a wider public and to younger Spaniards who have grown up unaware of their country's past.

Films and documentaries about the Spanish Civil War and its aftermath constitute a genre whose origin and development will be mapped out in this book. My work will trace an important segment of this tradition through an analysis of films that include *maquis* in their narrative, and which were produced in the context of the dictatorship (1939–75), the democratic era (1975–95) and the ensuing 'memory boom' (1996–2010). Besides redressing some gaps in our knowledge, I situate these works within the legal and historical debates vis-à-vis the 'historical memory' of those who fought the Franco regime or who supported that struggle in one way or another. These cultural productions are, therefore, grounded within the resistance and dissidence that culminated during the last years of the dictator's life, as well as the memorializing debates taking place in the twenty-first century.

The dimensions of the *maquis*' struggle and of a repression that was to last four decades have slowly seen the light, with a growing number of testimonies and books published as the last survivors rapidly started to disappear. This follows a 'memory boom', which has broken not just some long-held silences but also the earth covering many anonymous graves. These endeavours witnessed the creation of the *Asociación para la Recuperación de la Memoria Histórica* ('Association for the Recovery of Historical Memory') in 2001 and the passing of the *Ley de Memoria Histórica* ('Law of Historical Memory') in 2007.[14] The recovery of bodies has been accompanied by, and has often been preceded by, historical research, facilitated by the opening up of archives to the public since the mid-1990s. The memories, and the corpses that literally ground them, have set to rest the pretension of benevolent dictatorship that Franco tried to promote, especially during the Cold War and the subsequent opening up of the country for tourism and investment from 1960 onwards.

The idiosyncrasies of the Spanish 'memory boom' will be contextualized in relation to the international 'turn to memory' and the rise of Memory Studies in Chapter 1 of this book: 'Memory, History and "Historical Memory" of the Spanish *Maquis*'. This cultural and sociopolitical process now known as the 'recovery of historical memory' has stimulated, and has been stimulated by, the production of a number of documentaries and films on guerrilla fighters and their supporters, which refashion the struggle from their perspective. This contrasts with the Francoist stigmatization of insurgents as bandits and the silence surrounding the lives of their relatives and supporters.

The *maquis*' fragmented memories have been reconstructed from the scarcity of mementoes that they left and the words of the aging survivors, relatives, friends and supporters. This endeavour has been fronted by an organization, *La Gavilla Verde* ('The Green Sheaf'), which has fostered their memorialization in several ways, including a monument inaugurated in 1991 and a yearly conference, ending in a festivity, the *Día del Guerrillero* ('Day of the Guerrilla'), the first Sunday of October. The monument and the events are located in the remote mountainous village of Santa Cruz de Moya (in the province of Cuenca), in one of whose mountains, Cerro Moreno, a group of 12 armed men were killed in 1949 and where *La Gavilla Verde* is currently based.

While organizing cultural and social events has put the *maquis* on the political map, *La Gavilla Verde* has also taken an active role in digging up mass graves and fighting legally for the recognition of the rights of these men and women. A consequence of these activities was the removal of the decree that declared them bandits in 2001, when they were recognized as legitimate fighters, *guerrilleros*. *La Gavilla Verde* has also assisted in helping the survivors and relatives to attend events and to record their life stories and testimonies in books and documentaries, voicing their opinions about the way they are represented and wish to be remembered.

Cultural events such as the annual celebration of surviving guerrilla fighters at their monument in Santa Cruz de Moya attest to the creation of 'lieux de mémoire' in the meaning given to the term by Pierre Nora, as will be detailed in Chapter 1. These commemorative events and festivities celebrate these men and women while collecting information about them and their families. Bounded by the geographical location of the village in which the events are celebrated, Santa Cruz de Moya, these celebrations effectively link the present with the past, invoking the fighters' connection with the very mountains towards which their monument looks, Cerro Moreno. These events create a site of memory where *maquis* may be honoured, corroborating Ernest Renan's claim that victimization can be a powerful social cement.[15]

Film, Memory and the Legacy of the Spanish Civil War complements the work of grassroots organizations which, like *La Gavilla Verde* or the *Asociación para la Recuperación de la Memoria Histórica*, aim to reconstruct the long-lost memories of the Spanish *maquis* and the civilians who supported their fight. Like monuments or commemorations, the films investigated here will be treated as potential sites of memory, affording information which could not be otherwise expressed, especially in the early productions.

Throughout its exploratory narrative, this book historicizes the men, women and children who fought Francoism after the end of the Civil War, exploring the ways in which they are presented in films prior to and following the dictator's death. While many of these films are based on actual memories and sound research, all of them, including the productions released during the dictatorship, afford important insights into the social processes and experiences of the time in which they were created. The narratives thus constructed are inflected by the perspective from which they are narrated, which, in the case of post-Francoist cinematic reconstructions of Spanish guerrilla fighters, is often that of their supporters. This is the point of view given in Montxo Armendáriz' *Silencio roto/Broken Silence* (2001), Mario Camus' *Los días del pasado/The Days of the Past* (1978) or Guillermo del Toro's *El laberinto del fauno/Pan's Labyrinth* (2006). It is an approach that also inheres in documentaries about the subject, including Javier Corcuera's *La guerrilla de la memoria/The Guerrilla of Memory* (2002) and César Fernández' *La guerra de Severo/Severo's War* (2008).

By and large, the post-1975 cinematic men and women engaged in or associated with Spanish guerrilla warfare foreground solidarity and resistance as communal values. Supporters and relatives of guerrilla fighters are often deployed in post-Franco films and documentaries as protagonists from whom to view the events. The deeds of the actual guerrilla fighters thus become associated with those on whom they depended for support and sustenance. In this way, their filmic memories contribute to remembering important elements of the personal, local and national idiosyncrasies inherent in the vexed concept of Spanishness. This has been and remains a problematic notion because, inside Spain, it was appropriated by the Spanish right, including the neo-fascist groups ('ultras'). By contrast, outside Spain the concept remains stereotyped by the romantic 'orientalization' of the country which was further consecrated following on its commercialization as a mass tourist destination from the 1960s onwards.

At the time they were released, most of the films explored in this book sought to play a significant role either in the justification of the Francoist repression or in the recasting of collective identity in the aftermath of the dictatorship. In several instances, their reception at different historical times makes them significant for our understanding of the ways in which the past is rehearsed in order to bolster a particular view of the present. Furthermore, the outreach of these productions reveals important issues of cinematic, social and political interest, denoting people's beliefs, ideas or even the subtle ways in which they manage to negotiate their everyday lives in challenging circumstances. Although not limited to that era, this is more revealing in the films produced during the dictatorship and the onset of democracy studied in Chapters 2 and 3, when censorship and self-censorship were strongly enforced.

The Spanish Civil War and its aftermath have inspired many films with female characters used as points of identification for audiences, often as protagonists or in central roles. The films' reliance on a strong female presence is in itself interesting because women were traditionally marginalized from the war fronts. Arguably, this feminine presence corresponds to the reality that the films evoke because, during the conflict, women were active agents as part of the militia or in the so-called home front. From the trenches to the rearguard, Spanish women participated actively in the Civil War, as well as in the resistance that followed it. This is directly acknowledged by the photographs and posters issued to illustrate or advertise aspects of the conflict and in the films produced during the Civil War and thereafter. In spite of this, women's roles were ignored in history books up to the 1970s, making the films of the time more relevant vis-à-vis the dialectic between wilful amnesia and remembrance.

While women became more prominent in print in the later part of the twentieth century, it is in films that their presence has been constant, as they tend to be just as important in earlier productions. In fact, women are central even in the Francoist *cine de cruzada* ('crusade cinema'), which comprises a handful of proto-fascist films released in the immediate aftermath of the Civil War, when the Axis powers were in the ascendant during World War II.[16] This 'crusade cinema', whose melodramatic features influenced other films during the following decades, was devised as a celebration of the Nationalist victory and became a model for many subsequent productions. The pattern of these films, in which families, with women at their centre, configure an image of the country, became prevalent, even in productions that were not overtly political in theme.

Women are present in all Francoist films dealing with guerrilla struggle, including those classed as Spanish *noir* in the 1950s and 1960s in which they play secondary roles. In the remaining films, women either embody the homely roles that the regime promoted or act as *enlaces* ('links' or 'points of support'). The association of 'mothers' with the nation is one which Francoist films inherited from their predecessors and developed along the lines of Nazi melodrama, which centred on family life as an image and a constitutive part of the state.

Equally important for the present study is the way in which Francoism sought to embrace and dictate all areas of social and private life, concentrating heavily on the conscription and limitation of domestic roles. This provides the context for the cinematic correspondence between resistance fighters, women and the lower classes, whose agency Francoism felt as a threat to its notion of social order. As will be seen below, in films released during the first Francoist era the representation of women is intimately linked to that of the lower classes.

Essentially dramatic or melodramatic, Francoist films afford information about the intimate relationship between the domestic and the political realms. This is especially relevant because, during the Franco years, women were charged with being the repositories of 'purity' and were, therefore, required to observe and enforce social norms that largely obliterated their individuality and agency.[17] In fact, the Francoist regime differentiated sharply the roles of women and men, condemning the feminization of men who could not enforce control of their wives and families. They also outlawed the handful of rights that women had acquired during the Republic, including divorce and management of their own finances, classing them as a form of unnatural and corrupt masculinization. Women suffered during and after the Civil War not just by being incarcerated, shot or seeing their loved ones disappear, but because even the hard-gained, small advances made towards equality were ruthlessly taken away from them, as Shirley Mangini has noted.[18]

A focus of my investigation will be the extent to which the historical and fictional women appearing in films and documentaries embody alternative social visions. As will be seen, the regime's rhetoric of purity affected the way women were seen both physically and morally, while becoming an inherent component of its 'cleansing' policies. The quasi-ritualistic spilling of blood that was routinely visited on its opposition by the dictatorship grounded itself on religious notions that the Catholic Church propelled wholeheartedly and had a tragic effect on the lives of ordinary women.[19] This was reflected in the language of the victors, which celebrated murder and mayhem in an overt, at times sadistic manner. As Richards has observed:

> Purifying language derived, in part, from the discourse of 'cleansing' articulated via the Catholic Church. Catholic doctrine commended bloodshed in particular circumstances: in ascetic mortification of the flesh, as a voluntary act of self-imposed suffering, or as patriotic self-sacrifice ... The war, once it became clear that it would not be concluded rapidly, was depicted by the Church as a violent form of Lent, during which Spaniards would expiate sins and do penitence,

purifying themselves through the spilling of blood. This was seen as preparation of the 'Resurrection' which would come with victory. More important, it was the punishment of 'God's justice' upon a nation, 'so favoured in every way, and yet so ungrateful'. (Richards 1998: 50)

The spilling of blood so often shed and alluded to in the Spanish context has religious overtones that are underwritten with political and social significance. As René Girard's classic study, *Violence and the Sacred*, shows, blood can be a polyvalent signifier: 'Blood serves to illustrate the point that the same substance can stain or cleanse, contaminate or purify, drive men to fury and murder or appease their anger and restore them to life' (Girard 1989: 37). Of special relevance to this investigation is Girard's apprehension of violence as a type of language that can be socially constructive, even if that entails the obliteration of individuality, agency, ethnicity or alternative political, religious or social arrangements.[20] In this context, Girard argues, the search for a surrogate victim is unleashed in order to contain a potentially infinite need for sacrifice.[21]

The symbolism of blood is used cinematically to convey a conglomerate of ideas, some of which are related to one another. From war to horror films, blood is often deployed to mark rites of passage, as well as to appeal to our primal fears through an emphasis on the fragility of life. Not exclusively limited to the films studied in this book, it is precisely the ritual shedding of blood that, according to Marsha Kinder, differentiates the representation of violence in Spanish productions from their Hollywood counterparts. Tracing its origins and development to Counter Reformation aesthetics, Kinder has paid special attention to the way that violence, 'as remolded by the Fascist aesthetic' is 'eroticized as ritual sacrifice' in Spanish productions.[22] Blood rituals, even when enacting masculine rites of passage, are either associated with the feminine or entail the feminization of those on whom they are performed.

In spite of its peculiarities, such as the religious overtones of blood, Franco's National Catholicism was closely modelled on Italian fascism and German National Socialism. This was more obviously the case during the first years of the regime, when World War II was being fought and when the Spanish Falange were in control of many aspects of political life. As with fascism, National Catholicism conforms to what Emilio Gentile classes as the 'sacralization of politics' into a type of 'political religion' (1996, 2006). In the Italian case, Aristotle Kallis refers to the production of 'a vision of eschatological salvation for the entire community' that is relevant to the Spanish context. Here, Kallis observes, the concept of *political religion* 'denotes both a transfer of "sacredness" from the strictly religious domain to the emerging secular landscape and a relation of intriguing permeability between the two' (Kallis 2008: 3). It is precisely this 'permeability' between the secular and the religious that inflects Francoism's development during the rise and fall of Nazism, and which had an effect on the way in which women were cast in cinematic productions.

The representation of women in the films studied here is thus conditioned by the fact that blood, a symbol aptly associated with the feminine, can also be a sign of the sacred that is intimately woven with sacrifice and scapegoating. The centrality of women, especially in the earlier films, is also fraught with the many paradoxes inherent in their 'marianization'. On the one hand, their presence allows filmmakers to introduce aspects of everyday life that add coherence and nuances to our vision of war and resistance. On the other hand, however, the varied presence of women does not necessarily imply a liberal approach to the lives of real women. Indeed, the fact that some issues might be classed as domestic or feminine could be used to disempower women as subjects in their own right, as will be shown in relation to the earlier films studied in this book. Nevertheless, women's roles invariably illuminate significant aspects of the twentieth-century history of civil society, shedding light on the experiences of ordinary people.[23]

Closely related to the deployment of cinematic women is the use (or misuse) of emotions that are associated with the feminine in productions about Spanish guerrilla fighters. Traditionally, emotion has been coupled with women and with so-called feminine genres in both literature and film. This often meant a devaluation of significant human feelings and the classification of products in which they were central as a subcategory in terms of cultural or social value. Family dramas or melodramas were marked as being of lower quality than those genres allied with the masculine world of 'adventure', including westerns and war films. The reappraisal of cinematic melodrama, however, started in the 1970s, following the pioneering work of Thomas Elsaesser, who brought to the fore some of the contradictions inherent in the evaluation of the genre and its adjudication to the sphere of domesticity. By contrast, for Elsaesser, melodrama represents nothing but 'the struggle of a morally and emotionally emancipated bourgeois consciousness against the remnants of feudalism' (1987: 45).[24]

Following upon Elsaesser's work, analyses of melodrama have taken into account the political dimensions implicit in the cinematic gendering of the private world of emotions. Ben Singer's summary is worth quoting in this context, when he argues that: 'While several overviews have noted its semantic ambiguity, the term melodrama seems to have adopted a more or less stable meaning in contemporary film studies. Melodrama as it generally is used today refers to a set of subgenres that remain close to the heart and hearth and emphasize a register of heightened emotionalism and sentimentality' (Singer 2001: 37).[25]

Some criticism of the melodramatic genre can, therefore, show prejudices against women and popular culture by suggesting that emotion necessarily debases a cultural product.[26] Whereas the representation of women may be linked to emotional displays that can be exploited for cinematic appeal, it can also reveal some important undercurrents that are essential to a reconstruction of the past that takes into account civilian experience. From this perspective, the films studied here provide a privileged vantage point from which to observe the peculiar engenderment of filmic melodramas and their inherent paradoxes. More notably, the role played by emotions in cinematic representations of the anti-Francoist resistance allows these productions to be used as tools with which to reconstruct aspects of the everyday lives of ordinary people after the Spanish Civil War.

As in literature, the use of emotion in film straddles a difficult line which could involve the wilful manipulation of the audience. To stress the importance of human emotions, including love, compassion and solidarity, does not necessarily entail the vindication of a whole array of overwrought attempts to exploit the feelings of mainstream audiences. Nevertheless, in practice, it is often difficult to segregate what may be a cheap appeal to sentiment from the legitimate use of empathy and solidarity as tools to convey human, social or political messages.

Although melodrama is the favoured genre through which notions about the Civil War are conveyed in early productions dealing with the Spanish conflict and its aftermath, this is by no means restricted to films released during the dictatorship. Later films in which women act as points of identification for the audience also foreground the intimate connection between the domestic and the political, even if from a different standpoint or with alternative objectives. Consequently, the films which form the core of this study not only provide social and historical data. They also reveal the paradoxes inherent in the construction of films around emotive identification of audiences with civilian women as uncontroversial victims.

Most Spanish films about the political situation produced after the Civil War, including those made by the regime's supporters, embed in unambiguous terms the inextricable relationship between the intimate and the political or, to put it in terms of cinematic genres, the adventurous and the domestic. In this context, the role attributed to women as buttresses of the regime's notions of domestic enclosure and subservience is often unashamedly displayed, celebrated and promoted by Francoist films. Not surprisingly, the paradigm of interior versus exterior presented in those films is gendered within a division of spheres that conforms to Laura Mulvey's now classic formulation of the engenderment of this split in classical Hollywood films:

> [The] 'interior' also contains within it 'interiority,' the psychic spaces of desire and anxiety, and the private scenarios of feelings, a female sphere of emotion within the female sphere of domesticity ... Thus in the melodrama, the home is the container of narrative events and the motifs that characterize the space and place of the genre. But its emotional reverberations and its gender specificity are derived from and defined in opposition to a concept of masculine space: an outside, the sphere of adventure, movement, enclosed space, and confinement. The depiction of generic space is, in this sense, over-determined by the connotations implicit in the masculine/feminine binary opposition. (Mulvey 1992: 55)[27]

In spite of their deployment of exaggerated overtones, the melodramas studied here resist being classified only in terms of a concrete genre. Whereas many of them are centred on a romantic plot, others are set in a warlike situation, containing some elements of what we understand as War Films. However, these films do not contain basic elements of the war genre, such as a focus on men or dramatizations of battle scenes and trench life. Overall, films about the Spanish Civil War could be regarded as forming a genre, essentially dramatic but with the addition of both melodramatic and epic elements. Javier Juan Payán's remarks are worth quoting at length in this context:

> Se observa, por ejemplo, la incidencia e influencia del melodrama en todas las películas producidas en España sobre el conflicto, tanto en la etapa del franquismo como una vez establecida la democracia. Incluso en el denominado 'cine de cruzada', de marcada intención propagandística y donde con frecuencia se corteja la aventura y la gesta de corte épico, encontramos también un protagonismo esencial en el argumento de elementos propios del melodrama, lo que vuelve a manifestarse en las producciones de los años sesenta y setenta, incrementándose ese hecho aún más en las películas filmadas con posterioridad a la muerte de Franco ... Y es que, a nuestro juicio, el subgénero que componen los filmes sobre la Guerra Civil no pertenecerá nunca al territorio del cine bélico, sino más bien hará de las escenas bélicas un complemento para sus argumentos melodramáticos, de manera que, tanto a través de sus personajes como de sus historias, así como en la manera de contarnos las mismas, estará casi siempre más vinculado al género dramático, presentando, eso sí, una clara singularidad que viene dada por la propia naturaleza del conflicto y la implicación que en el mismo tuvo la población civil. (Payán 2006: 7)[28]

The presence and experiences of civilians thus inflect the dramatic or melodramatic tones of the films investigated here. Those elements show how the reconstruction of the memory of the Spanish Civil War necessitates the recognition of emotional displays as potential resistance tools in the struggle against enforced silence and conscious or unconscious forgetting. Moreover, these displays can denote the actual trauma of the civilian population who they purport to represent. Cinematic representations of the Spanish guerrillas become instrumental in the recuperation of a usable past and in the debate about the possibility of recovering repressed, ignored or disregarded aspects of the historical experiences of the era.

The films that form the core of this study will be approached from chronological and generic divisions that are largely coincidental. This analysis follows the aforementioned summary of the filmic underpinnings of the Spanish process that has become known as the recovery of historical memory, which is provided in Chapter 1, 'Memory, History and "Historical Memory" of the Spanish *Maquis*'. This chapter introduces the historical and political background of the cinematic representations of the Spanish *maquis* in the context of contemporary developments in Memory Studies.

Following this theoretical analysis, I explore the refracted representation of *maquis* and the women and children supporting them who have been variously interpreted in films dating from the 1950s, when the *maquis* were mostly presented as ruthless bandits and heartless criminals. By contrast, most films on the subject produced after Franco's death foreground the desertion of the fighters by international forces and the important role played by women who supported the guerrillas: their *enlaces*. These later films present how, especially during the first years of Franco's regime, the international struggle against fascism entailed the hope that the end of World War II would bring to Spain the logistic and material help that had been denied to its Republic. As the years passed, and the Francoist regime consolidated its stronghold in Spain, it became increasingly clear that no support would be given to an insurgency marked by a largely communist leadership. Their numbers dwindled during the second half of the 1940s, until they finally all but disappeared in the 1950s, following a protracted struggle that became more desperate and easier to suppress.

The first filmic representations of the *maquis*, which started to appear a few years after they were mostly eradicated, are traced in Chapter 2, 'Francoism's *Bandoleros* (1954–1964)', which outlines the films produced during Franco's regime.[29] Although guerrilla warfare could be a topic with remarkable cinematic potential, it is worth noting that only a handful of Spanish films on the subject were produced during that time, and the *maquis* appear as ruthless bandits with no political motivation in most of them. A number of other films dealing with raiders or common criminals are also relevant in this context, although the references to the conflict may be nonexistent or marginal, as happens, for example, in the Spanish *noir El cerco*/*The Siege* (1955), directed by Miguel Iglesias, or in José Rovira Beleta's *Los atracadores*/*The Raiders* (1962). Lastly, this chapter also studies two contemporary Hollywood films, Sam Wood's *For Whom the Bell Tolls* (1943) and Fred Zinnemann's *Behold a Pale Horse* (1964), as well as the earliest film in which the *maquis* appear marginally in order to support an otherwise flat romance in Iglesias' *Carta a una mujer/Letter to a Woman* (1963). In spite of the fact that this film offers a rather superficial view of the guerrillas, its female protagonist becomes the centre of a struggle within which some notions about national identity are disputed.

Most of the Francoist films about or with *maquis* centre on a patriarchal household as a microcosmic representation of the country and the people within it (or the model intended for it). Within this 'family', the roles given to women are either as mothers or girlfriends, or, when associated with the guerrillas, concubines or prostitutes. Besides promoting the Francoist National Catholic ideal of womanhood, these characters embed some societal paradoxes which this chapter seeks to unravel. This can be seen in Francoist films dealing with the guerrillas, which include some made by directors who wanted to spread the National Catholic doctrine, with eloquent titles such as *Dos caminos/Two Paths*, *Torrepartida/Broken Tower* or *La ciudad perdida/The Lost City*. The study of these Francoist films is completed with the two Hollywood films that deal with the guerrillas, Wood's *For Whom the Bell Tolls* and Zinnemann's *Behold a Pale Horse*. While Wood's adaptation of Ernest Hemingway's novel is set during the Civil War, Zinnemann's *Behold a Pale Horse* offers a portrait of the struggle from the point of view of one *maquis* living in exile in France. For this film, however, Zinnemann and his producers had to pay a hefty price by seeing all their productions banned from Spanish screens and losing millions of dollars.

By and large, the films produced during the early Franco era attest to the construction of a symbolic topography that associates the household and the patriarchal family with the state in a micro-macrocosmic correspondence. Consequently, female roles are clearly gendered along the paradigm of Catholic womanhood that became the hallmark of a regime that was buttressed by the victimization of the 'maternal', suffering 'good' woman. The imagery displayed to convey these ideas is obvious and unsubtle, and includes silent, discreet, modestly dressed mothers or girlfriends, located in church or at home, and even sewing in front of religious images.

Rabidly conservative, the 'Francoist' woman vindicates a passivity that was totally alien in reality not only to working-class Spanish women, but even to those given the task of disciplining them, the

Falange's *Sección Femenina* ('Feminine Section'). This unit of the fascist party was in charge of many aspects of female education, including cooking, modesty and gymnastics, until the end of the regime. In fact, as will be seen in Chapter 3 of this book, the notion of woman that Francoism and the Falange's *Sección Femenina* tried to uphold became rather anachronistic by the 1960s, when it started to accommodate alternative traits. The 'new' woman was still Catholic and subservient, though she could be increasingly seen in a number of public spaces in line with the image of openness that the regime wanted to present to the tourists then entering the country. This version of womanhood was, however, out of line with women's actual lives in the urban centres of Spain during the 1960s and 1970s and these contradictions can be seen in the films studied in Chapter 3 of this book, 'From *Apertura* to Democracy (1970–1980)'.

The films released during the last years of Francoism (1970–75), now normally known as *tardofranquismo*, and the first years of the Spanish transition to democracy (1975–80) display the changing attitudes towards the guerrilla fighters during the last years of the regime. These cinematic productions stride between the construction and contestation of societal notions that rely on the supposedly voluntary subjugation of women and of the working classes. As Chapter 3 shows, there is an intimate relationship between the representation of the lower classes, women and *maquis*, who are caricatured in films produced under the banner of Francoist ideas. These films thus chart the intricate link between misogyny, class prejudice and the repression of dissidence that pervaded Francoism, stressing the important role played by the Catholic Church in buttressing such a status quo.

A film based on a novel by Falangist Emilio Romero, José Antonio Nieves Conde's *Casa Manchada/Stained House* (1977), exemplifies some interesting continuities in the filmic portrayal of the *maquis* during the 1970s and is representative of the contradictions inherent in the era. The vicissitudes this film underwent since the time that it was planned, 1970, to the year it was released, 1980, five years after the dictator had died, illustrate the shifting attitudes towards the conflict that are traced in this chapter. The aptly named *Casa Manchada* concentrates on the lives and violent deaths of the male heirs of three generations who die in the house. Their deaths occur as a result of the various wars taking place on Spanish soil since the nineteenth century, with the *maquis* making a surreptitious appearance to kill the last of them. The survival of the posthumous unborn heir is ensured when the mother sets the house on fire at the film's end – a gesture reminiscent of the Francoist proclamations of the need to ritually cleanse the country by uprooting and extirpating all that was seen to be ill within it. In fact, this film rightly 'belongs' in an earlier era, as does another film of the period, Pedro Lazaga's *El ladrido/The Barking* (1977), which retraces the history of two guerrilla fighters from a point of view that is unquestionably Manichaean and misogynist. An alternative, though related, view of 1970s womanhood is given in José Antonio de la Loma's *Metralleta Stein/Stein Machinegun* (1975), which is only marginally about *maquis*, foregrounding instead the masculine rivalry between a 'bandit' and the policeman chasing him.

A more nuanced approach towards the insurgents was inaugurated by the fleeting appearance of a fugitive, in the first sympathetic presentation of a possible *maquis* on the screen. This takes place in Víctor Erice's acclaimed *El espíritu de la colmena/The Spirit of the Beehive* (1973), a film that has become the embodiment of the full extent of the desolation in 1940s Spain. Here the five-year-old protagonist, Ana, smiles briefly at a silent and solitary man who is immediately taken out of circulation by the Civil Guard in the night. Protagonists of the chase of resistance fighters in real life, Civil Guards, either in their own policing role or disguised as *maquis* in what became known as the *contrapartidas*, also figure prominently in the rest of the films produced on the topic from earlier to later dates.

Whereas Francoist films dealing with the *maquis* present women as mothers, wives, fiancées or prostitutes, this monochrome image started to change from the 1970s onwards. These productions often associate women with the guerrillas themselves, as happens in Mario Camus' *Los días del pasado/The Days of the Past* (1978), where the teacher, Juana, played by the famous Spanish actor Pepa Flores (also known as Marisol), appears in all scenes but five in the film. Similarly, Pedro Olea had recast a story of repression and black-market corruption in *Pim, pam, pum ... ¡Fuego!/One, Two, Three ... Fire!* (1975), which is seen through the eyes of a tragic cabaret girl, Paca, played by the charismatic Concha Velasco.[30] This film develops the unlikely love story between a *maquis* trying to run away and a cabaret worker who supports her disabled, Republican father, emphasizing corruption and the repression that resulted from the economic deprivation of the defeated. Olea offers an alternative approach to those presented before him in a film in which the role of the guerrilla fighter is secondary to that of the woman who befriends him. Likewise, a woman is also at the centre of the fragmentary, or surrealist, perspective on the plight of those who remained in the mountains given by Manuel Gutiérrez Aragón in *El corazón del bosque/The Heart of the Forest* (1979).

Chapter 3 thus sets out an analysis of the way female characters are used to represent ideas about social construction. Although Olea or Camus outline a sophisticated portrait of female resistance and courage, Lazaga or Nieves Conde invoke a notion of womanhood that harks back to Francoism's National Catholicism, with a touch of 1970s eroticism added to it. Altogether, these films reveal the difficulties of breaking the mould of received notions of womanhood and of the dismissal and stereotyping of the working classes and the *maquis*, whose representation as bandits is intricately woven with misogyny and class prejudice.

The study of the films produced during the 1960s and 1970s is followed by a scrutiny of the films released after the democracy was consolidated, from 1982 to the end of the first decade of the twenty-first century in Chapter 4, 'Democratic *Maquis* (1987–2010)'. Besides three films in which *maquis* are secondary characters, six films with *maquis* as protagonists were released at this time: Julio Sánchez Valdés' *Luna de lobos/Wolves' Moon* (1987), Sancho Gracia's *Huidos/Runaways* (1993), Antoni Ribas' *Terra de canons/Cannon Land* (1999), Armendáriz' *Silencio roto* (2001), del Toro's *El laberinto del fauno* (2006) and Lluís Galter's *Caracremada/Burnface* (2010). Curiously, the first film, Sánchez Valdés' adaptation of Julio Llamazares' novel, *Luna de lobos* (1985), echoes Gutiérrez Aragón's *El corazón del bosque* in its foregrounding of the abandonment of the guerrillas by the Spanish Communist Party. This film presents in unambiguous terms the paranoia and sheer despair that accompanied the dwindling numbers of guerrilla fighters after their desertion first by international forces and, subsequently, by their main organizer, the Communist Party. An alternative view of the *maquis*, and one based on a real story, is Gracia's *Huidos*, which, like *Luna de lobos*, focuses on the solitude of the fighters.

Like its two predecessors, the last fiction film of the twentieth century, Ribas' *Terra de canons*, travels in time, charting the trajectory of resistance in rural Catalonia from the Civil War until the 1950s. The focus of the film is the relationship of a woman, Contxita (Cristina Pineda), with an anarchist who later becomes a *maquis*, Lluís (Mario Guariso), and with an *enlace*, Eduard de Siscart (Lorenzo Quinn), whom she marries. As in other films about *maquis*, Ribas focuses on a woman, Contxita, who provides the main point of view from which the events are presented. By contrast, the last film of the first decade of the twenty-first century offers an alternative view, by centring on the isolation of a single *maquis*, Ramón Vila Capdevila. Galter's enigmatic biopic, *Caracremada*, is a largely silent film, where one learns little about the feelings or beliefs of its protagonist, concentrating instead on his association with the landscape.

Three more films released in the twenty-first century use the *maquis* to support a romantic plot, as had happened in Iglesias' 1963 film, *Carta a una mujer*, which is studied in Chapter 2. Surprisingly, there are some similarities between the ideas represented in the earlier and the later films which use the guerrillas as background. These similarities concern not just the nebulous and, at times, caricatured representation of the guerrillas, but also the use of female characters to bring forth alternative social settings. The films in which this is seen are José Luis Garci's *You Are the One* (2000), Gonzalo Suárez' *El portero/The Goalkeeper* (2000) and Jaime Chávarri's *El año del diluvio/The Year of the Deluge* (2004). As will be shown in Chapter 4, these films decontextualize the struggle, arguably diminishing its importance or even, as happens in *El portero*, serving an image that borders on farce. Nevertheless, I will propose that the treatment of the guerrillas in these films also recreates some salutary images that prevent us from mystifying or stereotyping them, effectively bridging the gap between the earlier Francoist films and the later films and documentaries on the subject.

The last years of the twentieth century and the beginning of the twenty-first witnessed the beginning of the aforementioned 'memory boom'. Stories about the personal and collective experiences of those defeated during the Civil War and oppressed thereafter have multiplied tenfold, as have the assessments of the short- and long-term effects of their trauma. The activities inspired by these tragic events have been wide and all-encompassing, ranging from the intellectual to the artistic. However, it is in historical books and documentaries that the memories of aging survivors have found the most important outlet. The way these testimonies trace the dialectic between memory and history is scrutinized in Chapter 5 of this book, 'Documenting "Historical Memory" (1985–2008)'.

'Documenting "Historical Memory"' investigates these testimonial accounts, which have been aired in cinemas and at festivals, as well as on local, regional and national television. These documentaries have started to fill some of the fissures in our knowledge, although they remain necessarily fragmented. This is the case not only because many of the actual witnesses have passed away but also because personal, historical or archival documentation was consistently purged throughout the best part of six decades up to and including the 1990s. In spite of these shortcomings, or often because of them, these works do not just contribute information but also, and more importantly, help us infer the meaning of events or attitudes during the conflict.

The titles of these documentaries illustrate the perspective and approach taken, emphasizing the sense of loss and the guilt inherent in the oblivion that first Francoism and then democratic Spain imposed on these men and women. These include *Las ilusiones perdidas/Lost Illusions* (2005), *Las fosas del silencio/Silence's Graves* (2004), *Rescatadas del olvido: Mujeres bajo el franquismo/Rescued from Oblivion: Women under Francoism* (1991), *Memoria recobrada/Recovered Memory* (2006) and, one title that probably sums up the approach taken by most of them, *La guerrilla de la memoria/The Guerrilla of Memory* (2002).

All of these documentaries set out to celebrate the survivors and honour the dead, rescuing them from the oblivion or misunderstanding which was thrown onto their images. Some of them trace single lives, such as Daniel Álvarez and Iñaki Pinedo's *Girón: El hombre que murió dos veces/Girón: The Man Who Died Twice* (2003), or César Fernández' *La guerra de Severo/Severo's War* (2008). The majority of them, however, deal with smaller groups, with some articulate speakers, such as veterans Eduardo Pons Prades and José Murillo, taking part in many of them.

Chapter 5 compares the ways in which these documentaries use the testimonies of the survivors or relatives to negotiate the gap between history and memory. From different points of view, these works illustrate Gutiérrez Aragón's claim in his presentation of *Los del monte/The Men from the Mountain* (2006). Gutiérrez Aragón remarks on the everlasting presence of the guerrillas in the mountainous landscape in which he was born, suggesting that these mountains will forever signify the *maquis* and their fight in our imagination. As this and other documentaries show, the *maquis* will remain a 'memoria viva' ('living memory'), surviving in the landscape and local lore, as well as in the historical traces that they have left with us.

My book thus surveys film and memory, taking into account the socio-economic constraints operating in cinematic production and reception. The films studied appeal to the sense of living history which has become commonplace in twenty-first-century Spain, and which was celebrated in David Trueba's adaptation of Javier Cercas' acclaimed book *Soldados de Salamina/Soldiers of Salamis* (2003 and 2001 for the novel). In fact, in its substitution of a male for a female protagonist, Trueba's film sums up some of the paradoxes which my book addresses regarding the relationship between representations of women and images of the fatherland. Similarly, the films signal the pertinacious survival of an inimical view of womanhood that still pervades the society in which these cultural representations have been produced and consumed.

The wish that the vanquished and silenced in the Spanish Civil War not be forgotten has stimulated many twenty-first-century films. It is a wish that was articulated by Julia Conesa, who was cast in Emilio Martínez Lázaro's *Las 13 rosas/Thirteen Roses* (2007). This film traces the arrest, indictment and execution of the young women that popular lore remembers as 'the thirteen red roses', who were shot in the Civil War's immediate aftermath. The fact that most of them were minors and none had ever held a gun did not prevent them from being accused of instigating a crime committed after they had been taken into custody. In her last letter written the night before her execution, Julia Conesa asked her mother to believe in her innocence and to be remembered: 'que mi nombre no se borre en la historia' ('may my name be never erased from history'). Hers is a posthumous wish that was belatedly taken on by Carlos Fonseca's book, *Trece rosas rojas* (2004), and has been recreated by Martínez Lázaro's film. It is also celebrated in the modest plaque that honours them in the place they were shot, and is now continued by the trust that carries their names, Fundación Trece Rosas Rojas, founded in 2005. Like these efforts, many of the productions looked at in this book trace the experiences of people who occupy an important place in twentieth-century Spanish history, and which were repressed or killed by Francoism and silenced thereafter.

All the films studied here differ in their cinematic accomplishments, and their appreciation has changed since they were released. While a number of them have inspired critics, others have been shown on television, at festivals or commemorative events, and are taught at schools and universities. Some preceded and others are part and parcel of the Spanish 'memory boom' with which they are hereby integrated in an archaeological work that could be said to mirror that of the 'memory associations' in twenty-first-century Spain. As with the work of those associations, this book is a long-overdue dig for the traces of men and women who fought in the Civil War's aftermath, and that have inspired some remarkable cinematic representations.

1
Memory, History and 'Historical Memory' of the Spanish *Maquis*

In contemporary historical interpretations, the Spanish Civil War marks the prelude of the tragedies that fascism would visit upon civilian populations during World War II.[1] The international dimension of the conflict was signalled not just by the ideologies on the ground but also by the logistic and human support received, which was unevenly shared by both warring parties. On the one hand, Franco's rebel army was heavily strengthened by the colonial Moroccan troops that he commanded, which crossed Gibraltar to leave a bloody halo of terror in the conquered zones. A determining factor in his final victory was the personnel and arms provided by the Italian and German governments, including the mighty Condor air force which became forever infamous after the bombing of Guernica and Durango in 1937.[2] By contrast, the Spanish Republic was defended by segments of the Spanish police and military forces that remained loyal to the government, as well as the civilian population who formed militias under party or union banners. From 1936 until 1938, loyalists were also supported by the 32,000 men and women of the International Brigades, who were enlisted through their unions and their local communist parties, and who remained in Spain during the first two years of the conflict.

By and large, the Republican 'army' was made up of people who had neither weapons nor military training.[3] In addition, the international Non-Intervention Pact ensured the Republican dependence on Russia for most of its deficient supplies, boosting the Spanish Communist Party at the expense of larger segments of Republican resistance, including the socialist and anarchist unions, *Unión General de Trabajadores* (UGT) and *Confederación Nacional de Trabajadores* (CNT).[4] As Sebastian Balfour observes, the price of the international alienation of the Spanish Republic was to be paid for by untold suffering on the part of millions of ordinary Spaniards for many years thereafter.[5]

The decision of the Western democracies not to sell weapons to the Spanish Republic was partly informed by the wish to appease Hitler, as well as the fear of a left-wing revolution which would threaten established commercial interests. Along these lines, following the victory over fascism in World War II, the Allies turned their back on the plight of Spanish insurgent fighters, endorsing implicitly and, eventually, explicitly Franco's dictatorship on account of his proclaimed anti-communism.[6] This abandonment, and the unabated repression unleashed after 1939, effectively sealed the fate of democratic, left-wing and ordinary Spaniards, who endured one of the most ruthless and long-lasting repressions of the twentieth century.

Most films that show Spanish *maquis* focus on the local context, often mentioning the international struggle within which their fight could be contextualized. The *maquis*, and the civilians supporting them, have been variously interpreted in these films from the 1950s, when they were mostly presented as ruthless bandits, heartless criminals or promiscuous women. By contrast, post-Franco films foreground the important role played by the women who acted as *puntos de apoyo* ('points of support') or *enlaces* ('links'). This chapter will contextualize the study of these cinematic representations within local and international developments in the study of memory. The rise of Memory Studies will situate the role of filmic characterization in the reconstruction of the lives of those who actively resisted Francoism after the Spanish Civil War and their incorporation into the country's 'historical memory'. This term, which often encapsulates the processes embraced under the label 'collective memory', will be defined to include their experiences, as well as the historical and cultural traces left by the struggle.

Post-Franco fiction films and documentaries about the Spanish guerrilla fighters are often based on recorded memories and testimonies of the struggle, as happens with Montxo Armendáriz' *Silencio roto/Broken Silence* (2001), whose scenes originate in actual events and attitudes of the guerrillas and which will be studied in Chapter 4.[7] To achieve a sense of reality in his film, Armendáriz went so far as to isolate his crew and actors, in order to recreate the atmosphere of the times, as Sánchez-Biosca remarks:

> En su afán por crear un ambiente propicio al realismo y fiel a los testimonios [de los maquis], Armendáriz instaló a su equipo en unos caseríos de la zona de rodaje (el Pirineo navarro) durante las dos semanas previas al inicio del mismo con el propósito de estimular la convivencia y recrear el clima de aislamiento y concentración que consideraba necesario para la interpretación de los actores mientras ultimaba los ensayos. (Sánchez-Biosca 2008: 42)[8]

In spite of Armendáriz' efforts, some aspects of the film were criticized as having more to do with cinematic conventions than with the actual experiences that the director sought to portray. Some such inconsistencies include the location of the *maquis'* fight close to their own homes, the use of a bar as a meeting point or the boldness displayed by the female protagonist, Lucía (Lucía Jiménez), in taking supplies to their camp on her bicycle in broad daylight.[9] Whereas some of these limitations are inherent in the limited scope and time constraints imposed by the medium, others are related to the need to create characters with whom the audience can identify. Although this means that the final result can be charged with Manichaeism, the focus of the present study is not to assess historical accuracy through film but to interrogate the parameters embedded in both the reproduction of the past from the privileged point of view of the present and the possible effects that the present can have in the reification of the past. From this perspective, these films offer unique insights into the history of the Spanish *maquis* and their 'historical memory', as will be seen below.

During the first years of Franco's regime, the international struggle against fascism entailed the hope that the end of World War II would bring to Spain the logistic and material help that had been denied to its Republic. As the years passed, and the Francoist regime consolidated its stronghold in Spain, it became increasingly clear that no support would be given to an insurgency marked by a largely communist leadership. The *maquis*, in turn, did not give up arms immediately after realizing that they would be without either Western support or a popular revolt in the urban centres of Spain. Their numbers dwindled during the second half of the 1940s, until they finally all but disappeared in the 1950s, following a protracted struggle that became more desperate and easier to suppress.[10]

Although the word and concept associated with guerrilla warfare are of Spanish origin, dating back to the popular uprising against the Napoleonic invasion of 1808, the Spanish fighters of the 1940s are known as *maquis* because they were closely related to their French namesakes. The word guerrilla, which was first applied in the struggle of Spaniards against Napoleonic forces, refers to a line of shooters, an avant-garde group or series of small groups, whose mission is to harass the enemy, provoking skirmishes designed to distract them. Guerrilla fighters have been either plain clothes or military, and their struggle is normally associated with resistance against invaders, wars of independence or social revolutions. The term *maquis*, on the other hand, comes from the Corsican word *macchia*, meaning shrub land, and was subsequently applied to the French Resistance fighters who struggled against the Nazi army in the early 1940s. In the Spanish case, however, the 'invader' was not external and outright support for the guerrillas was not forthcoming either within or outside Spain after World War II.

The relationship between the Spanish and French *maquis* is not just a chronological or political coincidence. Many Spanish insurgents fought in the two countries, playing an important role in the French Resistance against the Vichy government and entering Paris with the forces of General Leclerc in 1944. Some of those who passed into Spain after the victory of the Allies were subsequently captured and executed by Franco, even in cases in which they were claimed by the French government as war heroes, to no avail. This happened, for example, to José Vitini, who had been Lieutenant Colonel in the Resistance, who was executed in 1946 alongside six others, with a further 16 *maquis* executed the following day.[11] Likewise, Cristino García Granda, shot one year later, had been Lieutenant in the Republican Army and then took part in the liberation of Foix (south of Toulouse), the release of prisoners from Nîmes and the victory of La Madeleine in Normandy. Alongside a good number of others, both Vitini and García fought first in Spain between 1936 and 1939, then in France in the early 1940s, where they gained recognition as war heroes, and subsequently in Spain, where their lives ended. Even though there is no fiction film dedicated to their lives, they provided an inspiration for both the Francoist condemnation of resistance fighters as outsiders and bandits, and the subsequent vindication of their sacrifice. Their brief careers thus provide a pattern on which many productions hinge.

Originally from Madrid, José Vitini Flórez was born in 1913 and became a member of the Communist Party (PCE) in whose ranks he fought for the Spanish Republic before fleeing to France in February 1939. Following the Nazi occupation, Vitini joined the Spanish guerrilla groups that became part of the anti-Nazi struggle in the French Midi. Afterwards, Vitini became military chief of the French Interior Forces or FFI ('Forces Françaises de l'Intérieur'), where he reached the rank of Lieutenant General after several years of risking his life. At the head of the 168 Division, Vitini led guerrilla operations which helped liberate the area around the Tarn and Aveyron rivers and the cities of Albi, Rodez and Lourdes from the Nazis. Vitini also took part in the liberation of Paris in August 1944, before returning to Spain in December of that year. After the failed 'invasion' of Spain through the Aran Valley by guerrilla fighters in 1944, the Communist Party gave Vitini command of an urban guerrilla force, *Cazadores de la Ciudad* ('Urban Hunters'), which operated in Madrid, seeking to destabilize the regime while waiting for international support. After several successful raids directed against the offices of the fascist party, Falange, Vitini was arrested by the Spanish military police, alongside his lieutenant, Juan Casín Alonso, and the nine men under their command, between March and April 1945. They were immediately judged by a *Consejo de Guerra* ('War Tribunal') and summarily executed in the Campo de Tiro de Carabanchel on 28 April 1945.[12]

Cristino García Granda was born in Asturias in 1914, and took part in the Spanish Civil War as a member of the *XIV Cuerpo de Ejército Guerrillero* ('XIV Unit of the Guerrilla Army'), a special unit which attacked behind the Nationalist lines. After the Civil War he escaped to France where he was part of the French Resistance as a member of the *Agrupación de Guerrilleros Españoles* (AGE) ('Association of Spanish Guerrillas'). Highly successful fighting the occupiers, García returned to Spain at the end of World War II to work with resistance groups aiming to oust Franco. Captured on 15 October 1945, García was tortured and subsequently executed on 21 February 1946 in Alcala de Henares, aged 32, with nine other heroes of the French Resistance. One year later, in 1947, the French government posthumously awarded him the War Medal with a Silver Star and his memory is honoured with a street named after him in Saint-Denis in Paris. He also has a small obelisk in La Madeleine which reads: 'Honeur à Cristino Garcia, chef de maquis', and a district, the 'Quartier Cristino Garcia', in Aubervilliers, Paris. He is buried in the Carabanchel Cemetery, in the south-west of Madrid.

Even if guerrilla fighters like Vitini and García were active in urban centres, many of their contemporaries fought and sought refuge in the mountains. In fact, the word and concept of *maquis*, which is a short version of the word *maquisards*, was first coined in Corsica where it referred to the mountainous landscape that harboured the nationalist fighters on the island. Like their Corsican counterparts, during the 1940s most Spanish *maquis* fought from the mountainous areas of Cantabria, León, Asturias, the Levant and the Pyrenees.[13] Their association with the scenery of which they became an integral part makes the landscape an over-determined sign in films dealing with the conflict, including Gutiérrez Aragón's *El corazón del bosque*, Camus' *Los días del pasado*, Armendáriz' *Silencio roto*, del Toro's *El laberinto del fauno* and Galter's *Caracremada*. Throughout these films, a lush, mountainous landscape dominates the oppressive life in the village or compound, standing in for the men or adding to the meanings conveyed by the films' narratives. This environment provides an effective background for the action, as well as a coherent vehicle for the atmosphere represented.[14] Overall, however, unlike the deployment of the landscape in films belonging to genres such as westerns, open spaces in films about the *maquis* are not normally associated with a notion of freedom, accentuating instead a sense of enclosure and overall claustrophobia.

In spite of the fact that there were some remarkable women in their ranks, the Spanish *maquis* were, by and large, groups of armed men attacking from and hiding in the mountains of Spain, while depending on their families and local villagers whose safety and lives they risked. Their ranks were made up of returning exiles and *huidos* ('runaways') who had escaped to the mountains in the occupied zones throughout the Civil War, with the end of the conflict fostering the creation of a co-ordinated guerrilla movement that gathered momentum when the victory of the Allies appeared to be imminent.[15] After the fall of Paris, in 1944, the *Junta Española de Liberación* ('Spanish Liberation Junta') was formed in Toulouse with the objective of penetrating Spain via the Pyrenees and forcing the Allies to intervene on behalf of the defeated Republic.[16] Even if the guerrillas grew, with several *Agrupaciones de Guerrilleros*, created from 1944 to 1948, they had no external support in the form of weapons or ammunition and also lacked a base in the Spanish cities. This makes the Spanish *maquis* unlike the French Resistance, which was a movement against a foreign invader that was backed by the British Air Force and widely supported both in urban and rural France.[17] Moreover, the strict control of the media enforced at the time meant that the actions of Spanish *maquis* remained isolated incidents with little repercussion beyond the localities affected. In spite of their limitations, the *maquis* contributed to the regime's increased instability from 1944 to 1948, especially when they undertook a failed 'reconquest' of Spain via the Aran Valley in 1944 (Serrano 2002: 123–4). This period is thoroughly traced in *Silencio roto* by Armendáriz, who sums up the main developments of the guerrilla movement as follows:

> Efectivamente, la guerrilla fue desde sus inicios un movimiento de resistencia, como dice Manuel al principio de la historia. Esa fase inicial es la que más o menos simboliza el primer bloque de la película, correspondiente a una etapa que llega hasta el verano de 1944, cuando se ve ya – tras la caída de París en mayo de ese año – que los aliados van a ganar la Segunda Guerra Mundial. Los guerrilleros españoles que han colaborado con la resistencia francesa, y que tienen armas, las utilizan entonces para impulsar la invasión que se produce por el Valle de Arán ... Eso tiene unos momentos álgidos que van desde 1944 a 1945, que es la etapa en la que el maquis tiene más actividad ... Hasta que poco después, cuando empieza a quedar claro que los países vencedores no van a ayudar a la guerrilla, sino que se disponen a pactar con Franco, la Guardia Civil y el ejército comienzan a machacar indiscriminadamente a los puntos de apoyo, con lo que se produce la caída y el hundimiento del movimiento guerrillero. (Armendáriz 2001: 149)[18]

In a statement issued on 5 March 1945, the French, British and United States governments released a tripartite resolution in which they urged Spanish people to bring democracy to their country, while explicitly avoiding committing themselves or any resources to help those who were fighting the regime. Half a year after this document was released, the League of Nations made a public declaration recommending the exit of ambassadors from Madrid and an economic blockade of the country (Serrano 2002: 149–53). Franco then closed Spain's doors to all foreign trade, perpetuating the hunger, misery and corruption associated with rationing and the black market until the end of the 1950s.[19]

A few years after the United Nations condemned Spanish rule as fascist, the governments of the United States of America and the United Kingdom established closer ties with a regime whose anti-communist credentials were to them reassuring in the Cold War climate. Paradoxically, the lack of support from the Western democracies meant a closer rapprochement between the guerrillas and the Soviet-backed Communist Party, very much along the lines of the dependence on weapons and material from Soviet sources during the Civil War. This made both the war and the guerrilla struggle easier to crush, as it effectively separated them from the resistance to Nazism throughout the world. In the case of the Spanish guerrilla struggle it also alienated large numbers of Spanish Republicans, who were trying to negotiate with Franco using the mediation of the Western powers.

The dimensions of the *maquis*' struggle has been slowly coming to light in Spain, following the 'memory boom' that gathered momentum in the last years of the twentieth century. Like the Spanish Civil War, this 'memory boom' is in many ways a unique phenomenon within Spain because the country was isolated internationally during and after its conflict, and did not take an active part in World War II. On the other hand, there are aspects of the Spanish 'turn to memory' that are closely intertwined with international developments. The intersection between the local and global contexts is here of special interest because events taking place in other countries, such as Chile, Argentina or South Africa, have influenced those taking place in Spain and vice versa.

Holocaust Studies and the fall of the Berlin Wall were determining factors in the 'turn to memory' from the 1980s onwards. As the generation of Holocaust survivors started to reach the end of their lives, there was a renewed sense of urgency to preserve their testimonies.[20] This was facilitated by a temporal distance that enabled people to approach events in their lives from a less traumatic angle. In turn, this gave way to a renewed interest in the study of personal, public, cultural, social, historical or collective memory, as the phenomena are often called, as well as investigations of trauma at social and individual levels.

Beginning with the work of Maurice Halbwachs who introduced the concept of 'collective memory' and of social 'cadres' (or frames) for memory in the first half of the twentieth century, the study of memory has become increasingly common across different scholarly disciplines, including sociology, history, anthropology and psychology. A committed socialist scholar, Halbwachs published *Les cadres sociaux de la mémoire* in 1925, while his writings on 'collective memory' were issued posthumously, in 1950, five years after he died in the concentration camp of Buchenwald. The concept of collective memory that Halbwachs introduced has become part and parcel of social debates in academia, as well as in communities whose recent past has been one of conflict. In Halbwachs' understanding of the processes of memory, even though it is individuals who remember, the activity of remembering relies on social patterns that could not have developed in isolation:

> We can remember only on condition of retrieving the position of past events which interest us from the frameworks of collective memory. A recollection is the richer when it reappears at the junction of a greater number of these frameworks, which in effect intersect with each other and overlap in part ... Depending on circumstances, and point in time, society represents the past to itself in different ways: it modifies its conventions. As every one of its members accepts these conventions, they inflect their recollections in the same direction in which the collective memory evolves. (Halbwachs 1992: 172–3)

By appealing to a social framework for memory, Halbwachs relates individual experience to existing concepts or mentalities that make memory meaningful within a given social context, the framework or 'cadre' of memory. The images provided by 'memory' thus need the mental constructs that a given society or grouping constructs for itself in a reciprocal and dynamic relationship that is of relevance to its present. Memory and identity, in other words, rely on the fixing of images in our individual and collective imagination.[21] This is not to say that groups 'remember', as Halbwachs emphasized, but that individual memory is embedded within its social context, and is inflected by the sense of belonging to particular social groupings at a given time. This framework enables some memories to survive and deepen, while others are obliterated or relegated. 'The succession of remembrances, of even our most personal ones', for Halbwachs, 'is always explained by changes occurring in our relationships to various collective milieus – in short, by the transformations these milieus undergo separately and as a whole' (Halbwachs 1980: 49).

Highly influential in the study of memory has been the encyclopaedic undertaking led by Pierre Nora in 1980s France, which introduced the now widely used term 'lieux de mémoire', normally translated as sites or realms of memory.[22] For Nora, the current turn to memory reveals not just a renewed interest in the past but a type of nostalgia for something that is lost from our daily lives: 'We speak so much of memory because there is so little of it left … There are *lieux de mémoire*, sites of memory, because there are no longer *milieux de mémoire*, real environments of memory' (1989: 7). It is, therefore, the 'acceleration of history' that is mourned in the construction of memorials or the reification of other memory constructions as part of national consciousness. Nora defines these 'sites of memory' as 'bastions' which 'buttress' a sense of collective identity, which he sees under threat:

> *Lieux de mémoire* arise out of a sense that there is no such thing as spontaneous memory, hence that we must create archives, mark anniversaries, organize celebrations, pronounce eulogies, and authenticate documents because such things no longer happen as a matter of course … These bastions buttress our identities, but if what they defended were not threatened, there would be no need for them. (Nora 1989: 7)[23]

Nora's is a view that has been challenged from different standpoints by critics, including Andreas Huyssen, for whom it is not so much a sense of loss that inheres in the current memorializing efforts but a wish to counter the pace of change in the modern world. Memory is, for Huyssen, a form of resistance, rather than of mourning: 'an expression of the basic human need to live in extended structures of temporality' (1995: 7).

Nora's narrow understanding of 'history' and his split duality between 'history' and 'memory' have not been incorporated into the

Spanish context, where the potentially paradoxical term 'historical memory' is commonly used.[24] The term 'historical memory' can be seen to be an oxymoron or a tautology, depending on the definitions both of history and of memory. The fact that the term is used as a stable entity, seeking to recover the voice of those deprived of it, is, nevertheless, not unproblematic, as Michael Richards argues. It is not just that dividing people into two segregate categories, winners and losers, leaves out many for whom to be classed as 'the defeated' was rather more 'complex ... and therefore remains a challenging task for social history' (Richards 2006: 87). 'For the historian', as Richards shows, 'historical memory is more variable and subtle than is often assumed and ought therefore to be more precisely situated *between* Memory and History' (Richards 2006: 86; italics in the text).[25] This is due to the climate of fear, hunger and corruption that alienated civilians in multiple ways, even those who might not have defined themselves as 'the defeated'.

Also relevant to the 'turn to memory' is the fact that it concurs with the so-called 'turn to culture' which has led to the rise of Cultural History as a discipline (or sub-discipline) from the 1980s onwards. This follows from, and overlaps with, the development of Social History in the aftermath of World War II and the succeeding decolonization of the world. In this context, it is also pertinent not just to define what a society or individual understands about history and memory, but to question why and how people deploy them, even when their use becomes, to borrow Tzvetan Todorov's term, an 'abuse' of a right (Todorov 2001).

In the aftermath of the political transitions undergone by former communist states, Latin American countries, such as Guatemala, Chile or Argentina, and former colonies like South Africa, Rwanda and, to some extent, Northern Ireland, references to 'memory' have become intimately associated with issues of justice and human rights. Not surprisingly, Memory, as a 'field' or a discipline, has become increasingly congested and confusing, and there is often political capital to be gained from particular views or definitions.[26]

In the Spanish context, the need to construct and evaluate the 'memories' of the Francoist years has particular difficulties because of shadows cast by the failure to dissociate political debates from that past. The Francoist appeal to legitimacy through a physical, historical and rhetorical destruction of the Second Republic is thus echoed by a process whereby the main political parties align themselves with different points of view about that past and the way society should (or should not) address it. This has followed the consecration of the Transition to Democracy (1975–82), the Amnesty Law of 1977 and the Constitution of 1978 as foundational myths of the current state. Thus, in a movement that mirrors the exclusivity that Francoism attributed to itself, efforts to revisit the Civil War and its aftermath are often clouded by accusations of a desire to stir up old hatreds and dishonour the pact on which the current democracy is based. Such declarations, however, disregard the legitimate attempts to restore dignity and legality to those deprived of it in the past, forestalling the social dialogue that is still to take place, and dividing up the political spectrum along 1936 lines. Furthermore, it is a standpoint that evens out the responsibility for the military coup of 1936, disregarding the actual events and their long-lasting consequences.

Far from being assimilated or understood, therefore, the events taking place in twentieth-century Spain remain the subject of contention, and have the ingrained potential to be divisive along social and political lines.[27] This book seeks to contribute to that debate, opening it up through a cultural history of the real and imagined roles given to *maquis* and their supporters in post-Franco's Spain. It, therefore, traces the dialectic between voluntary and involuntary forgetting, and the need to select segments of the past for their present relevance in other post-traumatic contexts, taking into account studies related to the Holocaust. In this regard, the present work has benefited from Lawrence Kritzman's approach to memory within its 'sacred context', as it relates to the concept of ritual sacrifice:

> Memory, which also includes forgetting, can be understood in its 'sacred context' as the variety of forms through which cultural communities imagine themselves in diverse representational modes. In this sense, as a critical category 'memory' distinguishes itself from history, which is regarded as an intellectual practice more deeply rooted in the evidence derived from the study of empirical reality. (Kritzman 1996: ix)[28]

The films on the *maquis*' struggle produced during and after the dictatorship are part of the historical, cultural and social memory of twentieth-century Spain, as well as the European rise of and resistance to fascism taking place from the 1920s. Directly or indirectly, the productions studied in this book appeal to notions of sacrifice, victimization and redemption, participating in the tension between memory as transient and contestable and the creation of a monolithic view of history that is 'permanent and uncontested'.[29]

The investigation and interpretation of twentieth-century Spanish history has become the site of a struggle for social recognition as well as reconciliation in the twenty-first century. Memory has become a site of struggle not just to remember but to select what to re-present or to ignore, endorsing or challenging notions of individual and social identity. This 'struggle for historical memory', Georgina Blakeley reminds us,

> can help us to re-evaluate the process of democratization in Spain and the role of civil society within that process. It contends that the struggle to recover historical memory constitutes an attempt on the part of civil society to renegotiate the original pacts agreed upon during the transition to democracy in order to move beyond the narrow *political conciliation*, symbolized by the 1978 constitution, to a broader *social reconciliation*. (Blakeley 2005: 44)

Blakeley is alluding here to the aforementioned silence about the past that became a trademark of the Spanish transition to democracy. This 'pact of forgetting' meant that, for many, it became impossible not only to seek redress of previous injustices but even to remember or honour their loved ones. In this sense, many of the films studied here attest to the need for survival traced by Paul Connerton who, with regard to German 'acts of silence', remarks that:

> With the sole exception of Nossak, and some passages on ... Böll, no German writer was prepared to write or capable of writing about the progress and repercussions of the gigantic campaign of destruction ... Confronted with a taboo, people can fall silent out of terror or panic or because they can find no appropriate words. We cannot, of course, infer the fact of forgetting from the fact of silence. Nevertheless, some acts of silence may be an attempt to bury things beyond expression and the reach of memory; yet such silencings, while they are a type of repression, can at the same time be a form of survival, and the desire to forget may be an essential ingredient in that process of survival. (Connerton 2008: 68)

The work of 'unearthing' living memories in Spain, as well as the bones of those assassinated, has been taken up by a distant generation from that which suffered directly the trauma of the Spanish Civil War and its protracted aftermath. Not an isolated phenomenon, the recovery of the past by a generation that is physically removed from the conflict has taken place in different contexts, fitting in within the paradigm set by, for example, Paul Ricoeur, who refers to this process as 'secondary memory'. For Ricoeur, 'memory is re-presentation, in the twofold sense of re-: turning back, anew' (Ricoeur 2004: 39).[30] Similarly, Marianne Hirsch charts the second generation's efforts to access a past that cannot but be mediated by representation as 'postmemory'.[31] Along these lines, Jacques Derrida (1994) refers to the 'ghosts' of the past, using the term 'hauntology', whereas Alison Landsberg has developed the concept of 'prosthetic memory'.[32] For Landsberg, the contemporary access to a past that was inaccessible to earlier humans does not necessarily entail a sense of loss. Instead, it can undermine the sense of exclusivity or boundaries between certain groups, which may have been created by the appropriation of memory and its concomitant sense of belonging:

> Prosthetic memory, therefore, unlike its medieval and nineteenth-century precursors, is not simply a means for consolidating a particular group's identity and passing on its memories; it also enables the transmission of memories to people who have no 'natural' or biological claims to them. (Landsberg 2004: 28)

A generation that grew removed from the shadow cast by the Spanish Civil War has thus been the main catalyst for the renewed interest in the post or secondary memories of the Spanish Civil War. The incorporation in the country's 'official history' of memories that were forcefully erased is a way of reimagining the past, providing the basis for a culture to evolve. In this sense, it is salutary to remember that for many in Spain, the process outlined by Dominick LaCapra as 'working through' the past in order to come to terms with personal and social traumas is still to take place, and that this requires remembering and mourning (LaCapra 1994: 65).[33] In the Spanish case, articulating a past that was outlawed from public memory for more than 50 years remains unfinished business in the twenty-first century. Cultural products, like the films studied in this book, can facilitate the process of working through those memories, making them part of the social fabric.[34]

The attitudes of writers, directors and civil society vis-à-vis the Spanish Civil War corroborate Connerton's claim that memory and history are intricately woven in the exercise of power.[35] The study that follows takes as its point of departure Connerton's claim that memory is always already political, and that the past is and remains a battlefield for the control of power in the present. It is a point of view that is shared by most films dealing with the guerrilla resistance to Franco's Spain, and which relies on a traditional cinematic use of women and children, whose innocence as impartial observers or unwilling resistance fighters remains unquestionable. In this context, memory, whether real, 'invented', 'imagined' or reconstructed, becomes the site of a struggle to select what to remember and what to forget, as well as how to make sense of plural, contested and fragmented stories. Films, like books and the activities of civil society, contribute actively not only to historical interpretation but also, and more decisively, to social construction, political reconciliation and to a sense of individual and shared uniqueness. The result is a form of living history that, as Jean-François Lyotard affirms, 'is not satisfied with providing cognitive certainty about the event, but ... tries to "restitute", to "relive", to "make present", which is to say that it moves us by the evocation of lost time' (Lyotard 2004: 108).

Evocation and emotion are essential tools in the reconstruction of the cinematic memories of the Spanish *maquis* in post-Franco films. In order to make sense of this past, these films reify testimonies that can stimulate empathy and solidarity. By doing so, these productions foreground the plurality of individual and social memories, often inviting audiences to take part in the processes of reconstructing this as a 'collective memory'.[36] These works, moreover, enter into a dialogue not only with the historical period that they represent and the one in which they are constructed. They also contain references to and rehearse or challenge ideas from other films, including those produced during the years of censorship and repression in which guerrilla fighters were mostly portrayed as bandits with no possible redemption.

The Spanish 'memory boom' has stimulated the production of a good number of documentaries, all of which refashion the Civil War from the perspective of the vanquished. In their different ways, films and documentaries honour the men and women who risked or lost their lives in a doomed attempt to revisit Franco's victory. This fin-de-siècle's 'memory boom', I have suggested in this chapter, was triggered by the international context, as well as the efforts of second-generation descendants of Civil War veterans to recover the memory, as well as the remains, of their ancestors. It is a 'boom' that spurred on the work on the Spanish *guerrilleros*, with films, books and documentaries being the main vehicles through which the voices of these belated fighters have been heard. As will be seen below, the resistance that many of these films celebrate is an unambiguous condemnation of the oppression that fascism means socially and politically, as well as culturally, personally, emotionally and imaginatively.

By and large, however, cinematic productions are primarily designed to entertain audiences, even when they also seek to inform them through the reconstruction of a silenced past or by contesting previous historical interpretations: in this case, the Francoist stigmatization of Spanish *maquis* fighters and the plight of their supporters. Films and books, like the activities of groups within civil society, make present what is (apparently) forgotten and can contribute to political reconciliation or to the reconstruction of a sense of individual or collective identity that may have been marginalized or obliterated. In the Spanish case, this is the vision of those treated as vanquished in the Spanish Civil War, which was deleted by the 'official' history disseminated during the nearly 40 years that Franco was in power, and remained largely subdued for 20 years afterwards. The 'telling' of these stories through the cultural products in which they are embedded can enable a society to access its own past, making 'living memories' into a usable narrative that can have the function of including within it those hitherto excluded. They can also allow traumas to be expressed and thus worked through or prepare the ground for apologies or to challenge judicial impunity. Emotion and evocation therefore become essential tools in this investigation into ways in which social cohesion may be facilitated by creating a particular narrative about the past.

Overall, the present study shows that thinking about modern identity relies on exploring the relationship between individual and social, cultural and collective memories, and the way these overlap, contradict one another and constitute the material on which history is written. Indeed, the films investigated here attest to the relationship between a threatened notion of national belonging and the role played by individuals and social groups in shaping the past and giving it meaning in the present. They therefore constitute attempts to fill in some of the 'holes of memory' left by the silencing of testimonies during and after Francoism. These films are part of the cultural history of Spain, often articulating the trauma left by the breach of human bonds of solidarity and the deep wounds caused by a past yet to be worked through. In this way, they open up a social dialogue within a cultural arena in which cinematic productions have occupied a privileged position, as will be seen in the following chapters.

2
Francoism's *Bandoleros* (1954–1964)

By the time that the first Spanish films portraying the 1940s guerrillas were released, the *maquis* of rural Spain had all but disappeared, having maintained intermittent focus of resistance for the first decade of the totalitarian regime. These films can be seen as the first cultural attempts to memorialize the conflict, furthering the notions of religious crusade in ways which were relevant to their contemporary endeavour to incorporate Spain into the international world order. As this chapter will show, these productions offer a transparent window into the 'sacred context' of memory outlined in my previous chapter, showing the intricate relationship between the regime's self-presentation and its manipulation of public opinion and historical interpretation.

The intertitles of the second film released, Pedro Lazaga's pro-Franco *Torrepartida/Broken Tower* (1956), offer an eloquent summary of the regime's view of resistance fighters, disclosing its position vis-à-vis the *maquis* during the 1940s and situating the struggle within international developments. After indicating that the characters and events to be depicted 'are not all imaginary', Lazaga stresses their historical context and relevance to 1950s Spain as 'fragments of our history ... fortunately overcome':

> Las personas y los hechos que aparecen en esta película no son todos imaginarios, las más de las veces, son un pedazo de nuestra historia, aun no lejana, aunque afortunadamente superada. Todas las guerras dejan tras sí, como sedimento amargo, la lepra del bandolerismo. La desunión entre hermanos, fomentada por pasiones

e intereses bastardos, conduce inexorablemente a la ruina y a la muerte. (*Torrepartida* [1956])[1]

Referring to the *maquis* as 'banditry', they are then classed as 'leprosy' and the war's 'bitter sediment'. The Civil War itself is then portrayed as a fratricidal conflict, a 'division between brothers', which, 'spurred on by illegitimate passions and interests, leads inexorably to ruin and to death'. As this chapter will show, *Torrepartida*'s intertitles sum up the ideas which Francoism mobilized during the 1950s in order to legitimize its usurpation of power and its continuing oppression of the country's citizens. These ideas, moreover, have had a long-lasting effect, remaining the subject of political contention in the twenty-first century.

While the historical segment to which the epigraph refers might not have been as 'happily overcome' as the regime would have liked during the 1950s, its 'bitter sediment' remained ingrained within Spanish society. Indeed, the Civil War was still present in the lives of the millions marked by the regime's long-lasting repression, as well as the fear, hunger and deprivation that it left in its protracted aftermath. Another important aspect highlighted by Lazaga's words is that the guerrillas, hereby dismissed as 'banditry', were the outcome of a fratricidal struggle spurred on by passions or interests which Lazaga renders 'illegitimate'.[2] The vision of a harmonious, traditional family broken up by foreign forces became the prevalent official view of the Civil War from the mid-1940s onwards. This was emphasized during the 1950s, which witnessed the international acceptance of Francoism as first and foremost an anti-communist regime, very much in tune with contemporary Cold War politics.

This chapter will investigate how the films about the *maquis* of the fifties articulate the projection of an 'alien' enemy within the family with degraded images of women, workers and resistance fighters. In line with Nazi melodrama, this vision of the 'nation' is one that excludes from its 'body' all possible dissidence, rendering it alien and therefore obliterating it from public memory. This applies to the areas that Franco's National Catholicism saw as a threat to its integrity, including the rights of women and the working classes, non-Catholic beliefs and the expression of regional identities. Republicans, liberal, left-wing and revolutionary Spaniards were thus paradoxically classed as outsiders, the 'other', as well as 'the enemy within'. This vision is one that demonizes the lower classes, making them often appear subhuman, and articulates notions of Catholic and submissive womanhood as inherently patriotic, thus stigmatizing and grouping all forms of resistance and dissidence, excluding them from the social fabric.

Dismissive of all possible nonconformity, the Franco regime's monolithic view of a Catholic and backward-looking Spain had serious implications for Spaniards, especially those who had supported actively or passively the elected Republic. It had a markedly retrograde effect on the lives of women, whose few rights regarding control of their finances, access to the workplace, divorce or abortion were completely eroded. Now utterly dependent on their menfolk to be allowed to join the workforce, travel or even receive and dispose of their own income, women also had their reproductive capacity under the control of a regime that classed as criminal activities all forms of birth control. Along those discriminatory lines, adultery, which was 'reprehensible' in men, was a criminal offence for women, as was the abandonment of the marital home, even in cases of domestic violence.[3]

The regime's oppression of women was signposted by its peculiar perspective, only distinguishing between 'good' and 'evil' women. This view, which pervades films up to and including the last years of Franco's life, is essential to understanding the type of national identity that was enforced through the strict policing of every aspect of public and private life, as well as the estrangement of the opposition to the regime's political, social or religious ideology. Paradoxically, this is a vision in which women both embodied and were excluded from the very fatherland that they were meant to nurture. These images are dominant in films dealing with guerrilla fighters up to the 1960s and survive in diverse forms thereafter.

This chapter's investigation of the *maquis* thus highlights their presentation alongside roles given to women, either as mothers or girlfriends or, when associated with the guerrillas, concubines or prostitutes. By and large, these productions foreground a Catholic and conservative family on which the state would be modelled and upon which it would rest. Besides promoting the Francoist National Catholic programme, these films embed some societal paradoxes contained within the genre many of them fit into: 'fascist melodrama'. As Kinder proposes, fascist melodrama has certain peculiarities:

> Yet rather than suppress the political plane by focusing entirely on the private sphere as in most classical Hollywood melodrama, Fascist

melodrama acknowledges and politicizes the connection between the domestic and public realms. Like subversive melodrama, it proclaims the family as a legitimate site for effective political action, mobilizing 'the people' around universal issues of morality, generation, and gender that cut across class lines. (Kinder 1993: 72)

Fascist melodrama is, therefore, a useful tool through which to foreground the familial and Catholic notions that the regime sought to impose during the Spanish *posguerra*. The genre concurred with the Francoist moral dualities of good and evil, as Kinder further argues.[4] This division packs important ideas prevalent in the Francoist productions with *maquis*.

The images of women promoted by Francoism were in part modelled on those from Nazi Germany, and bear some resemblance to those of fascist Italy due to its Catholic structures. This aspect of the regime's projection is very much in line with its overall similarities to and differences from the two prototypically fascist governments of Europe. It is a difference that Franco himself magnified after the fate of the Axis powers was sealed at the end of World War II, and which subsequently ensured the endurance of his regime for nearly four decades. Although for strategic reasons Franco did not participate in World War II, he openly supported the Axis powers by sending a battalion, the Blue Division, in 1941 to fight alongside Hitler, who posted them on the Russian front. However, from 1943 onwards, when the dominance of the Axis started to wane, the regime first relegated and subsequently all but deleted the fascist credentials it had so proudly shown until then, including fascist salutes and insignia. It did this by foregrounding its Catholic and anti-communist beliefs, while gradually silencing its allegiance to the fascist governments that had helped Franco win the Civil War and sidelining from important posts prominent members of the Spanish fascist party, Falange, then known as FET y de las JONS.[5] This transformation, which was also shown in the replacement of Falange ministers by Catholics and Monarchists, can also be traced in contemporary films, and can be seen in those figuring *maquis* that are studied in this chapter.

In spite of the remarkable cinematic potential that the guerrilla conflict could have had, only a handful of films were produced in the years encompassed by this chapter. In fact, films with *maquis* at the centre of the plot could be reduced to a mere four: Arturo Ruiz-Castillo's

Dos caminos/Two Paths (1954), Lazaga's *Torrepartida* (1956), Margarita Alexandre and Rafael Torrecilla's adaptation of Mercedes Fórmica's novel *La ciudad perdida/The Lost City* (1955) and the adaptation by León Klimovsky of the Planeta Prize novel by the famous Falangist journalist Emilio Romero, *La paz empieza nunca/Peace Never Starts* (1960). Not surprisingly, the *maquis* are, by and large, cast as bandits with no political motivation in these productions. Four more films of the time, including two by Miguel Iglesias: *El cerco/The Siege* (1955) and *Carta a una mujer/Letter to a Woman* (1963), and José Rovira Beleta's *Los atracadores/The Raiders* (1962), deal with bandits, raiders or common criminals as accessories to a central narrative in which the references to the resistance are either non-existent or totally marginal. The study of Spanish releases in the 1950s and 1960s is completed with the two films on the topic produced in the USA: Sam Wood's famous adaptation of Ernest Hemingway's novel, *For Whom the Bell Tolls* (1943) and Fred Zinnemann's *Behold a Pale Horse* (1964).

The four films in which *maquis* figure as central characters are by no means solely propagandistic of the regime's values. In this, they reflect the broader cinematic trends of the time, for not all cinema produced and released during the early years of the dictatorship reproduced the regime's monolithic view of society. This happened in spite of the fact that they were made under the constraints enforced by a stringent censorship, as well as an economic autarky that closed the country to cultural or commercial exchanges. Nevertheless, in terms of both genre and style, the 1950s was a period of vitality and experimentation, notwithstanding the famous accusation levelled at the industry by Juan Antonio Bardem. During the Salamanca Congress (1955), Bardem alluded to the industry's decay in every possible aspect, using the most often cited words of Spanish cinematic history.[6] However, even filmmakers from the old school, including the previously mentioned Ruiz-Castillo and José Antonio Nieves Conde, as well as pro-Franco directors such as Rafael Gil and José Luis Sáenz de Heredia, produced a number of remarkable films, not all of which can be classified as outright endorsements of the regime's policies.[7] Significantly, these men were joined by a new generation of filmmakers, many of whom were influenced by Italian neorealism, as was Bardem in his most famous films: *Muerte de un ciclista/Death of a Cyclist* (1955) and *Calle Mayor/Main Street* (1956). Probably the most important of this period is Luis García Berlanga, who worked with Bardem on two productions and who put censors to the test in his famous parody, *Bienvenido Mister Marshall!/Welcome Mr Marshall!* (1953), as well as *Los jueves milagro/Miracles of Thursday* (1957), *Plácido* (1961) and the caustic *El verdugo/The Executioner* (1963). These productions, and the contradictions inherent in them, illustrate Carlos Heredero's claim that the decade ought to be treated not simply as a monochrome era in which cinema acted as a voice for the regime's values. It should, instead, be seen as a 'crossroads' which embeds the trends that Spanish cinema would develop during the following decades (Heredero 1993: 15). Ironically, it was Falangist Nieves Conde's acerbic film *Surcos/Furrows* (1951) that stands out as a symbol of the era because of its dim vision of black-marketeering, corruption, migration and malice. Besides its interesting social criticism, of relevance to the present study is the fact that *Surcos* focuses on a family that can be seen as a microcosm of society's underprivileged and that the film 'adopts melodrama as its unifying system of narration' (Kinder 1993: 42).[8] Indeed, the vicissitudes that this neorealist film underwent show some of the most important contradictions of the time. While it was initially lined up for the coveted accolade of being a film 'Of National Interest', it became so controversial that its selection forced the resignation of the director of the Film Institute, José María Gómez Escudero.[9] Following this controversy, the prize was given to Sáenz de Heredia's chauvinist *Alba de América/Dawn of America* (1951), which represented Columbus' discovery of the New World as a heroic enterprise, rightly sponsored by the Catholic King and Queen of Spain, Ferdinand and Isabella.

Like *Surcos*, then, many of the films produced during the first years of the dictatorship deploy a patriarchal household as microcosmic representation of the country and the people within it (or the model intended for them to follow). In this context, the paradigmatic example of the time was given by the film scripted by Franco himself under the pseudonym Jaime de Andrade, *Raza/Race* (1941), which, like *Alba de América*, was directed by Sáenz de Heredia. *Raza* sublimates the Caudillo's ancestry by tracing it to a famous naval officer killed in the Battle of Trafalgar, Cosme Damián Churruca.[10] The father in the film, Pedro Churruca (José Nieto), is a liberal womanizer, while the suffering mother, Isabel Acuña de Churruca (Rosina Mendía), was closely modelled on Franco's own. After tracing the genealogical tree of the film's protagonist, José Churruca (Alfredo Mayo), *Raza* channels Churruca's heroism in the form of self-abnegation and through the association of service to the family and to the fatherland. The family thus becomes the embodiment of the country's 'race', and Franco's alter ego, Churruca, is symbolically placed as the heroic male and rightful father of the *patria*.[11]

While this took place in the early 1940s, the direction of World War II meant that there were changes in the regime's self-presentation, dealing a final blow to the so-called *cine de cruzada* ('crusade cinema') that had celebrated the Nationalist victory in unambiguous terms since 1940.[12] An important film by Nieves Conde, *Balarrasa/Reckless*, which was released in 1951, clearly exemplifies the variations, by focusing on priests and religious people, thus eliding the military and Falangists.[13] Interpreted by the charismatic Fernando Fernán Gómez, *Balarrasa*'s protagonist finds his vocation as a missionary who sacrifices himself in the wild steppes of Alaska attempting to convert Inuit while contributing to the redemption of his own divided family.[14] A symbolic embodiment of the country, *Balarrasa*'s materialistic family represents an environment in which corruption has become endemic, as seen in the father's relinquishing of his patriarchal duties and his daughter's penchant for nights out drinking and flirting. Nieves Conde's family drama presents a disjointed and uncommitted family as an allegory for the country as a whole.[15]

The familial division among brothers to which *Balarrasa* alludes was often attributed in films to a 'father' relinquishing his authoritarian duties over his family, a reading that is historically intertwined with the regime's efforts to dissociate itself from the fascist establishment on which it had relied to access power. From the 1950s onwards, the prevalent rhetoric becomes one of 'reconciliation', even though the term was understood as the unquestioning acceptance of the winners' values and policies, including the delegitimation of the Republic. As Román Gubern puts it, this reconciliatory note was nothing but 'una llamada a la sumisión de los vencidos que persistían en luchar por la democracia, mostrando en cambio como contraste la pacífica integración ciudadana y profesional de los vencidos dóciles' (Gubern 1986: 114).[16] This particular meaning of 'reconciliation' is ubiquitous in the handful of films dealing with the struggle of the *maquis* that were produced in the 1950s. The first film representing a *maquis* who returns from France to continue the war in Spain, Ruiz-Castillo's *Dos caminos*, encapsulates the features so far outlined.[17]

The Francoist path of reconciliation was paved with the acceptance of a defeat that embraced all aspects of life for those who had not fought with the rebel army of Franco. This line is seen in *Dos caminos*, in which director Ruiz-Castillo rehearses the jingoistic style that he had used a few years before in the rabidly militant *El santuario no se rinde/The Sanctuary Does Not Surrender* (1949).[18] A filmmaker trained in the Republic, Ruiz-Castillo presents here a propaganda film that offers no avenue for negotiation with the defeated, exemplifying both the regime's attitude towards the past and its wish to cleanse that image with a view to its integration into the international community. As its title suggests, *Dos caminos*, which was released when only a few isolated fighters remained in the mountains, focuses on two Republican friends who at the end of the Civil War choose one of the two available paths: home or exile (Figure 2.1). The film was released at the time that the US signed a pact with Spain and that Spain after long negotiations signed a Concordat with the Vatican, which awarded Franco the 'Order of Christ'. Only two years later, Spain became a member of the United Nations that had urged countries to withdraw its ambassadors from what it classed as a fascist regime in 1946.[19] This eventually led

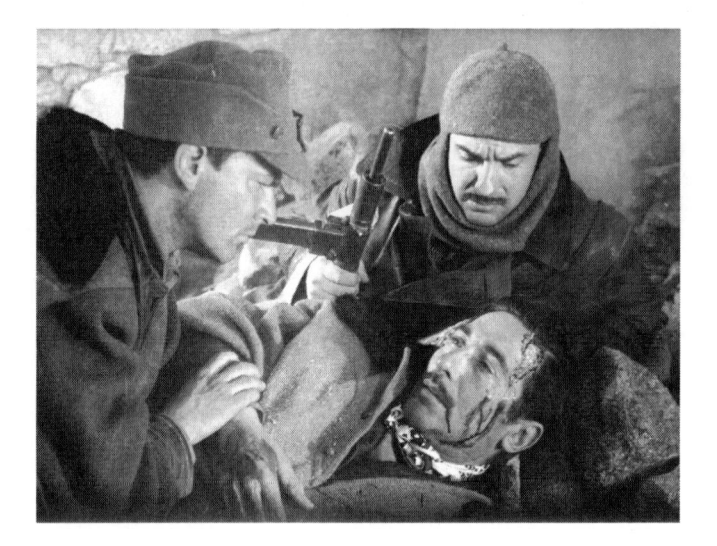

Figure 2.1 Dos caminos/Two Paths (1954). The destiny of Republicans who chose exile is death

to the full integration of Spain into the International Monetary Fund and signalled the beginning of the end of the country's autarky, which would follow the 1959 *Plan de Estabilización* ('Stabilization Plan') at the end of the decade.[20]

As with the remaining films of the period, *Dos caminos* uses a family drama to convey the dimensions of the existing socio-political conflict. The film strives to convey an image of a benevolent regime, capable of accepting those who 'never left their land', even if they had chosen the wrong side in the Civil War. By the same token, *Dos caminos* suggests that it is precisely some ignorant lower-class supporters of the regime, embodied by an illiterate black-clad old woman, who prevent the social reincorporation of those capable of embracing its tenets.

This intolerance contrasts with the image of goodness embodied by the submissive and understanding young woman, Carmen (María Luisa Abad), who supports the Republican doctor, Antonio (Ángel Picazo), in his duties, thus embodying literally the possibility of 'reconciliation'. Suitably, after Antonio successfully improvises an operation on her bigoted father, Carmen becomes his devoted wife, thereby transmitting the image of the regime's desirable norm for women. With this familial stereotype, *Dos caminos* projects the image of a country happily submissive and willingly subjected to a father figure that dominated Francoism's domestic and public politics.

Representations of women in this and other family dramas of the time carry therefore a double significance. On the one hand, they stand in for an idealized image of Catholic motherhood that is selfless, devoted, silent and obedient. On the other hand, this woman also signifies a motherland on whose body the struggle for possession of the body politic is fought. The references to this 'body' accord with the notions of physical pollution, which were so often used in public discourses of the regime, and the implicit fragility of the body politic. As Mary Douglas' classical study has demonstrated, this symbolism can give the female body and its 'boundaries' or orifices an added significance, reifying notions of possible pollution that are associated with social breaches. To quote Douglas, 'as we examine pollution beliefs we find that the kind of contacts which are thought dangerous also carry a symbolic load. This is a more interesting level at which pollution ideas relate to social life. I believe that some pollutions are used as analogies for expressing a general view of the social order' (Douglas 1989: 3).[21]

The correspondence of the body politic and female cinematic presence is corroborated in the films associated with guerrilla warfare following Ruiz-Castillo's *Dos caminos*. If only some lonely fighters continued in the mountains when *Dos caminos* was released, even fewer remained in 1956, when the next film dealing with the guerrilla war was released, Lazaga's *Torrepartida*.[22] In this film, Lazaga, a director who dedicated a good number of cinematic releases to the Civil War, firmly establishes his credentials vis-à-vis contemporary politics, femininity and social cohesion.[23] Like *Dos caminos*, *Torrepartida* rehearses the paradigm of fratricidal war that became the entrenched interpretation of the conflict from the 1950s onwards.[24] Like *Dos caminos* too, in *Torrepartida* women, in this case a girlfriend and a mother, embody and foreground the conservative traits of Spanish National Catholicism. These films also, and more importantly, stand in for and represent the regime's idea of nationhood, reified in a female body whose purity is deemed to be absolute. This corroborates the integration of bodily and social boundaries studied by Douglas, Peter Stallybrass (1986) or René Girard (1989). In fact, Girard's comment on the impossibility of mixing purity and pollution is especially relevant to the Francoist intransigence with those who were described as 'alien' or the enemy within. As Girard notes, 'As long as purity and impurity remain distinct, even the worst pollution can be washed away; but once they are allowed to mingle, purification is no longer possible' (Girard 1989: 38).

The notion of a polluting and fratricidal war, with its Biblical connotations of the Cain and Abel story, announced in Lazaga's epigraph for *Torrepartida*, is central to the film.[25] Not surprisingly, the two alternative paths are here followed by two brothers: a good one, Ramón (Javier Armet), who had fought with the rebel army of Franco, and the bad seed, the Republican Manuel (Germán Cobos). The brothers not only take opposing sides in the conflict but also fight over the same woman, significantly named after the Virgin Mary, María (Nicole Gamma).[26] In this case, masculine rivalry is focused on one woman, as well as on the country that she embodies. This masculine struggle is then perceived as part of the battle to define national identity in terms of homosocial relations. It is, moreover, a notion of 'Spanishness' that is not only clearly divided along gender lines, but also implies that masculinity is victorious over 'the rival'. The paradigm of rivalry outlined by Girard, for whom the desire of the rival stems from a wish to possess that which a subject has and not the other way round, illuminates this context:

> The rival desires the same object as the subject, and to assert the primacy of the rival can lead to only one conclusion. Rivalry does not arise because of the fortuitous convergence of two desires on a single object; rather, *the subject desires the object because the rival desires it*. In desiring an object the rival alerts the subject to the desirability of the object. The rival, then, serves as a model for the subject, not only in regard to such secondary matters as style and opinions but also, and more essentially, in regard to desires. (Girard 1989: 145; italics in the text)

In *Torrepartida*, moreover, the fraternal rivalry is punctuated by explicit references to Cain and Abel, with the added implication that 'reds' refusing to change their beliefs are 'bastard' brothers who cannot possibly be redeemed. *Torrepartida* therefore choreographs a fight between brothers witnessed by two women who project the Francoist model of femininity: the girlfriend, María, and their mother, whose goodness and modesty are emphasized whenever they appear on screen. As expected, both women are largely situated within the walls of their home, and are framed by domestic implements and furniture. The safety of this domestic sphere is guaranteed by the armed forces protecting the village from outside forces, the *maquis*. The *maquis*' territory, by contrast, is the open space, which is here presented not as an attractive space of adventure, as in western films, but as the habitat of danger. As will happen in many subsequent films, here the mountains surrounding the village are offered as a metonym for the guerrillas, adding an aura of menace and mystery whenever the camera points at them.

Along the lines thus described, the 'closed' female body has its social projection in the 'good', honest and upright society that these women represent, while the 'open' woman is associated with a corrupt society. To convey the latter, *Torrepartida* cast Manuela (Maite Pardo), whose presentation leaves no doubt as to her sexual promiscuity. She is an *enlace* or link, which, in this case, also means that she provides sexual relief, embodying the social and sexual stereotyping that dominated Francoism's ideology. Named as a representative of the 'lowly' people, Manuela is introduced when a wounded fighter, Tomás El Alicantino

(Fernando Sancho), reaches a house in the mountain and calls out her name. After Manuela asks him about the fate of the rest of the group, he falls asleep to be woken up by her kisses, which are then cut at the point of a lustful embrace that suggests their immediate sexual liaison.

By contrast, María, the woman sought by the two brothers, is always framed as an 'angel in the home', with her presentation on screen taking place as she hangs freshly washed clothes.[27] María's image of 'perfect' womanhood is complemented by that of the brothers' mother, who is cast in her elegant house, surrounded by very stylish paintings, and often appears near a hearth, whose centrality to the scene conveys the warmth of her home, and whose modest attitude is sealed with the demure scarf that protects her hair. As the brothers' rivalry progresses, María marries the 'good' son, Ramón, and soon becomes a mother herself, thus furthering the association of familial and patriotic duties by means of procreation, complying with the regime's celebration of women as maternal vessels. María's image of perfect motherhood and her association with the Virgin Mary are framed when she is seen sewing in her elegant, austere stately home beneath a sculpture of the child Jesus.

These peaceful scenes end when the space of the mountains and that of the village intermingle as the *maquis* kidnap the son of the local policeman. This leads to the final clashes and the death of the bad brother, who realizes his errors before dying at the hands of his own colleagues. In this way, *Torrepartida* expounds one-dimensional views about the regime and the anti-fascist struggle within the context of a familial arrangement that conforms with the National Catholic notions of womanhood. The film offers a peculiar compromise with no possible negotiation beyond the total acceptance of the regime's ideals by the losers, and their removal from society, which was the regime's response to the Spanish Communist Party's appeal for 'national reconciliation'.[28] Not surprisingly, Lazaga is one of the directors who has made more films about the Civil War and its aftermath, up to and including the last year of Franco's life, as will be seen in Chapter 3.

More unusual in its contemporary context is the approach taken by Margarita Alexandre and Rafael Torrecilla in a film based on the novel by Mercedes Fórmica, *La ciudad perdida* (1955 and 1951 for the novel). In this noteworthy film, a solitary man, Rafael (Fausto Tozzi), wanders into and observes a city, Madrid, during the last hours of his life, considering what he could have achieved had it not been for the causes, outbreak and consequences of the Civil War (Figure 2.2). Even though the film's ending is as conservative as the other films on the topic, *La ciudad perdida* itself is rather fragmentary and offers glimpses of a possible alternative. This is something that can be partly attributed to the censor's cuts, especially centred on the warm relationship that develops between the *maquis* and the wealthy woman that he kidnaps, María (Cosetta Greco). Alexandre, who went on to work in Cuba, reflected on the censor's intervention after the end of the dictatorship, in an interview held in 1991: 'Fíjate tú la censura. Cómo un terrorista iba a hablar de tú a una señora de ciudad. Cambiaron todo, porque no podían tolerar el acercamiento entre ellos. Nos dieron los diálogos escritos de nuevo, de tal forma que expresiones determinadas fueron sustituidas por estupideces' (Alexandre 1991: 24).[29]

Although the film's title alludes to a 'lost' city, *La ciudad perdida*, it is, in fact, the lost protagonist who arrives at and wanders into a Madrid that is inhospitable and seemingly cold. On arrival, Rafael walks past different landmarks until he reaches the front of an old and elegant building. From a distance, he stares at its windows, suggesting an

Figure 2.2   La ciudad perdida/The Lost City (1955). Rafael enters Madrid through its Puerta de Hierro, which here imprisons him through its iron bars

affectionate relationship between himself and the house. As Rafael watches the house, a dissolve takes us to a re-enactment of the past, and we see his father (Alessandro Fersen) insisting that he become a professional like him, a doctor, while his mother (Emma Barón) witnesses the scene in silence. Rafael remembers a lost past in which his life is presented as having been wasted for no apparent reason, although the book on which this film is based ends up blaming the Civil War, thereby exonerating Rafael from his crimes. Nevertheless, *La ciudad perdida* shows clearly that dissidents could not possibly be reinserted into society, even when, as in this case, they are endowed with a degree of humanity. This concurs with Franco's own view that: 'the suffering of a nation at a particular point of its history is no caprice: it is a spiritual punishment, the punishment which God imposes upon a distorted life, upon an unclean history'. For Franco, only those 'capable of loving the Fatherland, of working and struggling for it, of adding their grain of sand to the common effort' would be tolerated. The others could not be allowed back into 'social circulation'. Those others were simply classed as 'Wicked, deviant, politically and morally poisoned elements ... those without possible redemption within the human order' and of being of 'inferior national and human quality' (Qtd Richards 1998: 50).[30]

La ciudad perdida also exemplifies the regime's notion that redemption could only be reached through sacrifice and the shedding of blood, through a death that might possibly clean the sins of having defended or being otherwise involved with the Spanish Republic. Consequently, and in order not to compromise the safety of the woman he has kidnapped, María (Figure 2.3), when surrounded by the police, Rafael comes out of the old train coach where they were hiding and is shot. As María is taken away by the police, Rafael's lonely corpse on the rail tracks is the film's last shot, highlighting the cruelty of a system in which he could never find a place again.[31]

A few years after *La ciudad perdida* another adaptation of a novel dealing with the *maquis* was released, León Klimovsky's *La paz empieza nunca/Peace Never Starts* (1960), based on the Planeta Prize novel by Emilio Romero, which had been published in 1957.[32] Although Klimovsky was an Argentine filmmaker who had moved to Spain, Romero's ideas of guerrilla fighters and women shine through his production. In this film, moreover, the plurality and contradictory significance of female roles within the patriarchal 'household' are captured,

Figure 2.3   La ciudad perdida/The Lost City (1955). Rafael and María talk in a bar

as we witness the transformation of a childlike village girl, Paula (Concha Velasco), into a prostitute after she becomes involved with a Republican. Although Paula eventually becomes a police informer, she dies at the hands of a *maquis*, pinpointing the regime's notions of purity and social cleansing. Paula is seen to be indelibly tainted by being the girlfriend of a Republican soldier, even though this takes place after her right-wing lover and the film's protagonist, Juan López (Adolfo Marsillach), is publicly proclaimed dead. Nonetheless, as happens with 'bandits' who repent their past in the films studied so far, Paula cannot be effectively reincorporated into the society that the regime imposed and her death is her only possible redemption, as happens to Miguel in *Dos caminos*, Manuel in *Torrepartida* or Rafael in *La ciudad perdida*.

Although *La paz empieza nunca* shares much with the three films analysed above, in political terms Romero's propositions were meant to offer a corrective to a government which had lost its true 'fascist' leanings. Besides rejecting the possibility that the lower classes could be anything but servile,[33] Romero foregrounds the regime's rejection of its fascist underpinnings in order to court international acceptance. Those thus abandoned by the regime, according to Romero, are the 'Falangist lads', like López, who were 'fascistas puros, de verdad, integrales … la única gente que se batía por aquel entonces, que eran los muchachos falangistas' (Romero 1979: 77).[34] Romero thus felt that 'Falangist lads' had been sidelined by a government which strove from the mid-1940s onwards to dissociate itself from its fascist origins. Indeed, this proved a successful tactic, embraced by the democratic powers that saw the threat of communism to be as considerable as that of fascism. This assumption not only erased the distinctions between the many different political and unionist ideologies that came together to form the Spanish Republic, but it also separated the Spanish opposition to Francoism from contemporary resistance to fascism. As Paul Preston identifies:

> An eagerness to exonerate the Franco regime from the taint of fascism can go with a readiness to forget that, after coming to power through a civil war which claimed hundreds of thousands of lives and forced hundreds of thousands more into exile, the dictatorship executed at least a quarter of a million people, maintained concentration camps and labour batallions and sent troops to fight for Hitler on the Russian front. Under any circumstances, the confident exclusion both of prewar Spanish rightists other than the Falange and of the Franco regime from a discussion of fascism could be justified only if fascism is taken to be synonymous with Nazism at its most extreme, complete with racialist bestiality. (Preston 1990: 12)

López is not only one of the victors in the Civil War, he also singlehandedly infiltrates an important *partida* of *maquis* to destroy them (Figure 2.4), while his wife, Carmina (Kanda Jaque), procreates at a fast pace and, by the film's end, has no fewer than four children. Carmina thus contrasts with Paula, who becomes a prostitute and, in spite of her innocence and López' belated awareness of her plight, is stabbed to death in the street (Figure 2.5). At the film's end, Paula becomes the scapegoat, having been tainted through her involvement with 'reds' and thus irrecoverable for normal life. Unsubtly, then, the film shows that there is no possible room for those who were 'outside' the rank and file of the rebel army of Franco, even civilians who did not take any direct part in the struggle. Her association with the Republic makes Paula an 'internal outsider' to a fascist regime intent on cleansing. Like German and Italian fascism, Spanish

Figure 2.4 La paz empieza nunca/Peace Never Starts (1960). López (centre) infiltrates a *partida* of *maquis* in order to destroy their threat to the established order

Figure 2.5 La paz empieza nunca/Peace Never Starts (1960). Paula's corpse is held by the policemen who arrive too late to save her

National Catholicism added idiosyncratic notions of blood sacrifice and scapegoating to the fascist process of 'rebirth-through-cleansing' that Aristotle Kallis sums up as follows:

> The fascist discourse of 'rebirth-through-cleansing' united the idealization of the nation with the most aggressive notions of ethno-exclusivity, and recast 'others' as incongruous and detrimental to the national regenerative project. Those 'others', particularly internal ones ... were identified as dangerous aliens that stood in the way of national self-fulfilment. As menacing 'others' they had no place in a future ideal national community and nation-state; and as 'internal outsiders' they epitomized a visible, threatening anomaly at the heart of the community's living space, to which they did not and should not belong. Therefore, violence against them could be a legitimate expression of the nation-state's historic sovereignty over its own destiny. Fascist ideologies offered the opportunity to enact a future without 'others', dominated by the regenerated and cleansed national community in a powerful, complete, and homogeneous stage. (Kallis 2008: 312)

Innocence or repentance, the Spanish films of the era suggest, could guarantee a grave in one's homeland or even an eternal life, but a polluted past precluded social integration. In this way, these films illustrate the politics of revenge and exclusion that dominated life in Spain. These notions ran hand in hand with the segregation of those whose status as legal citizens was effectively removed by the Law of Political Responsibilities of 1940, which outlawed those who worked for the legal government of the time, the Republic, with retroactive effect to 1934, effectively removing from their posts not only those from the armed forces and politicians but also teachers and civil servants.

The four Spanish films with *maquis* as central characters corroborate Girard's dictum that '[s]acrificial violence can ... serve as an agent of purification' (Girard 1989: 40). The women and the *maquis* appearing in productions figuring the guerrilla fight show the regime's implacable resolution to uproot all dissidence, classing them as 'internal outsiders' and linking them with an 'alien' campaign against the fatherland. These 'bandits' and the women who were in any way linked to the Republic had to be purged, finding their sole redemption through death. Meanwhile, the 'Falangist lads', even when relegated from the regime's National Catholic discourse, found their solace in their 'angels in the home', designed as vessels for procreating the next breed of 'lads'. The vision that films like *La paz empieza nunca* foreground embeds the notion that the war against 'internal outsiders' had to be fought both in the field and in a domestic arena. In this private sphere, female 'purity' embodied an idealized notion of femininity, materialized in unquestionable devotion to 'the fascist lads' and to an idea of motherhood as service to the fatherland.

The two Hollywood productions which deal with the guerrilla struggle offer an interesting alternative to these notions. These two films, Sam Wood's adaptation of Ernest Hemingway's novel *For Whom the Bell Tolls* (1943) and Fred Zinnemann's *Behold a Pale Horse* (1964), exemplify some of the problems of remembering and forgetting, as well as the distortions imposed for commercial, cultural or political reasons.

The book on which Wood's film was based was published in 1940, only one year after the Civil War ended, and the narrative is set during the war. This makes its protagonists not guerrilla fighters, strictly speaking, but *huidos* (runaways) who sought to undermine the advances of the Nationalist Army. It is, furthermore, an approach to the conflict that fits within the context of an adventure film, with the protagonist, Robert Jordan (Gary Cooper), who is cast as an International Brigader, appearing very much like a cowboy. Also, as he would demonstrate before the Committee on Un-American Activities in 1947, Wood's sympathies were not on the side of the Spanish Republic. Nonetheless, the film, which was released during World War II, became 'the' view of the Spanish Civil War and its aftermath for many outside Spain for a long time, in spite of its stereotyping of bandits and Hispanics in its casting of Russian actors as guerrilla fighters.[35] The film does not contain a single political reference, which, for Gubern, makes it an example of the 'trivialization' of the conflict by removing all possible social connotations (see Gubern 1986: 105). Unlike the complexities of Hemingway's book, the cinematic version of *For Whom the Bell Tolls* is unambiguous in its presentation of the fighters as mostly ignorant and cowardly villains, ready to turn against one another when the occasion demands. Nonetheless, through the presentation of the girl, María (Ingrid Bergman), the film offers an image of the 'violated' country. In this case, however, she represents the 'raped' Republic that the corrupt guerrilla fighters cannot possibly defend.

While Wood's film deploys stereotypes that associate the Spanish resistance against the onslaught of Franco and his fascist supporters with Hollywood's vision of Mexican bandits, Fred Zinnemann's *Behold a Pale Horse* (1964) offers a sympathetic portrait of the struggle from the point of view of one *maquis* living in exile in France. The film, shot in black and white, was based on Emeric Pressburger's novel *Killing a Mouse on Sunday* (1961), while its protagonist, Manuel Artiguez (Gregory Peck), was inspired by urban guerrilla fighter Quico Sabaté. For this film, however, Zinnemann's producers had to pay a hefty price for it was banned in Spain by the Minister for Information and Tourism responsible for the censorship board, Manuel Fraga Iribarne, who also banned all releases from its producing company, Columbia Pictures, from the country, where it was only released in 1979 (Gubern 1986: 139).

Behold a Pale Horse uses an epigraph from the Book of Revelation to situate its plot. It also deploys footage from the Civil War in 1936 and a voice-over commentary that informs viewers that the whole world was then looking at Spain. It then transports the audience to the late 1950s ('twenty years later'), with the image of a boy, Pedro (Paolo Stoppa), who crosses the Spanish border in order to find a guerrilla leader called Artiguez. When the boy finds Artiguez, he asks him to revenge his tortured father by killing a policeman called Viñolas (Anthony Quinn). In the meantime, Viñolas, on finding out that Artiguez' mother is dying, prepares himself for the encounter with Artiguez. The mother seeks the mediation of a priest, Padre Francisco (Omar Sharif), to save her son, but Padre Francisco's efforts are thwarted by the boy Pedro. After a relentless pursuit, Artiguez is finally killed and placed on a bed next to his mother in the hospital. As in *Dos caminos*, the fighter, Artiguez, fulfils his desire to die in the land in which he was born, alongside his own mother, thereby associating mother and motherland.

The unlikely heroism that Jordan embodies in *For Whom the Bell Tolls* is comparable with Falangist López taking on and defeating several *maquis* in *La paz empieza nunca*. However, whereas Jordan sacrifices his life, López risks his but it is Paula who dies. Paula, who represents civilian Republicans unable to be incorporated into civil society, could thus be compared with María in *For Whom the Bell*

Tolls, who survives at the film's end. By contrast, it is the masculine rivalry presented in *Behold a Pale Horse* that can be compared to films such as *Torrepartida* and which would be echoed in José Antonio de la Loma's *Metralleta Stein/Stein Machinegun* (1975), studied in Chapter 3. Interestingly, though, the 'mother' next to whose body Artiguez is laid in *Behold a Pale Horse* disappears from the Spanish films of the 1970s. As will be seen in the next chapter, these women, like the *maquis* with whom they are associated, present a different concept of a fatherland where they remain 'internal outsiders'.

Although Wood's and Zinnemann's films are rather different in essence from the films produced at the same time in Spain, they nonetheless contain some similarities. This is evident with reference to the notion of heroism embedded by Wood's Jordan and the masculine rivalry in Zinnemann's production. Nevertheless, it could be argued that the presence of the *maquis* in these two films is circumstantial, and their fight is dispensable from the narrative, as happens with other films in which *maquis* are marginal to the plot. In both films, however, women and land are closely associated, providing an image of the country and of the fight to 'possess' it, as in *For Whom the Bell Tolls*, or return to its 'maternal' womb, as in *Behold a Pale Horse*. Absent from these films is, however, the notion of the country as a family, and the role of the father as essential to the maintenance of its internal order. This is a role that is emphasized clearly in the remaining Spanish films figuring *maquis* at the time, where the fight against the regime is accessory to the plot.

Most of the films in which the *maquis* are only marginally invoked focus on raiders and can be largely classed as detective stories or Spanish *noir*. These films also project an intimate connection between the domestic and the political domains, in line with the associations traced so far in this chapter, and are inflected by social and gender parameters. Curiously, the first two films which include veiled references to *maquis* were by the same director, Miguel Iglesias. Dealing with social misfits or common criminals, Iglesias' oblique *noir El cerco/The Siege*, released in 1955, inaugurates the handful of films in which urban *maquis* figure as low-life bandits within a plot in which their role as resistance fighters is occluded or largely irrelevant. These films are: José Rovira Beleta's *Los atracadores/The Raiders* (1962), Iglesias' *Carta a una mujer/Letter to a Woman* (1963) and Francisco Pérez-Dolz' *A tiro limpio/Clean Shooting* (1963), which was remade by

Jesús Mora in 1996. As a whole, these films decontextualize the struggle, recreating images that prevent us from associating the men with any political outlook.

By and large, these films feature social outcasts with a further dimension added to this formation: that of the 'lost' father. This is especially prominent in Rovira Beleta's *Los atracadores*, where the film explicitly indicates that the leading young man at the centre of the story, Vidal (Pierre Brice), becomes a hardened criminal because of his father.[36] As Kinder notes, these patriarchal figures are embodiments of a type of oedipal triangle which is peculiar to Spanish *noir* ('negro'), within which she classes *Los atracadores*: 'Spanish cine negro does not focus on erotic desire for the woman. It expresses its cultural specificity by operating primarily as a discourse on fathers and sons. Most of the criminals become deviant because there is something wrong with their father: either he is a dead idol impossible to equal ... or too weak ... or too strict ..., or, if he is a good father, then he inspires heroic imitation' (Kinder 1993: 60). Along those lines, the notion of masculinity foregrounded in these productions is one in which signs of humanity are potential flaws that could threaten social stability and must therefore be eradicated, like the absentee husband in *Carta a una mujer*, who is significantly devoid of offspring.

The first Spanish *noir* in which *maquis* are indirectly invoked as low-life criminals, *El cerco*, is inspired by the deeds of the legendary anarchist guerrilla fighter Josep Lluís i Facerías, who was active in Barcelona during the 1940s and 1950s. As in the remaining films to be studied in this chapter, Iglesias recreates here an atmosphere of danger and criminality, with the sole peculiarity that the raiders' base is Marseille, which was, alongside its close neighbour, Toulouse, a departing point for *maquis* entering Spain from France across the Pyrenees. The protagonist of *El cerco*, Conrado (José Guardiola), comes into Spain with the purpose of pursuing his criminal life and escaping with his booty to France, which he does until finally caught. After one of their raids goes fatally wrong, Conrado and his men flee in different directions and are besieged until the death of the last of them closes the film.

In many ways, *El cerco* rehearses the argument of Hollywood's gangster films, foregrounding egotism and division among criminals, leading to their ultimate destruction. Juan Bosch's script did not enter into conflict with contemporary censorship precisely because the film is largely presented as a police thriller in the style of contemporary detective films (Figure 2.6). Likewise, low-life robbers with only tenuous links to the guerrillas are central to the second film in which guerrilla fighters appear, Rovira Beleta's *Los atracadores*.[37] As in the previous film, it is through references to the French city of Toulouse, a centre from which *maquis* entered Spain, that a veiled relationship between these bandits and guerrilla fighters is suggested.[38] We hear in the corridors of Madrid University's Law Faculty, where one of the robbers, Vidal, studies, that 'Activistas procedentes de Toulouse' have raided a factory. The reports indicate that, while some refer to them as anarchists, others say that they are communists or simply sadists (see Sánchez Agustí 2006: 251–2).

Based on a book by Tomás Salvador, *Los atracadores* charts the lives of three young men who become criminals when they try to exact revenge for an attack on the sister of one of them. The leader of the band, Vidal, is the upper-middle-class son of a lawyer who leads a double life with his mistress. Young Vidal joins forces with two other boys: Carmelo (Julián Mateos), who is the son of a factory worker, and Ramón

Figure 2.6 El cerco/The Siege (1955). The raiders of this film *noir*, with Conrado in black in their midst, aim their guns at the camera, standing in for the workers of the factory

(Manuel Gil), a petty thief (Figure 2.7).[39] The trio start their criminal career robbing pharmacies but things go wrong when they try to raid a cinema and kill a worker. After a while on the run, they are finally caught by the police and face justice (Figure 2.8). While the leader, Vidal, dies in the street, Ramón is taken to jail to serve a long sentence and Carmelo, who had fired the criminal shot, is condemned to death. The last scene shows him on his way to being garrotted, which was the punishment inflicted on political criminals, the last of whom was Salvador Puig Antich in 1974. Although we do not see Carmelo being actually killed, the scene is quite explicit, with the camera zooming out from the point at which his head is covered with a hood, sitting on the chair about to be executed. Ferran Sánchez Agustí, who sees the film along the lines traced by Italian neorealism, remarks that:

> Con diversos cambios en la resolución final respecto al argumento de la novela anterior se reconstruyó en la realización cinematográfica

Figure 2.7 Los atracadores/The Raiders (1962). The three robbers, Carmelo, Ramón and Vidal, contemplate the murder weapon they will use in a scene with obvious religious symbolism

Figure 2.8 Los atracadores/The Raiders (1962). The two surviving raiders, Compare Cachas and Ramón, hear their fate in court

Los atracadores ... película neorrealista cuestionada en Francia y amputada en la Berlinale alemana por la crueldad de su última escena, una ejecución al garrote, fotocopia de alta resolución de la pena capital gracia de Fernando VII. Era ordinario para homicidas normales, vil para delitos infamantes y noble si se trataba de estrangular a personas de sangre azul. La diferencia ... consistía en la manera de conducir al cadalso al reo. (Sánchez Agustí 2006: 251)[40]

If *Los atracadores* puts the blame for the son's deviance squarely on the father's shoulders, the next film to include references to *maquis*, Pérez-Dolz' *A tiro limpio*, makes the social misfits the centre of a narrative which distils an unusual degree of empathy towards them.[41] The film, set in post-Civil War Barcelona, is a mixture of *noir* with traces of French Nouvelle Vague. This was Pérez-Dolz' first feature; it conveys a harsh atmosphere with political undertones which, surprisingly for the time in which the film was made, overcame the censors' hurdles. We hear in this film Castilian, French and Catalan spoken and the deeds evoke those of anarchist fighters Facerías and Quico Sabaté. The film was remade in 1996 by Jesús Mora, who set it in Santa Cruz de Tenerife.

In *A tiro limpio*, the robbers, Martín (Luis Peña) and Antoine (Joaquín Novales), arrive from Toulouse to commit 'unsettling deeds' ('acciones desestabilizadoras'). Once in Barcelona they contact their old comrade, Román Campos (José Suárez), to scale up their actions. Román Campos then requests the help of his friend, Jorge Abad, *El Picas* (Carlos Otero), who lends him machineguns as well as expertise. The four men, following Martín's plan, raid a bank in broad daylight, but their booty is not what they thought it would be. They meet again to plan further action, with Martín setting his sights on a betting office, the Patronato de Apuestas Mutuas, in Barcelona. Román and *El Picas* raid the office on a Sunday afternoon, while Martín and Antoine rob the customers of a club to distract the police. This time around, the band gets a good booty, but *El Picas* is recognized and wounded by the police in a routine inspection at the harbour. Upset because Román had assured him that *El Picas* was not in the police files, Martín strangles *El Picas*. To take revenge on his friend, Román strangles Antoine and, while the police besiege them, Martín and Román fight. Martín is killed and Román is finally shot by the police who pursue him as he tries to run away. His corpse travelling upwards on the escalator of an underground station is the film's very last scene.

A more explicit part is played by another contemporary *maquis* on the screen, who this time features in a 'romantic' plot and is cast by Iglesias in the unusual role of being the carrier of a love letter in *Carta a una mujer*. In Iglesias' *Carta a una mujer/Letter to a Woman* (1963), the fighting men provide a background of danger to a sentimental story, with few or no references to the political context surrounding the events. As in twenty-first-century films with *maquis* in secondary roles, Iglesias' is a cinematic adaptation of a literary work: in this case, a play by Jaime Salom, *El mensaje*.[42] Very much as in the earlier film adaptation studied, Alexandre and Torrecilla's *La ciudad perdida*, the protagonist of *Carta a una mujer* is an upper-class woman, Flora (Emma Penella), who is placed at the centre of a political conundrum. Iglesias' adaptation, however, deploys a *maquis* as messenger in order to highlight female vulnerability and perviousness. Flora's sense of betrayal towards a long-lost husband whose love she did not reciprocate mirrors some of the regime's ideological stance vis-à-vis its social status quo. Within this familial arrangement, women would be a model for a wider civilian society, and both were seen as inherently futile, volatile, infantile and in need of management, protection and strong, masculine leadership. Thus the film denigrates women's failure to fit into the National Catholic framework, as well as the wider society's incapacity for loyalty to its 'father'. Eventually, however, Flora falls in love with her (late) husband's memory, and decides to wait faithfully for his impossible return, abandoning her lover.

The structure of *Carta a una mujer* is also reminiscent of Alexandre and Torrecilla's film in that the relation between the *maquis* and the woman begins after he stalks her for some time. This places the camera in the position of a male voyeur, thus making the female a 'field of vision', object of a voyeuristic camera and, by implication, the audience's desire. Such a location is conveyed from the film's initial sequence, where, following the intertitle that locates the action in Barcelona in 1954, we meet Flora and the *maquis*, Germán Fernández, also known as 'El Asturias' (José Guardiola) (Figure 2.9). We first catch sight of them when we see their fragmented images refracted through a shop window where Flora realizes that she is being followed. This suggestive duplicity also projects a degree of reciprocity between both characters and the camera, rejecting the cinematic 180-degree convention of shooting two characters at such an angle to show that they are or will be related to one another

Figure 2.9 Carta a una mujer/Letter to a Woman (1963). El Asturias addresses Flora in the street

throughout the film. Through the use of the window, moreover, audience and protagonists take part in a potentially infinite game of mirrors, in which they exchange positions as viewers and objects of sight. This ambiguous and unusual presentation of the film's main characters also inflects the oblique representation of the guerrillas, which contrasts with the four contemporary productions with *maquis* as central characters described earlier on in this chapter. The climate of anxiety created by Flora's stalking continues until we see her car disappearing inside a metallic gate from the standpoint of the partly disguised voyeur, marking Flora as the audience's main point of identification.

Carta a una mujer is set in 1954 in the city that became the main focus of urban guerrilla activities at the time, Barcelona, and was released some ten years later, after this type of struggle had largely disappeared. Also gone were the two decades of economic autarky that followed the end of the Civil War until the Stabilization Plan of 1959 started to open up the country for investment and tourism. As such, Iglesias' film gives an indication of the changing position vis-à-vis Spanish exiles more than 20 years after the end of the conflict that had drawn many to abandon the country. While the film is as unforgiving towards dissidence or any form of resistance as its forerunners, it offers a glimpse of possible reconciliation between the two sides of the conflict, although this is restricted to the time when the Blue Division right-wing fighter, Carlos, and the *maquis* meet on foreign soil. In this way, this production reaffirms the notion of 'illegitimate' interests that Francoism had already attached to its opponents, as though all form of opposition was inherently alien. In other words, it corroborates the regime's defensive creation of enemies as 'outsiders', the enemy within or 'insider aliens', invoking the threat of foreign invasion to its own insularity as an effective way to rally and unite all citizens behind its banner. This was the line regularly adopted after the death penalty for political dissidents led to protests abroad, especially in neighbouring France, where many Spanish exiles lived. At these junctures, the regime sponsored demonstrations of 'mass support' in Madrid's Plaza de Oriente, where Spaniards of all classes and political outlook would render homage and pledge loyalty to the dictator. These demonstrators, who were often bussed together from their workplaces, were plastered on newspapers and flagged as the endorsement of the atavistic concept of Spanishness defined and bound by Francoism's National Catholicism. It was, moreover, a set of ideas presented as the leitmotif that united all Spaniards under the banner of a dictatorship which needed to protect its 'difference' as a cause for celebration within its borders. Interestingly, one such demonstration is staged in Romero's novel *La paz empieza nunca*, where it is pointedly used to urge the regime to forgo its attempts to pay attention to the international scene, and focus instead on its populist fascist origins.

The concept of assailed Spanishness was thus bandied about by the regime whenever there was some sign of solidarity with the repressed or any criticism of Francoism. It was this Spanishness that was insistently projected onto the cinematic screens of the time and that was firmly embodied in its female characters, as happens with the besieged Flora in *Carta a una mujer*. After Flora is followed, we learn that she lives with her partner, the conductor Augusto Briz (Luis Prendes), and both are friends of the chief constable, Comisario Ruiz (Rafael Durán), whom Flora visits to talk privately about her stalker. There, we learn the background to Flora's story, as she indicates that she knows her stalker because he worked in a factory with her husband, Carlos, who is believed to have died fighting abroad. Although we are not given any location for Carlos' whereabouts, her stalker, El Asturias, indicates that he met him in jail and refers to him as a 'divisionario' who fought during World War II in the Blue Division sent to help the Axis powers against Soviet Russia. Flora tells Ruiz that her persecutor could be seeking revenge, as he might believe her husband to be the cause of his having been sacked from his job. Ruiz shows Flora some pictures of El Asturias, indicating that he has entered the country from France, which is the sole reference in the film to his being a *maquis* returning to fight in Spain. Ruiz gives information about his background, indicating that he was arrested twice and was a criminal who had 'political positions' ('cargos políticos') before and during the Spanish Civil War and suggesting that he may belong to a *partida* of *maquis*.

Divided between guilt and love, Flora's characterization is surprisingly similar to that of other females in the handful of films released in the first decade of the twenty-first century that use the guerrillas as background romantic stories. These similarities include the deployment of women to enhance or question the existing status quo while representing a rather nebulous version of the *maquis* and their struggle.

Arguably, as will be seen in Chapter 3, this type of representation has the potential to contribute either to a humanization of their struggle or to a mystification that deletes them from the historical record. At the film's end, Flora abandons Augusto, having fallen in love with the memory of a heroic husband who had joined a voluntary force in order to remove himself from her life, while El Asturias, who had fallen in love with her on hearing her husband talking about her, is shot in the back in a tunnel. The fact that Flora chooses to live in the hope that Carlos may return, and that she will wait for him belatedly redeems her earlier volatility, showing loyalty to a dead cause that she chooses to honour and keep alive in her thoughts and life. The film's last shots overlap newspaper clips with views of Flora waiting for the impossible return of her lost husband in every ship arriving, suggesting repetition and constancy.

The complexities of the films studied in this chapter reveal that, during the 1950s and 1960s, whenever the *maquis* appear, the victory over Republicans in the Spanish Civil War is evoked to buttress the regime's legitimation as an anti-communist regime bent on its incorporation into the international arena as a paladin of law and order. Within this context, alternative social or political views are neither contemplated nor given expression, either than as sources of disorder or pollution of the body politic. More subtly than the outspoken speeches in which Francoists claimed the blood of their enemies as sources of cleansing, these are still outsiders, whose repentance does not mean social incorporation. Likewise, female characters display those notions of social purity in blatant terms, either as clean vessels to transfer the name of the father domesticated through their reproductive ability, as loyal and devoted mothers, or as tainted outcasts unfit to belong socially. They thus become, like the *maquis*, an enemy within, regardless of whether they did or did not take arms against the regime. Their mere emotional or familial association with Republicans rendered them unfit elements for the future to be constructed within the 'nation'. It is with regard to the roles of men and women within the earlier films studied here that we can elucidate the crucial role played by the Francoist patriarchal family in strengthening its social arrangements, and its association with the Nazi melodrama whose parameters now become subtly, rather than openly, invoked. The films released during the late years of the regime and the transition to democracy expand and at the same time contest those ideas in ways to be studied in my next chapter, signalling the pertinacious survival, as well as the contestation, of an inimical view of womanhood, resistance fighters and the lower classes that pervaded the society in which these cultural representations were produced and consumed.

3
From *Apertura* to Democracy (1970–1980)

Years after the last *maquis* disappeared, the attitude towards their cinematic and fictional portrayal started to undergo some transformations.[1] These changes are already noticeable in the last ten years of the Franco regime, from 1965 to 1975, which are normally grouped under the label *tardofranquismo* ('late Francoism'), and became more explicit during the first years of the Spanish transition to democracy, or *Transición*, which is the name by which the years of 1976–82 have become known. These films are clearly divided between the endorsement and contestation of the exclusive notion of Spanishness in which dissidence is classed as alien. This notion, which had been hammered home throughout the previous decades, is reflected in the way the *maquis*, women and the lower classes are represented in films, along the lines established throughout the early twentieth century, although with some significant deviations from those models. In many ways, therefore, the films produced during the 1970s stand at the crossroads not just of a significant political and social change, but also of a perception of familial life, as well as labour relations. As will be seen throughout this chapter, this meant a rapprochement with some of the secularization processes started during the Republic and recognition of the agency played by women in the construction of everyday life and the resistance to Francoism.

During the 1960s, and after 20 years in power, Franco started to face opposition from within his own ranks, and many members of the Catholic Church began to voice publicly their dissent with the regime, offering its support and infrastructure for the growing opposition. Also, a new generation with no direct memory of the Civil

War spurred on an exponential growth in clandestine opposition to the regime, with the Spanish Communist Party (PCE) becoming prominent among many groups ranging from Christian Democrats to anarchists. Intellectuals, artists and students routinely showed solidarity with the growing number of strikes in the industrial sectors, leading to the closure of the Madrid and Barcelona universities in 1967 and Valladolid's in 1973. This dramatic increase in social unrest also extended to the 'cinema of opposition', which developed in the middle of a cinematic crisis of unprecedented proportions.[2] It is within the context of the difficult industrial environment created first by television and subsequently by the advent of VHS that the six films studied in this chapter were showcased, during the last years of Franco's life and the transition to democracy, between 1970 and 1980.[3]

Altogether, the films produced during the 1970s associate cinematically and dramatically the guerrilla fighters with female characters, as happened with their predecessors. Two out of the six productions released hark back to the Manichaean view of a past of good winners and evil losers that Francoism used to legitimize itself, as explored in the previous chapter. By way of contrast, the remaining films present an overtly anti-fascist perspective, even though some were conceived at a time when the dictatorship and the censorship attached to it were still very much alive.[4]

The films produced during the last years of Francoist censorship reveal the paradoxes inherent in the screening of a monochrome Spain where the struggles of the 1940s guerrillas are associated with that of women and the working classes during the 1960s and 1970s. An analysis of the particular portrait of female and lower-class characters in these films thus becomes essential for understanding the *maquis'* struggle, as well as some dimensions of the resistance to Francoism during the last year of its existence. Productions dealing with the *maquis* reveal the intricate links between guerrillas, women and class politics, exposing the regime's efforts to project a different image of the country to both tourists and investors during its last years.

The late 1960s and 1970s were, for Spanish women, a time of stark contrasts, where they could be cast as semi-defective beings compliant with their subservient roles or as 'new women' very much in tune with the ascendance of feminism in the 1960s and 1970s. Both in real life and in cinematic representations, these women appeared either as totally subjected or submissive or as full human beings able to exercise a degree of agency beyond their sexualized personae. Consequently, women's cinematic treatment reflects the contradictions inherent in the lives of Spanish women at the time, where an exponential rise of feminism clashed with the atavistic notion of domesticity that the regime had espoused. In cinema, therefore, women could be active and sympathetic protagonists or be cast in ambiguous roles, including scenes of seduction that obliterate consent. In many ways, this could be seen to be an integral part of *tardofranquismo*'s peculiar take on the sexual liberation of the 1960s, which came to be known cinematically as *destape* ('unveiling'), and which offered naked and compliant female bodies for masculine viewing and consumption.

The films showing *maquis* in the 1970s often express these sociopolitical concepts through female characters, who become central protagonists in many of them. Whereas Pedro Lazaga's *El ladrido/The Barking* (1977) projects the Francoist equation of the *maquis* and women with bandits and whores respectively, its contemporary, Pedro Olea's *Pim, pam, pum ... ¡Fuego!/One, Two, Three, ... Fire!* (1975), announces the more nuanced approach to the resistance fighters and their supporters that would follow upon the death of the dictator. Lazaga's *El ladrido* makes use of the facile stereotyping of the lower classes that became an essential ingredient of his mainstream cinematic comedies, and which was best embodied by Paco Martínez Soria in his role of country bumpkin.[5] This type of comedy relied heavily on slapstick humour to demean urban snobbery through the exaggerated and banal casting of those migrating to the urban centres, the *paletos*.[6] By contrast, Olea's film can be firmly placed in the context of the so-called Nuevo Cine Español (New Spanish Cinema), whose inspiration came from the French Nouvelle Vague. Like Olea's, the two films that followed it, Mario Camus' *Los días del pasado/The Days of the Past* (1978) and Manuel Gutiérrez Aragón's *El corazón del bosque/The Heart of the Forest* (1979), expose the regime's subjugation of all dissidence during the 1940s. A further film, the 'frontier-western' *Metralleta Stein/Stein Machinegun* (1975), directed by José Antonio de la Loma, figures *maquis* in a context in which their socio-political outlook is very much elided along the lines of the Spanish *noir* films of the 1950s and 1960s mentioned above.

In the two films produced under the banner of the regime's standpoint during this time, Lazaga's *El ladrido* (1977) and José Antonio Nieves Conde's *Casa Manchada/Stained House* (1977), the presentation of the fighters as ruthless bandits remains intricately woven with sexism and class prejudice. In fact, these films denote the resilience of National Catholicism in buttressing social and sexual injustice. This is a perspective that runs parallel to the classification of all dissidence as immanently alien, as investigated in my previous chapter. While the films of Olea, Gutiérrez Aragón or Camus showcase an image of female courage against adversity, Lazaga's and Nieves Conde's invoke a notion of womanhood that is clearly linked to the *tardofranquista* version of National Catholicism. Interestingly, however, all the films, including those that present an anti-Francoist stance, figure women prominently as foils for the *maquis*.

From the last years of Franco's life many books, films and documentaries started to revisit Spanish history, often paying attention to a past that had not been represented until then, including the history of working-class movements and the plight of the vanquished in the Spanish Civil War both during the conflict and throughout its aftermath. There were also a good number of books and films that represented earlier historical periods, including some that had previously been either ignored or misrepresented. This was the case with the eighteenth and nineteenth centuries, which Francoism had deleted from its official history on account of their 'decadence' or class conflict, foregrounding instead the 'imperial' grandeur of Spain during the sixteenth and seventeenth centuries.[7]

Throughout this time, however, acolytes of the old regime, the so-called 'bunker', held important positions of power, including commanding roles in the police and armed forces. Their influence stretched from the political to the cultural life of the country, including famous events such as the failed coup of 1981 or the treatment accorded to Pilar Miró's film *El crimen de Cuenca/The Cuenca Crime* (1979/81), which was banned for two years on account of its portrayal of the Civil Guard's torture of a peasant in the late nineteenth century. Like Miró, many filmmakers and intellectuals of the time were fully committed to the democratization of Spain and many of them overtly displayed this through their work and in public speeches. This is clearly the case in three out of the five directors that show *maquis* in this period: Olea, Camus and Gutiérrez Aragón, as well as the actors in some of the films, especially Pepa Flores and Antonio Gades who were protagonists of Camus' film.

The vicissitudes of the time can be neatly mapped by the treatment of a film which opens and closes the decade, Nieves Conde's *Casa Manchada*. Like a film studied in the previous chapter, León Klimovsky's *La paz empieza nunca*, Nieves Conde's was based on a novel by Falangist writer Emilio Romero, entitled *Todos morían en Casa Manchada* (1969). *Casa Manchada* concentrates on the lives and violent deaths of the male heirs of three generations, which take place in the eponymous house. The sequential presentation of their demise is seen to be the result of three conflicts taking place on Spanish soil from the nineteenth century's Carlist wars (1833–40, 1846–49 and 1868–72) to the Spanish Civil War and to the *maquis*' surreptitious appearance in the film's last sequence, taking place in early 1970s Spain.[8] The survival of the unborn, posthumous heir, implied to be a boy, is ensured by the fact that the mother sets the house on fire at the end – a gesture clearly reminiscent of the Francoist ritual cleansing of all that was seen to be ill within the country. These are parameters closely aligned with those investigated in my previous chapter and which also inform Lazaga's *El ladrido*, which retraces the history of two guerrilla fighters probably inspired by the lives of Cantabrian *maquis* Juanín and Bedoya.[9]

Both *El ladrido* and *Casa Manchada* make use of what became known as *destape* or unveiling, including titillating bed scenes with partial female nudity. These erotic touches, which fit in within the climate of sexual and political *apertura* ('opening') of the late 1960s and early 1970s, reveal the unsubtle and deep-seated misogyny that dominated the dictatorship's discourse.[10] Perversely, however, the association of sexual and political freedom allowed the regime's 'aperturistas' to project an image of openness which was belied by the contemporary political environment, as well as by the subservient role of women. Instead, the 'freedom' that the display of women's bodies illustrates was firmly grounded in the regime's conception of women as chaste mothers and religious girlfriends versus wanton concubines such as left-wing activists or feminists. As in the earlier Francoist views of the *maquis*' world, the women cast by pro-Franco directors are apprehended as objects for masculine consumption, in spite of the incorporation of some 'new' traits, or of their increasing centrality to the plot's development.

A prolific director with strong links to the regime, Lazaga was well known for many popular comedies and his conservative stance vis-à-vis the political situation of Spain. Not surprisingly from the director of pro-Franco films such as *El frente infinito/The Infinite Front* (1956), *La fiel infantería/The Proud Infantry* (1959) or *Torrepartida* (1956) (discussed above), *El ladrido* sets out to stigmatize guerrilla fighters and, with them, peasants and women. The film does so through an unsophisticated association of 'banditry' with corruption and greed in the lower classes and with the sexual availability of their women.

El ladrido's plot, which contains echoes of the last days of two legendary *maquis*, Juanín and Bedoya, takes place in a remote country house where two ruthless bandits take refuge when one of them is wounded. When the runaway men, Valentín (Manuel Tejada) and Mauro (Juan Luis Galiardo), offer money to their hosts, the sight of bank notes in their rucksack awakens the greed of the wife, Ramona (Lina Canalejas), which is immediately echoed by the dreams of grandeur of her husband, Juan (Antonio Ferrandis) (Figure 3.1).[11] The presentation of the couple's corruption is completed with that of their only daughter, Luz (María Luisa San José), who, displaying

Figure 3.1 *El ladrido/The Barking* (1977). Ramona tries to convince her husband, Juan, to rob the *maquis*

80 *Film, Memory and the Legacy of the Spanish Civil War*

a striking lack of feelings, offers herself to both bandits in sequence (Figure 3.2) in scenes which could easily invoke rape were it not for the suggestion of Luz' implicit consent for the benefits to be had. The lowliness of the kidnappers is thus matched by the selfishness and greed of the *campesinos* and the debauchery of their daughter. All the action is watched silently by the grandmother, who represents the censoring eye of the audience and who will be, at the film's end, the sole survivor along with her granddaughter.

As often happens in films about the *maquis*, the mountainous landscape in which we hear the dog barking soon becomes associated with the *maquis* themselves, who shoot a guard at point-blank range as the opening credits, with the film's alternative title, 'human beasts' ('bestias humanas'), appear.[12] As one of the bandits, Valentín, is wounded, the men run away until they reach the country house in which most of the film takes place. This is the setting to which Civil Guards, after hearing the suspicions of the local priest, arrive at the film's end only to find three corpses. These 'tragic' final scenes are triggered by the ambition of the family, with the mother calling her

Figure 3.2 El ladrido/*The Barking* (1977). In a *destape* scene, Luz offers herself to the wounded *maquis*, Valentín

daughter a 'zorra' ('whore') while asking her to bed Mauro so that she and her husband may kill and rob the sick *maquis*, Valentín. While Luz entertains Mauro, her father hacks Valentín to death, and is thereafter killed by Mauro. His wife takes her turn to shoot and is also killed, while the wounded Mauro goes downstairs only to be finally killed by the guards who have rushed into the scene. While the dog that reminds audiences of the proximity of death barks, Luz takes the rucksack with the money. A shot of the grandmother is replaced with one of the barking dog, with which the film ends, leaving a scene of death with no sign of hope for the future.

The presentation of Luz' depravity is thus associated throughout *El ladrido* with her parents' greed and the ruthlessness of the bandits. All are elements which hark back to the Francoist ideas of womanhood and its stigmatization of the lower classes that resisted its advances during the Civil War, both in the urban centres and in the large landholdings of southern Spain, where the semi-feudal system of serfdom kept peasants on the edge of starvation throughout their lives. A similarly depraved view of the humanity of the lower classes is given in a film that could be said to be the first and last production of the 1970s which figures *maquis*, *Casa Manchada*, which was conceived in 1970, shot in 1974 and only released in Spain in 1980.[13] *Casa Manchada* offers a rather dated view of the era in which it was set, and one in which the fleeting appearance of guerrilla fighters merely acts as a catalyst for the events, providing a background for the film's characterization of women. In fact, the film projects the image of a 'new woman', Rosa (Paola Senatore), who is, paradoxically, perfectly cast in the Falangist mould. Rosa, an active, well-educated mother-to-be eventually supersedes both the childless blonde wife, Elvira (Carmen de la Maza), who in timely fashion dies of cancer, and the passionate dark lover, Laura (Sara Lezana), whose unexplained disappearance leaves an uncertain vacuum. The contradictions embodied by these women signal *tardofranquismo*'s projection of an image of 'modernity' bounded by its deeply conservative 'difference'. In many ways, therefore, this film conveys the paradoxes of an 'opening up' that was largely circumscribed by the fascist ideals that had inspired the coup and the dictatorship.

Casa Manchada begins ominously with a summary execution taking place in 1876 in the courtyard of the large country house of the film's title, when an elegant man, assumed to be its master, surrounded by Carlist militia, the *requetés*, is shot beside the garden's stone cross.[14] A cut transports viewers to an analogous situation, this time 1905, following a riotous mob whose shouts of 'Viva la libertad' ('Long live freedom!') and 'Viva la anarquía' ('Long live anarchy!') identify them with early twentieth-century working-class movements.[15] Another siege of the house ends with the shooting of Don Álvaro, in 1936, at the beginning of the Civil War. Next, the same man, Álvaro (Stephen Boyd), dressed as a Falangist soldier, and obviously a descendant of those executed, returns home, and the film's action starts.

Besides its complex historical setting, the film's plot is a straightforward analogy for the country as a 'stained house' whose inhabitants kill their 'masters', the last of whom is the film's protagonist. The film follows Álvaro's relationships with three women: a dutiful but sterile wife, Elvira, an attractive and enigmatic lover, Laura (Sara Lezana), and his intellectual young ward, Rosa (Paula Senator), who survives him at the film's end. While the *maquis* only appear at the film's end to catalyse the events, the three women can easily be seen as models for a motherland for the 'new Spain' that the Falange preached from the 1930s up to the end of the regime. While the subservient wife, Elvira, is disposed of with a timely disease, the attractive lover, Laura, whom Álvaro had discovered when hunting disappears without trace for no apparent reason.[16] An accessory to the plot, this dark woman becomes his lover, meeting him in the night, while his dutiful wife, Elvira, observes and suffers in silence (Figure 3.3). After Laura departs, confirming the casualness of the relationship conveyed through the film's titillating *destape* scenes to which she is central, Álvaro marries Rosa, whose education he and Elvira had financed (Figure 3.4). It is on his return from their honeymoon, in the last segment of the film, that the anti-Franco guerrilla fighters finally make a fleeting appearance when they kidnap and try to ransom him. An unsuccessful attempt to liberate him leads to his untimely death. Rosa then adds his portrait to those of his family in the house, before locking it. As she drives away, the local doctor who accompanies her urges her to stop on hearing the church bells tolling, only to see the house rapidly consumed by flames, obviously the result of Rosa's arson. Her words, and the moral that closes the story, are that her unborn son will not be added to the house's victims: 'quiero cerrar la lista de víctimas de esa casa, mi hijo no morirá en Casa Manchada'.[17]

Figure 3.3 Casa Manchada/*Stained House* (1977). Elvira, the good wife, suffers in silence

Figure 3.4 Casa Manchada/*Stained House* (1977). The 'new woman', Rosa (left), replaces the wife, Elvira, and the lover, Laura (right), in Álvaro's affections

Casa Manchada thus closes the 1970s with references to purging and to 'cleanliness' that are very much reminiscent of the ideas explored in Chapter 2. This time, however, it will not just be the dark blood of reds that can clean the country of its pollution. For the novelist Romero, the 'house' has also been stained by the 'treason' of those who had abandoned the ideals of the 'Falangist lads', for whom, as the previous chapter has shown, 'peace never begins'.

A contemporary film, *Metralleta Stein/Stein Machinegun* (1975), whose masculine rivalry echoes Zinnemann's eventful *Behold a Pale Horse*, is the last release of the Franco era. Both the genre and tone of this film are signalled by its poster, which offers a low-angle shot of the shirtless and muscular Mariano Beltrán (John Saxon) holding the weapon alluded to by the title. The credits, shown as a car approaches the screen, insist on the fact that this is all fiction: 'Esta película no está basada en hechos reales. Sus personajes son fruto de la imaginación de su autor. Cualquier semejanza entre ellos y personas vivas o desaparecidas será mera coincidencia.'[18]

From the beginning, *Metralleta Stein* stages the male rivalry in the parallel lives of a 'common criminal', Mariano, and his relentless prosecutor, the *Comisario* Emilio Mendoza (Francisco Rabal). This is done through their presentation in two very similar scenes in which both characters are central. In the first one, Mariano wakes up among fellow criminals with his partner, Ana (Blanca Estrada), whereas in the second, Mendoza does likewise with his lawful wife. We then learn that their rivalry has already taken 12 years of their lives, and we hear Mendoza talking over slides shown to his colleagues (and the audience) about the setting for this chase, which had begun in 1956, locating the film in 1968. Through the slides, we hear how Mariano enters Spain in 1956 to raid a *meublé*, the Catalan name for a high-class brothel, which alludes to one of the most famous deeds of anarchist urban guerrilla Facerías. We also learn that Mariano kills children at random and relies on peasants' fear to escape his fate, thus stigmatizing guerrilla support and making it the product of fear. Mendoza asks for one month to bring Mariano to justice, which sets the film's pace against a deadline of time running out.

Mariano's attitude is shown when, fearing to be recognized, he kills a policeman on the toilet of a train, shooting him at point-blank range and discarding his body in a tunnel (Figure 3.5). In a significant gesture that evokes a perverse inversion of domesticity, Mariano

Figure 3.5 Metralleta Stein/*Stein Machinegun* (1975). Mariano kills a policeman in the train's toilet at point-blank range

asks Ana to clean the blood splattered in the mirror; Ana dutifully obeys, and follows him into the mountains. After a tireless pursuit, Mariano is finally killed by a policeman who happens to do so by mere chance. As Mendoza contemplates the body, it is the pregnant Ana who rounds up the symmetry by killing Mendoza with the machinegun. In fact, her attitude offers an interesting rehearsal of the contradictions vis-à-vis women's role in 1970s Spain. Whereas a degree of 'opening' up had meant more freedom for the exposure and consumption of naked female bodies, reciprocity was nowhere on the horizon. A woman with more agency than her predecessors, Ana is still bound by the roles dictated to her by her man and her role as a subaltern who obeys orders. Whereas Mendoza's wife is a model rehearsed endlessly in films from the 1940s onwards, Ana is the 'new' woman who, like Rosa in the contemporary *Casa Manchada*, is able to exercise a degree of agency, although circumscribed by her patriarchal environment. Ana, in other words, embodies the contradictions of her contemporaries, who were able to access higher education in greater numbers than ever before but who were still limited by inequalities that included their inability to open bank accounts, remaining minors for longer than males (23 and 21 respectively), and being largely unable to access contraception, collect their salaries or control their finances. While Ana follows orders to clean blood or cook, she can use a machinegun, ultimately exacting revenge in the name of her unborn child.

As suggested in this book's Introduction, the different approach towards the insurgents that the other films of the era display was inaugurated by the first sympathetic presentation of a fugitive on the screen in Víctor Erice's *El espíritu de la colmena/The Spirit of the Beehive* (1973). Erice's film has become symbolic of the Spanish *posguerra*, encapsulating in its yellow light and slow pace the silence and the desolation of defeat. It is relevant in this context not only for its important place in Spanish film history but also because the oblique reference to a possible *maquis* introduces the role played by the Civil Guard in their annihilation. Equally important is the role played by the innocent civilian or bystander, in this case a child, to foreground the immanent innocence and rupture of social and familial ties that the Civil War's aftermath meant for those growing up in its shadow.

Set only one year after the end of the Civil War, in 1940, *El espíritu de la colmena* was released in 1973, two years before Franco's death. In this film, the five-year-old protagonist, Ana (Ana Torrent), smiles briefly and warmly at a nameless, quiet and lonely young man who has jumped off a train and taken refuge in a dilapidated barn. To Ana's dismay, this man is immediately killed by the Civil Guard in the night, in a scene that is remarkable for being as static and economical as it is poignant and eloquent. Focusing on the barn that Ana has left, the change of light from day to night and a few flashes indicate that he has been shot in the dark. A distressed Ana discovers this the following day in the traces of blood that signal her friend's absence, while her father is summoned to identify the corpse on account of the watch and jacket that Ana had given the soldier.

Protagonists in the pursuit of fighters in real life, Civil Guards figure prominently in other films about the struggle, including Camus' *Los días del pasado*. Traditionally posted in rural Spain, Civil Guards were instrumental in the repression of the guerrillas, as well as of those who acted as *enlaces* or as their sympathizers and relatives. Their active role, first in hunting the *maquis* in open fight and then disguising themselves as guerrilla fighters in the so-called *contrapartidas*, led to the final uprooting of the guerrillas' *partidas*. In the final stages of the fight, by posing as *maquis*, the Civil Guard ensured that those who did not denounce their presence immediately would be classed as points of support and punished accordingly.

Erice's film compresses emotionally and stylistically the long-lasting damage that the Civil War and the repression that followed it meant for those growing up at the time, highlighting the shadows and the immense sadness that they cast over Spaniards. Above all, from the time that it was first shown, the film has been taken to represent in an effective manner the overwhelming and enduring silence of the times. More importantly for the present study, it created a platform for the emotional representation of the war's effects which would be echoed in other films, including three studied in this chapter: Olea's *Pim, pam, pum ...*, Camus' *Los días del pasado* and Gutiérrez Aragón's *El corazón del bosque*. The stillness, so aptly portrayed in the film through characters, setting, photography and camera movements, affected deeply the lives of many who, like Erice and some of the directors studied in this chapter, grew up after the Civil War and whom Marsha Kinder calls the 'children of Franco'.[19] For Erice, growing up at this time was a process deeply affected by the silence and the 'absence' of parents, which carried with them indelible scars, 'something deeply mutilated':

> A veces pienso que para quienes en su infancia han vivido a fondo ese vacío que, en tantos aspectos básicos, heredamos los que nacimos inmediatamente después de una guerra civil como la nuestra, los mayores eran con frecuencia eso: un vacío, una ausencia ... hubo en ellos, para siempre, algo profundamente mutilado, que es lo que revela su ausencia. (Qtd Pena 2004: 59)[20]

Indeed, Erice's film conveys the 'absence' that the Civil War left, and which was still part and parcel of daily life in 1970s Spain, living under a regime that effectively extended the climate of revenge that inspired it throughout its duration.

A time of alternative opening and tightening of the strict censorship and repression imposed by the regime, the 1970s were still largely shrouded in fear and witnessed increasing resistance from many sections of society, including writers, filmmakers and intellectuals. In spite of its supposed 'apertura', the regime closed as it had started, shedding the blood of its opponents with the detention, torture and execution of political prisoners.[21] Within this context, the Civil War and its aftermath had immediacy for audiences 30 years after the events that it describes that would be all but lost some years later with the advent of a democratic parliament and universal suffrage.

Of especial relevance to this book is the fact that Erice's film has become the prism from which the Spanish Civil War and its aftermath have been filtered by many. This is surprising because the film neither contains one scene about the war nor explicit references to it. Nevertheless, three decades after it was released, at the onset of the twenty-first century, the film remained the most significant revision of the war and its aftermath, and was even voted by critics as one of the best productions about an event that is addressed only through the psychological scars that it left on people.[22] Jo Labanyi's summary of the film's multi-layered allusions to 'the monster', which she associates with the 'ghosts' of the past, illustrates how this film conveys the effects and experience of the war:

> As critical studies of the film ... have noted, the monster stands as an allegory of the violence of the civil war and its repressive aftermath, which Ana's parents do not want to talk about and which in 1973 the censorship did not allow Erice to tackle directly. At the end of the film, little Ana refuses the doctor's injunction to forget the horror she has indirectly witnessed ... and goes out to face the night, summoning the monster to appear to her. In so doing, Ana breaks with the traumatized silence into which she has fallen as a result of her experiences – and which marks her parents throughout the film. (Labanyi 2007: 98)

In many ways, Erice's brief inclusion of the fugitive Republican is furthered in a quasi-contemporary interpretation of the conflict's sequel, Olea's *Pim, pam, pum ... ¡Fuego!*, which was also produced and released during the years of censorship. In Olea's film, the central protagonist, Paca (Concha Velasco), meets her death after she decides to help a runaway *maquis*, Luis (José Luis Flotats), with whom she falls in love. Paca is a representative of the many post-Civil War women who could not find work to survive and she first has to accept the gifts and then the sexual advances of Julio (Fernando Fernán Gómez), a wealthy Falangist who profits from the contemporary *estraperlo* ('black market'). The film is unambiguous in its cruel portrayal of the means used by Julio to control Paca's life, which are echoed by his abuse of rationing. In this case, Julio's right-wing credentials give him access to scarce building materials, from which he benefits economically, and he is able to manipulate those in need of them. This facilitates his management of Paca's life when he unsubtly orders theatrical managers to either hire or sack Paca at his whim. Julio's eventual discovery of Luis, who has become Paca's secret lover, leads to his immediate decision to dispose of them. Forging papers that send Luis to his death, he shows Paca a newspaper clip where his death is recorded, before shooting her at point-blank range and leaving her body on the side of the road, the infamous *cunetas* where many victims were routinely dumped in the years following the Civil War.

Pim, pam, pum ...thus projects a love story that places side by side the daily struggles faced by two of the vanquished: a *maquis* and a cabaret worker. Luis' fight is echoed by Paca's efforts to survive and to support her disabled father, Ramos (José Orjas), who is said to have been a Republican. This setting emphasizes black-market corruption, and the repression that resulted from the economic deprivation of the defeated.[23] The *estraperlo*, which became endemic during the autarky, was a direct result of the economic grip that Francoism imposed on the country. It was, moreover, a powerful weapon used by those in power against the civilian population, especially deployed to further humiliate and deprive the vanquished, who were condemned to a life of outright poverty and deprivation. As Richards observes, 'Scarcity was used to control the population' and '*estraperlo*, as it was known, was popularly considered as a central part of the Francoist terror'.[24] The resulting poverty was one of the greatest silences of the Civil War's aftermath, affecting dramatically those on the losing side. To quote Richards again, during the early 1940s, the US Red Cross found 'appalling conditions of starvation and need of every kind' in Madrid, where more than 20,000 had to be fed daily and around 30–40,000 were homeless (Richards 1998: 143). Thus, Paca's father, knowing the plight his daughter faces daily, tells her that their lives have been shattered by the winners. Ramos' intentional use of the collective pronoun, 'our', associates the victimization suffered by Republicans like him, guerrilla fighters like Luis and those who took no direct part in the struggle, like his daughter Paca, who has no choice but to accept the protection afforded by Julio.

Olea's film thus contains echoes of Erice's, which also includes the use of a train, deployed to similar effect in Camus' *Los días del pasado* three years later. The setting of Olea's film and the use of popular songs to underpin its message are two features that link his production with those which preceded and followed it, making the film a veritable crossroads in the representation of *maquis* and the women related to them. Suitable for the climate that it purports to represent, *Pim, pam, pum* ... begins at sunset in a barren landscape reminiscent of that of *El espíritu de la colmena*, described in the script as 'A bare, cold and yellowish landscape of the plateau' (Azcona and Olea 1974: 1). The film opens in a train in which the protagonist travels, significantly traversing the distance between the capital city, Madrid, and the eastern town of Cuenca, whose provincial mountains were one of the guerrilla hotspots during the 1940s. The credits, which appear on the rail tracks, are immediately followed by a steam train coming into the frame, which reminds viewers of the scene in *El espíritu de la colmena* in which Teresa cycles along a desolate road to the train station to post a letter addressed to the International Red Cross. As with the famous train scene of *El espíritu de la colmena*, everyone in the frame in *Pim, pam, pum* ... appears to be sad and cold as the police move from seat to seat asking for identification papers.[25] To signal the prevalence of poverty and of a black-market economy, people are seen to throw parcels out of the train for others to collect and sell or to avoid being caught with the parcels. (The exposure of the black market is one of the film's central themes.) With the non-diegetic sound of a popular song in the background slowly increasing its volume, the camera 'enters' the train and, after tracking some silent passengers, it focuses on an old couple sitting next to one another. The music then becomes diegetic, as we see that a man, who appears to be blind, is singing one of the tunes most closely associated with the *posguerra*. This song, 'Tatuaje' ('Tattoo'), punctuates the film up to its end, when the ominous words 'muero por él' ('I die for him') become literally true. With its reference to a strange sailor's name tattooed on the singer's skin, 'Tatuaje' rightly 'embodies' the action that follows. Thus, the four lines of the song that are used as an epigraph in the script become oblique statements that foresee Paca's doom: 'Mira su nombre de extranjero/escrito aquí sobre mi piel./Si te lo encuentras, marinero,/dile que yo muero por él' (Azcona and Olea 1974).[26]

For Spanish audiences, songs like 'Tatuaje' evoke the sadness, poverty and intense sense of longing associated with the *posguerra*. However, as Manuel Vázquez Montalbán remarks, the song's allusions to lost love were also potentially subversive, and not just on account of displaying deep sadness during a time of 'victory'. Their potential for subversion is precisely what the regime saw when they prohibited Basilio Martín Patino's montage of *posguerra* songs with documentary footage in his *Canciones para después de una guerra/Songs for after a War* as late as 1971.[27] Throughout this remarkable documentary, Martín Patino superbly used these songs as non-diegetic sound to accompany selections of newsreels of the period. Oblique though it may seem, the result ignited the censors, who saw the very images that the regime had released turned against them through a juxtaposition that relied heavily on the melancholy of the melodies to sharpen their effect. Within their historical background, as Vázquez Montalbán has eloquently traced, these popular songs contained implicit and explicit signs not so much of resistance as of the desperation of a generation blighted by the relentless repression and fear that the Franco regime instilled.[28]

The climate of repression is first embodied in the film through the silence of its occupants, who are interrupted by the intrusion of two Civil Guards asking them for their 'papers'. At this point, the film's central character, Paca, who has already been singled out by the camera because of the gayness of her attire against the neutral colours in her environment, helps a young man, Luis, hiding him in the train's toilet with her. When the guards knock on the door, Paca opens it, at the same time rearranging her clothing, and boldly addresses the intruders, who go away unaware that Luis is concealed behind the door. This marks the beginning of their relationship, after Paca agrees to hide Luis until he receives papers to enable him to leave the country. This situates the film in the late 1940s, after the guerrillas received orders from the Communist Party to abandon the armed struggle in 1948.[29] The resolution followed their gradual isolation during the Cold War years as a result of which, as Luis tells Paca, guerrillas were relentlessly hunted: 'No hay nada que hacer. Nos estaban cazando como a conejos.'[30]

Pim, pam, pum ... is, then, a film inflected by the *posguerra*'s climate of hunger, fear and degradation that are obliquely invoked by the contemporary *coplas* ('popular songs') used throughout, including 'Tatuaje'.[31] The *posguerra* songs used throughout Olea's film include 'Tatuaje' as well as the popular 'Perfidia' ('Perfidy') and 'No te mires en el río' ('Don't Look at Your Reflection in the River'). These are tunes which talk about faithlessness and contain forewarnings of death, as well as images of cruelty, sadness and trepidation, and all are immediately obvious in the opening train scene.

The film also offers an unusual perspective of the time through the eyes of a woman living on the social edge who is in every scene of the film. The film's politics are more clearly shown in the scenes with Paca's seedy suitor, Julio.[32] Unknown to Paca, Julio uses his leverage to ensure that she is sacked from a singing job that she had fought hard to obtain and then pushes her into another position, again using his influence. Finally, Julio buys a flat for Paca to use on condition that she becomes his lover, an offer which someone in her position cannot possibly reject. It is in this flat, as Julio shows it to Paca, that she finally gives way to his advances, rendering the notion of consent meaningless when Paca is heard to say 'no' as Julio gropes her on the floor (Figure 3.6).[33]

Figure 3.6 Pim, pam, pum ...¡Fuego!/One, Two, Three ... Fire! (1975). Julio rapes Paca on the floor of the flat he makes available to her and her father

The film's main song, 'Tatuaje' ('Tattoo'), is heard at this point in the film, as background music in a café in which Paca sits with Luis (Figure 3.7). Paca stresses her lack of options for survival if she does not become Julio's lover, indicating that Julio had threatened to evict her and her father from the *pensión*. Ominously, however, the scene ends with the segment of 'Tatuaje' that mentions that 'él se fue una tarde, con rumbo ignorado ..., se dejó olvidado un beso de amante que yo le pedí'.[34] The film's omens are fulfilled when Luis receives the documents he believes will ensure his safe passage to France, where he will wait for Paca. It is after he departs that Julio takes Paca to a night club from which he drives at dawn to the desolate road in which he kills her after showing her a newspaper where she reads that Luis has been killed. In the film's last shot, the camera zooms out of the car to see its door opening and Paca's body thrown out, discarded and abandoned. As the car departs, Paca's lifeless and bloodied corpse remains in the frame for a few seconds before the credits announce the end of the film. We then realize the meaning of the last words of 'Tatuaje', begging a faraway sailor to listen, which corroborate that Paca 'dies for him' ('muero por él'), ambiguously meaning either for Luis or for Julio.

Figure 3.7 Pim, pam, pum ... ¡Fuego!/One, Two, Three ... Fire! (1975). Luis and Paca talk about a possible future for them in France

Throughout *Pim, pam, pum ...*, therefore, the role of Luis, the guerrilla fighter, becomes an accessory to that of the woman who befriends him, as happens in most films on the topic that follow. The struggle is seen from the perspective of the civilian population suffering directly or indirectly from a repressive regime that did not discriminate between armed or unarmed opposition to it. The same position is taken by another film on the topic that, according to Casimiro Torreiro, was produced at a crossroads that inaugurated the 'historical revision' of the experiences of the defeated, which started to take place during the last years of the regime (Torreiro 2000b: 352–3).[35]

The films about the *maquis* produced during *tardofranquismo* thus show a spectrum that encompasses the prototypical Francoist prejudices and biased vision of the guerrilla fight, which is often embodied by their female characters. These films were contemporary to (and some were part of) the movement that would become known as Nuevo Cine Español, whose practitioners were variously committed to changing the country's political repression.[36] Whereas some did it in an oblique and obscure way, having limited outreach beyond arthouse cinemas, their productions and the audience's participation were part and parcel of the myriad challenges to the establishment that also included workers' strikes and the student protests.[37] It is, therefore, significant that the two pro-regime films treating *maquis*, Nieves Conde's and Lazaga's, were produced by directors trained and consecrated during Francoism's early years. By contrast, the remaining films were directed by men who grew up in the Civil War's immediate aftermath.

Cinema witnessed and participated in the events of a time of social unrest prior to the long-awaited death of the dictator and the onset of democracy.[38] Following Franco's death, a number of new directors, such as Fernando Trueba and Pedro Almodóvar, started to transform cinema, moving the plots away from their familial referents to talk about social issues, including unemployment and drug consumption, while also showing a more overt approach to showcasing sexual relations. This is a decade represented in films such as José Luis Garci's *Asignatura pendiente/Unfinished Business* (1977), Jaime Camino's attempt to recover the past in *La vieja memoria/Old Memory* (1979) or Jaime Chávarri's incisive interpretation of the family life of Falangist poet Leopoldo Panero in *El desencanto/The Disenchantment*

(1976). As Ferran Gallego has noted, it was Garci who encapsulated the desires of spectators, eager to share their feelings of a time wasted and of a mutilated past, by creating 'una *nueva memoria personal* que se vivía en común' in his famous film, *Asignatura pendiente* (Gallego 2008: 692; italics in the text).[39] It is precisely to the remembering of this 'mutilated' individual and collective history that the anti-Francoist films of the 1970s sought to contribute.

The Spanish *Transición* was accomplished by what is often today referred to as a 'pact of oblivion' vis-à-vis the previous 40 years of history. Although exemplary as regards its peaceful process and felicitous outcome, by definition the Transition meant that there was no clean break with the previous authoritarian regime. This came at a cost, as those who had been repressed for decades were once more enjoined to keep their grievances under a blanket of silence. The compromise not to redress past injustices was consecrated in the Amnesty Law of 1977, which brought the Spanish Civil War effectively to an end.[40] It also meant the total absence of any public apology or recognition of the manifold and long-lasting injustices committed as a result of the military coup led by General Francisco Franco on 18 July 1936. Silence, however, should not be equated with conscious or unconscious oblivion but with a desire to forge a democratic and fair future for all. As Labanyi posits, it was a conscious decision not to allow the past to stall the process: 'The obsessive memorialization of the Nationalist war dead throughout the Franco dictatorship led, at the time of the transition to democracy, to a desire to break with the past; it was not, as is often argued, a determination to forget, but a decision not to let the past affect the future' (Labanyi 2007: 89).

It is also worth remembering that, in practical terms, 'silence' about the Spanish past was also due to the fact that the Francoist power structures, defended by police and armed forces trained to fight the dissidence within its own borders, remained very much intact for a good number of years. Furthermore, the judiciary, and the laws that they represented, were precisely the same that had been put in place during the 40-year dictatorship of the self-proclaimed *Generalísimo*, or Caudillo, of the country's armed forces. Thus, for pragmatic reasons that have been scrutinized in great detail by Gallego (2008), the opposition consented to an agreement designed by those who, from the rank and file of the regime, saw compromise and dialogue as the only way forward for a country in which discontent, largely fuelled by a different generation from that which had witnessed the Civil War, had been on the increase for over a decade.[41] The result, as Stephanie Golob sums up, was that both individual and collective memories were kept under wraps: 'Keeping individual memory out of the public sphere and collective memory in the "deep freeze" was widely viewed as the formula which produced the Spanish success story: reconciliation without truth, transition *without* transitional justice' (Golob 2008: 127).

As Ruti Teitel's study of transitional societies shows, the Spanish 'model' was one that provided an inspiration for other countries, especially in Latin America, during the 1980s.[42] Among the many problems faced by countries' transitional contexts, as Teitel highlights, is the issue of responsibility, both social and judicial. The debate over transitional impunity or punishment is fraught with paradoxes, including: 'Whether to punish or to amnesty? Whether punishment is a backward-looking exercise in retribution or an expression of the renewal of the rule of law? Who properly bears responsibility for past repression? To what extent is responsibility for repression appropriate to the individual, as opposed to the collective, the regime, and even the entire society[?]' (Teitel 2000: 27). Transitional countries thus vary in the way they address issues of truth and reconciliation, as the Conclusion of this book will debate.

Nevertheless, even if examples like South Africa show that it is possible for the generation that has imposed or suffered widespread injustice to revisit its recent past, this is, more often than not, undertaken by a second generation removed from direct access to the events. Publicly, therefore, the Spanish Transition, and the democracy that followed it, were largely peaceful but did not entail a revision of the past. Thus, a legitimate government chosen by the people that had been disestablished by a coup was neither vindicated nor alluded to in contemporary documents or political speeches. The Spanish Second Republic and its defenders remained 'delegitimized' according to the insidious exercise that the right wing had begun in the 1930s as a justification for military intervention and the triggering of a civil war, the causes of which were retroactively attributed to those deposed. The 'rebels' needed to legitimize their violent overthrow of the Republic, first by declaring the Republic retroactively illegal, and subsequently by associating the Franco regime with what they described as the economic 'miracle' of the 1960s, which could largely be attributed to the increase in tourist revenues and the remittances sent by the two million Spanish workers who migrated to European countries (see Gallego 2008: 23).

The monolithic and harmonious Spain that the regime sought to create was also projected as the image of 'difference' from the rest of the civilized world that was attached to the country's touristic promotion from the 1960s onwards. This was a policy that blatantly disguised the existing repression and the fate of dissidents in order to present a country happy with the regime's anachronistic social, political and religious structures and strictures. Those who inherited this legacy, the 'new' right arising from the 1970s onwards, therefore, re-presented themselves as the 'cause' of democracy through a historical revision that remains part and parcel of twenty-first-century political discourse in Spain.[43]

The first film produced during this 'transitional' era, Camus' *Los días del pasado* (1978), figures dogs barking prominently, thus echoing Lazaga's *El ladrido*, which had been released one year earlier.[44] These two films cannot, however, be more different in their approach to the memory of the Spanish guerrilla struggle. In *Los días del pasado*, Camus firmly places the audience's sympathies on the side of a woman, Juana (Pepa Flores), a schoolteacher who travels to work in an isolated northern village in order to search for her *maquis* fiancé, Antonio (Antonio Gades).[45] For a Spanish audience, the film's main actors, Flores, better known by her earlier screen name Marisol, and Gades, were an important aspect in the apprehension of the film's message (Figure 3.8). A self-taught and outspoken communist who spoke publicly against the regime during the years of the *Transición*, Gades was to make his presence felt in the artistic arena of the 'new' flamenco and the political debates of the time.[46] Also forthright in her opposition to the regime was his then-partner, Flores, a household name who had been a famous child prodigy in 1960s Spain, starring in the most successful films of the time.[47] Flores, who had divorced Carlos Goyanes, the son of her producer during her early films, became increasingly politicized throughout the early 1970s. Her trajectory exemplifies the rejection of the regime by her own generation of Spanish 'baby boomers' belonging to the rising middle classes, unhappy with the anachronistic climate of repression that dominated all aspects of political, social and cultural life in the country. The presence of these two actors in the main roles

Figure 3.8 Los días del pasado/The Days of the Past (1978). Juana and Antonio meet surreptitiously

of the film is, therefore, illustrative of the active stance that many singers, intellectuals, artists and professionals assumed at the time, when they made their opinions public and, because of their relative immunity, were expected to be outspoken embodiments of the fight for democracy.

As in *Pim, pam, pum ...*, it is from a woman's perspective, in this case Juana, that we see and attempt to understand the guerrillas' fight. As in the earlier film, a train is again central to the character's introduction, emphasizing the notion of time passing and creating an atmosphere reminiscent of *El espíritu de la colmena* both in its long silences and in the sense of introspection that goes with them, likewise heightened by the washed colours of the photography. The poetic epigraph chosen, a segment from the Bible, adds a poetic tone to this melancholic outlook on days that, in the 1970s, were as far away in time as they were close in setting, with Franco's long rule still continuing. To tell and to count merge in the Spanish sense of 'recounting' grains of sand, drops of rain or days of the past in the poetic words: 'Las arenas del mar, las gotas de lluvia, los días del pasado, ¿quién podrá contarlos?'[48] This epigraph leads to the film's credits on a white screen, at the end of which the noise of a train, first seen and heard far away and then approaching the screen, announces the beginning.[49] On the train, silent, tired, poor people seem to stare at a vacuum, as does the figure of a lonely young woman on whom the camera stops, Juana (Figure 3.9).

As in Olea's film, a song, this time the most emblematic tune of the Civil War, ¡Ay! Carmela, is heard, this time extra-diegetically.[50] Over it, a male voice-over, which the close-up of Juana indicates to be in her mind, locates its narrator as an exile in a concentration camp in Jaifa (Algeria), a destiny for many Republicans. The letter read by the voice-over begs the reader and, by implication the audience, to answer how many wars one must fight to be able to live with dignity ('¿cuántas guerras más tengo que hacer para que podamos vivir con dignidad?'). These words associate the Spanish Civil War with World War II and the 1940s guerrilla warfare, informing us that the speaker had fought consecutively the three of them. The mention of 'seven years' locates the film in 1946, a year of hope for the guerrillas, soon after the victory of the Allies. As in Olea's film, here the Civil Guard's presence on the train reminds viewers of the climate of persecution and control the population at the time were forced to endure.

Figure 3.9   Los días del pasado/The Days of the Past (1978). Juana travels on the train to take up her appointment as teacher in a remote village

The night spent on the train suggests that Juana is going to a remote location, corroborated when she gets off the train only to board a regional bus and then completes an arduous walk up a hill to reach an isolated village. The atmosphere in the village is nebulous, with the dim palette of colours reinforcing the feeling of sadness and introspection. Overall, Camus' *Los días del pasado* uses a washed-out tonality that inflects the darkness of the time, with rain accentuating the sense of grief that underscores the film.[51] Within this context, the forest, which has, for Sánchez Noriega, 'its own personality' within the film, is now first seen as a mysterious environment as Juana walks towards the village.[52]

As happens in other fiction films presenting a sympathetic view of the Spanish *maquis*, civilians, this time a young woman and a boy, are used to accentuate the innocence of the struggle and to canvass the audience's sympathy. Juana is a schoolteacher who has moved to a northern village, the coldness of which is stressed from the film's beginning when she wraps herself up before going to sleep, only to get up a few moments later to put on even more clothes.[53] Once in her classroom, presided over by the portraits of Franco and the Virgin Mary, Juana meets the boy through whom she will establish links with the fighters, Ángel (Gustavo Berges). Complicity soon develops between Juana and Ángel, after Juana helps him learn to read and write.

The *maquis* are introduced via posters pinned up in the local shop-cum-bar with the words 'Se busca' ('Wanted'), and further located as fighting 'the war' by the use of the non-diegetic tune. As Juana approaches the wall to see them closely, the tune, *¡Ay! Carmela*, locates the men as fighters from the Spanish Civil War, who are now 'wanted' criminals.[54] Juana emphasizes the legality of their struggle when she uses in her teaching references to past rebellions against Roman invaders as an oblique criticism of the regime. Associating them with the local environment, Juana explains to her pupils the local (Asturian) resistance to the invasion led by Marcus Agrippa, who had been sent by Octavius Augustus.[55] With an obvious reference to the guerrillas, Juana remarks how time, cold and hunger weakened the local 'fighting spirit' until the winners elegantly conceded that the battle had ended not so much in 'victory as with the extermination of a people'.[56] Along those lines, Juana hears the actual guerrillas with whom she is seeking to establish contact described as the 'men up there' ('los hombres de arriba') who are 'still waging war' ('los que todavía hacen la guerra').

That the *maquis* are fighting a legitimate war is suggested the first time that they are introduced to the audience. We see an anonymous group preparing some dynamite and, in one of the handful of scenes in which Juana is not present in the film, we learn about the reasons for their fight. One of them, Pepe (Antonio Iranzo), comments, as Luis does to Paca in *Pim, pam, pum* ..., that they will be killed 'like rabbits'. The argument is settled when Antonio affirms that they simply are there ('estamos') so that others would realize that the fight is still ongoing and contribute to the struggle: 'Vendrán los que están fuera y daremos la cara. Pero ahora somos muy pocos ... Me conformo con que los de abajo sepan que estamos aquí. Que no nos hemos rendido. Que la guerra va a durar mucho más tiempo del que nosotros duremos.'[57]

Following a shootout with Civil Guards that results in one fighter dead, Juana is called to the guards' barracks for questioning about a letter that she has received in which Antonio says that he will try to see her on her birthday. Ominously, the guard asks Juana for her papers, paying attention to her date of birth (given in camera close-up), so that when Juana travels to a house on the coast to meet Antonio we foresee that she will be followed. After Antonio refuses to give up the fight, he is ambushed with his colleagues on the way out of the village and some of them are killed.

Juana arrives back at the school to find that she has been replaced by a teacher from the Sección Femenina of the fascist party (Falange), who talks to the children about the Reyes Católicos, Isabel and Fernando, the Inquisition and the importance of Spain's unity and past imperial glories. The teacher asks the children to chant the words: 'unidad religiosa y política de España'.[58] Accepting the situation, Juana tells Ángel that she will leave the village, and a scene with the film's epilogue completes the narrative in a different setting. The northern rain gives way to a bright sunny environment following a white dissolve, and we see Juana wearing pale green and white and teaching in a different school, with children also dressed in light colours. The children repeat Juana's teachings about Spanish geography, speaking with Andalusian accents, while Juana looks out of the window at a dazzling but pale bright sun, which underscores the sombre mood of the scene. A close-up of her sad face is followed by a cut and a shot of an autumnal forest, suggested as part of her imagination. The sounds of guns and dogs barking are backgrounded once more by the non-diegetic music of ¡Ay! Carmela with which the film closes as it started. The howling, signifying death, stands both for the demise of the guerrilla struggle and for the lifeless environment created during the Civil War's aftermath.[59]

Los días del pasado thus legitimizes the guerrilla struggle, which is seen from the perspective of someone sympathetic to it but not directly involved in it. This is the view that pervades most of the films released after Franco's death, most of which have little to say about the tactics or political outlook of the guerrillas themselves. Along these lines, Camus' film ends on an ambiguous note, with Juana departing and remembering the men and the past that she has left behind.

The end of the guerrillas, this time signalled by the presence of a bird of prey, and the role played by the Spanish Communist Party in its demobilization are central to the next film on the topic, Gutiérrez Aragón's *El corazón del bosque/The Heart of the Forest* (1979). The main protagonist of this film, Juan (Norman Brisky), is a card-carrying communist who comes back from France in search of the last *maquis*, known as 'El Andarín' ('The Walker') (Luis Politti), with orders to urge him to abandon the fight or to kill him. Although Juan's search for El Andarín punctuates the action, his sister, Amparo (Ángela Molina), becomes the link between the film's main characters: Juan, El Andarín and her husband, Suso (Víctor Valverde). The film's action is choreographed among mountains and forests which further aspects of the plot with the characters often shown veiled by the thick fog that dominates the photography and that often makes them indistinguishable, while adding an aura of mystery to the film's symbolism.

A sense of obscurity is an apt metaphor for Gutiérrez Aragón's individual vision of the guerrilla fight and of the mystery surrounding it for those who, like him, grew up in its shadow. In fact, the script's main drivers were the childhood memories of the guerrilla struggle that the producer, Luis Megino, who co-wrote the script with the director, shared with Gutiérrez Aragón. These memories remove the guerrilla fighters from their particular historical period to render them, in their minds, as timeless and legendary figures: 'el punto de partida del guión escrito con el productor Luis Megino fue su recuerdo infantil de esas figuras de la resistencia anti-franquista que, temidas, admiradas y magnificadas por las gentes montañesas, quedaban impresas en la mente de un niño como héroes no de una acción guerrillera contemporánea, sino de una gesta inmemorial' (Qtd Molina Foix 2003: 68).[60]

Although some scenes in *El corazón del bosque* appear wilfully dislocated in terms of time and space, the action is grounded in actual historical events surrounding the end of the post-Civil War guerrilla struggle. This followed the ruthless and effective use of Civil Guards disguised as *contrapartidas*, the indiscriminate repression of relatives and supporters, and the decision of the guerrillas' main organizer, the Spanish Communist Party, to call the armed struggle off in 1948. In the film, an envoy of the Communist Party, Juan, is sent from his exile in France with orders to kill El Andarín if he does not agree to give up the fight, as he will be treated as a 'traitor'. As Vicente Molina Foix observes, in this film the enemy is now not so much the regime as the Communist Party: 'Gutiérrez Aragón remarca el carácter mítico [mythical character] de un maquis ya abandonado por la Historia' because now 'el enemigo no es la fuerza de represión franquista sino un Partido Comunista para quienes los guerrilleros ya no son de utilidad' (Molina Foix 2003: 68).[61]

In its relentless search, which occupies the greatest portion of the film, *El corazón del bosque* recalls the book which it honours in its title, Joseph Conrad's *Heart of Darkness* (1902), whose plot is also centred on a manhunt and a final murder. In Gutiérrez Aragón's film, the solitary *maquis* who has become mythical for the locals remains in the mountains in spite of his party's resolution. Although this motif could suggest a film about a desperate fight, the film only addresses its topic obliquely, concentrating instead on the maze of semi-incestuous relationships among the four main characters, all set against the misty and mysterious environment that surrounds them.

From start to finish, the film is punctuated by the flight of birds of prey shot against a foggy landscape (Figure 3.10). Their sounds are heard during the opening credits, which appear in red against a black screen, suggestive of the darkness of the time and the blood and passion that we are going to witness.[62] Through this rainy and autumnal scenery we are given an image of a guerrilla clouded in mist, mystery and mystique. The intertitle informs us that we are in 1942 when, during a village *romería* ('fair'), a *maquis* appears, as he has been

Figure 3.10 El corazón del bosque/The Heart of the Forest (1979). Birds of prey flying over a misty landscape punctuate the action

doing year after year in defiance of the Civil Guard. After he dances with a few women, including his girlfriend, the man disappears uphill into the fog that envelops him, while a black dissolve transports us to a different time, ten years later. The intertitle now informs us that in 1952 El Andarín, the man whom we assume we met in the first scene, is the last man fighting fascism from the mountains. The scene is set for the hunt for this last man in what becomes, rather than a representation of the guerrillas' desperate fight, more a vision of their memorialization as part of the mountainous environment in which they lived and died.

The same nebulous treatment that surrounds the life and deeds of El Andarín also encapsulates others, including the Civil Guard's *contrapartidas*, who, on one occasion, appear clad in old women's black clothes. When they are discovered, they start running, creating a surreal image that evokes priests hunting. As 'the hunt' was immediately related to Franco's favourite pastime during his rule, these images bring home in an uncanny manner the association of the Church with the military during his uprising and dictatorship. The fact that both Juan and El Andarín are, in different sequences, seen in parallel montage running either from the guards or from one another also confuses pursuers and pursued, corroborating the film's coda about the implicit treachery embedded in the human condition.

Overall, *El corazón del bosque* projects an atmosphere that is dreamlike and uncertain, and in which the public and the domestic dimensions of the guerrilla struggle become embedded in the incestuous subtext that underlines the relationship between Amparo, Juan and El Andarín. Pessimistically, the film evokes a sense of failure and meaninglessness that is as personal as it is familial, emotional and political.[63] This is clearly conveyed by the film's end, when El Andarín's corpse disappears behind the mountainous fog, suggesting that he has become part of a landscape of which the *maquis*' memories were already a part. This is an elliptic perspective on the plight of those who remained in the mountains who, as Molina Foix observes, appear to be 'chimerical and arbitrary forces' guided by 'the spirit of the forest' and not by 'political reason' (Molina Foix 2003: 68).

The last treason that we witness is that of Amparo's husband, Suso, who gives the location of the wounded Juan away. According to the director, this gesture of self-protection and denunciation is not only based on historical fact but also furthers the merger between the political and familial in this peculiar representation of the struggle's layers. This is especially the case when we learn from the final intertitle that Amparo abandons her husband to live with her brother once he comes out of jail. The last filmic image, the bird of prey that frames the film flying below an overcast sky, furthers the dim outlook that we have been given so far, transmitting again the pervasiveness of human betrayal.[64] In this way, the film can be seen to represent not just the transition between hope and despair of the *maquis* between 1942 and 1952, but the *desencanto* ('disenchantment') that followed the long-awaited *Transición* to democracy in Spain.

The final question that Juan poses when El Andarín accuses him of treachery – 'Is there anybody who isn't a traitor?' – provides the film's epigraph, as well as a suitable epitaph for El Andarín, who answers in unambiguous terms: 'nobody' ('nadie'). The film thus questions the blurred line between treason and heroism, as Molina Foix observes (Molina Foix 2003: 71). It also projects a rather critical outlook on the last years of the guerrillas' struggle against fascism and the role of the Communist Party in calling the struggle off. In this context, Amparo's presence is the link between the men in the film, and she is central to keeping El Andarín alive, through the milk and bread that she leaves out for him, which suggests a relationship of mothering. In this context, the enigmatic intertitle at the end, suggesting that she abandons her traitorous husband in order to live with her murderous brother Juan, acquires political overtones with a clear referent in the political situation of the *Transición*. Standing in for the body politic, Amparo is both at the centre of the new social grouping and outside it, marked by a relationship that is considered illegitimate, blurring the lines between sibling and marital love. The Spanish Communist Party that ordered the murder of the last fighter of the Civil War is thus a winner of sorts in a victory that means relinquishing their beliefs. Its former member, the plague-ridden El Andarín, is forgotten after his death, while Amparo's former husband is simply abandoned to a fate unknown to the audience.

It becomes, therefore, significant in this context to note that the film was conceived, produced and released during the years in which the Spanish political parties were meeting with those in power to discuss, among other things, political and social liberties, as well as an amnesty for political prisoners. Negotiations were mostly held between members of the government of Adolfo Suárez and the then-outlawed left-wing parties, some of which had formed the *Junta Democrática*, under the auspices of the Socialist Party, PSOE, and the then important Communist Party, PCE. These talks eventually led to their legalization and the Amnesty Law of 1977, whereby political prisoners were released and prosecution for all the possible crimes related to the Civil War and its aftermath was foreclosed.[65] Whereas this was clearly a pragmatic measure to enable the country to move forward, for many of those who had suffered and were still suffering the regime's repression directly, this pact was seen as 'treason', especially as it was led by the PCE, the major political force in the clandestine 1970s. Altogether, therefore, Gutiérrez Aragón's film participates in the climate of 'desencanto' that followed the advent of democracy, both for its shortcomings and for its failure to address issues of restorative justice, which would return to haunt the country 20 years later.

Whereas all the films that present *maquis* in their plots from 1970 until 1980 read the past in the light of their present historical juncture, they do so from different perspectives. These range from the hardships faced by 'red' women, such as Paca, Juana or María in *Pim, pam, pum ...* , *Los días del pasado* or *Luna de lobos,* to the sexual and filmic abuse suffered by Luz in *El ladrido*. Likewise, the portraits of *maquis* extend from the dignified, humane projection of Luis' or Juan's impotence in *Pim, pam, pum ...* and *Huidos*, to the anonymous brutality of the 'bandits' in *Casa Manchada*. By and large, however, this time opened the door for a different representation of *maquis* and *enlaces*, foregrounding the plight of civilians who, thereafter, would be considered part and parcel of the fight.

While showing a degree of continuity with what had gone on before, most of the films studied in this chapter also demonstrate a marked departure from the model of the family as an image of the country exploited before. These films bridge the gap between the earlier Francoist melodramas and the films and documentaries on the subject produced following the 'memory boom' that started towards the end of the twentieth century. Although the film industry remained in crisis throughout much of this time, collaborations with national and regional television gave way to a number of films and documentaries, many of which revisited the Spanish past from different perspectives. The question that haunts these films, and the time in which they were produced, is the extent to which it was possible and desirable to revise the memories of those silenced during the regime's 40-year repression to become 'living memories'.

This chapter has shown how the films in which *maquis* appear during the 1970s, either as central or as marginal characters, appeal to a sense of living history or, to use the contemporary Spanish usage, 'historical memory', which is intrinsically related as much to a sense of closure after a social trauma as to the judicial and moral restoration of Francoism's victims. The dimensions of this concept were visibly delineated in David Trueba's cinematic adaptation of Javier Cercas' acclaimed book *Soldados de Salamina/Soldiers of Salamis* (2003 and 2001 respectively). Appealing to the immediacy of a recent past that had become alien to many, this film and book resurrect some of the 'ghosts' of the Spanish twentieth century. As Trueba indicates, the protagonist of the story first thinks about the Civil War as part of Spain's remote history, but the subsequent investigation leads him (or, in the case of the film, her) to consider it to be intrinsic to the present:

> [A]t the beginning, Cercas thinks, like the majority of people of our generation [born in the 1960s] that the Civil War is something

that belongs in the past, as distant and alien as, say, the Battle of Salamis, something that does not affect us ... But at the end of the novel, the protagonist ends up discovering that the Civil War is our present; that it is the beginning of the present, something which affects him directly and that is alive; something which, like it or not, has conditioned the lives of just about everybody in this country, including his own. (Cercas and Trueba 2003: 27)

Trueba's words are a suitable epilogue for a chapter that shows the immediacy of the Civil War, and the use of its distorted memory during the *Transición*. The films and documentaries released after this date stand at different crossroads, for they already have to contend with the fact that the *Transición* effectively sealed the past legally and, to some extent, morally too. In this way, it consecrated the divisions that the Civil War had created, and these would resurface in cultural and political discourses before the end of the century.

4
Democratic *Maquis* (1987–2010)

After a failed coup in February 1981 and the victory of the Socialist Party (PSOE) in the parliamentary elections of 1982, the forces involved in the consolidation of democracy in Spain concentrated their efforts on a future of 'progress' and European integration. This period, from the time of the *Transición* until the mid-1990s, has come to be identified as one of 'oblivion' or 'amnesia' vis-à-vis a past that was seldom invoked in political discourse. The cultural production of the time participated in that trend, prominently expressed by music, where the 'protest song' of the 1960s and 1970s gave way to an upsurge of local pop and rock groups, many modelling themselves on New York and London mods and punks. While books on the time continued to appear, there were fewer films made about the Civil War or the 1940s guerrillas up to the defeat of the Socialist Party in 1996, when the victory of the right-wing Popular Party witnessed the onset of the 'memory boom'.

The fact that there were only two films on *maquis* released during the years that the Socialist Party ruled Spain (1982–96) is, therefore, highly significant, as this was a time largely devoted to consolidating the country's democracy, forestalling the efforts of right-wing extremists and terrorist groups to wreck the process, and integrating Spain into Europe.[1] Within this context, not to revisit the past was a price many were willing to pay, even though this left unresolved issues of justice and human rights violations that would start to resurface from the fin-de-siècle. Unsurprisingly, the two films produced during this time had limited success, although they depart significantly from the Manichaean representations inspired by the regime's division of winners and losers, while refraining from idealizing the fight. The first, Julio Sánchez Valdés' *Luna de lobos/Wolves' Moon* (1987) is based on the novel of the same title written by Julio Llamazares (1985), who also co-wrote the script. This film, and the book on which it is based, present in unambiguous terms the paranoia and sheer despair that accompanied the dwindling numbers of guerrilla fighters after their abandonment, first by international forces, and, subsequently, by its main organizer, the Communist Party of Spain. Also unusual in this context is the second film of the time, Sancho Gracia's *Huidos/ Runaways* (1993), which, like *Luna de lobos*, focuses on the fighting men who ran to the mountains during the Civil War, stressing their solitude and the contradictions that they faced. Interestingly, neither of these two films figures fighters returning from exile to fight in Spain, as did so many of their predecessors, although *Luna de lobos* contains specific references to them. By contrast, three out of the four films on *maquis* released from the mid-1990s onwards – Antoni Ribas' *Terra de canons/ Cannon Land* (1999), Montxo Armendáriz' *Silencio roto/Broken Silence* (2001) and Guillermo del Toro's *El laberinto del fauno/Pan's Labyrinth* (2006) – focus on the plight of women. The same applies to the three films featuring *maquis* as background for a (mostly romantic) plot, José Luis Garci's *You Are the One (Una historia de entonces)/You Are the One (A Story of the Past)* (2000), Gonzalo Suárez' *El portero/The Goalkeeper* (2000) and Jaime Chávarri's *El año del diluvio/The Year of the Deluge* (2004). Thus, only the last film of the first decade of the twenty-first century, Lluís Galter's biopic of Ramón Vila Capdevila, *Caracremada/ Burnface* (2010), focuses on a *maquis*, although there is no fighting represented throughout the narrative.

Unlike *Luna de lobos* and *Huidos*, three fiction films that follow upon the 'memory boom' – Antoni Ribas' *Terra de canons* (1999), Montxo Armendáriz' *Silencio roto* (2001) and Guillermo del Toro's *El laberinto del fauno* (2006) – showcase explicit references to the international context within which the Spanish guerrillas operated. As this chapter will show, this is one of the aspects that contextualizes these three films firmly within a time in which, paradoxically, Spain 'recovered' its links with a Republican past which remained unacknowledged in political and judicial discourses. Willingly or unwillingly, this political position effectively situates the representation of the Spanish Civil War in these films at the crossroads of being a 'national' or an 'international' conflict.

In many ways, the films produced in democratic Spain embed a sense of historical proximity, as well as political distance from the events thus memorialized, constituting a dialogical process that has been grouped under the term 'historical memory'. The apparent contradiction between closeness and distance reveals the conflicting process of remembrance versus oblivion that inheres in twenty-first-century Spanish debates about its 'historical memory'. The rapprochement with an earlier historical period of which only a dwindling number of people have immediate experience links the present with the past, reifying a continuity that had been severed during Francoism. This continuity is coherently expressed by the term 'memory', though ambiguously or tautologically termed as 'historical memory', signalling the temporal gap that separates the events from their remembrance. While establishing familial and political links with the past, the recovery of this 'historical memory' is a process undertaken by a generation removed from any direct contact with the events thus memorialized.

The first film of this time, *Luna de lobos*, is set in the mountainous landscape where writer Llamazares was born, in the north of León, bordering Asturias and Cantabria. *Luna de lobos* charts the decadence of a small group of left-wing *huidos*, who become *maquis* when they realize that there is no going back for them. Both book and film follow the lives of these men from the time that their area is taken by the Nationalist Army, in 1937, until the main protagonist, Ángel (Santiago Ramos), who is the last surviving member of the group, leaves in a train, hoping to reach a safe destination. The numbers of these *maquis* diminish as the narrative progresses, with their fight being first met with ruthlessness and subsequently rendered so meaningless as to make the men a burden on their friends and relatives. This diminishing group of *maquis* survive like the wolves of the title, risking the lives and livelihood of those who support them. Compared repeatedly to wolves and referred to as being already 'dead', they are also impotent to help their family and friends, who suffer directly as a result of the fight, with constant questioning and torture, accompanied by economic deprivation and solitude (Figure 4.1).

A familial context provides the frame of *Luna de lobos*, which grounds the fight in events taking place during the Civil War, extending them into its aftermath as a direct consequence of the repression unleashed in the areas taken by the rebels. Initially, with the war still being

Figure 4.1 Luna de lobos/Wolves' Moon (1987). Civil Guards arrive to harass the relatives of the men in the mountains

fought throughout the rest of Spain, Ángel visits his father and realizes that he had previously been arrested and taken in for questioning. In spite of this, the father gives him money and asks him not to hand themselves in, as they would be killed 'by the roadside' ('en la cuneta'), like others who had been 'at the front', meaning the Republican lines. Presciently, Ángel indicates that it is as though they were already dead ('es cómo si estuviéramos muertos'), a claim that is subsequently reinforced throughout the remaining sections of the film.

The repression of the fighters is again centred on their familial background in the next time recorded, 1940, when the victim is Ángel's sister, Juana (Cristina Collado), who has been taken away to be tortured. In this way, the desperate plight of the men is evenly matched throughout the film with the no-less-hopeless predicament of those related to them, for whom hardship and torture become part of everyday life. This can be seen not only in the treatment accorded to Ángel's family. Exemplifying the struggle faced by many who did not take up arms and could not easily be classed as 'winners' or 'losers' of the Civil War is Ángel's girlfriend, María (Kiti Manver), whose plight shows how the Francoist repression lumped together fighters and civilians who were somehow caught in the struggle in the category of 'losers'. People like María thus became part of the 'defeated', following a classification that embraced many whose lives were simply framed by their social, geographical or familial relationships to the struggle. Initially, María helps the men with food and accompanies her boyfriend before becoming the mistress of a local Civil Guard, Sargento Argüello (Fernando Vivanco). By the third timeframe of the film, however, in 1943, María spells out what the struggle in the mountains meant for those like her, who see in the men's death their own release.

The key moments of the Nationalist usurpation, repression and subsequent consolidation of the regime at the end of World War II are traced in *Luna de lobos* through the four segments of the narrative: 1937, 1940, 1943 and 1946, which are indicated on intertitles. At the film's end, in 1946, the sole survivor, Ángel, decides to leave and, hiding his mutilated arm, catches a train. This is where the film ends, ambiguously occluding his destiny from the audience.

The remaining films of the era are equally explicit in their temporal location in the 1940s, with only one, del Toro's *El laberinto del fauno*, taking place in a single year, 1944. The next film on the topic after *Luna de lobos*, Sancho Gracia's *Huidos* (1993), is set initially during the Civil War, stretching to the end of World War II (1944–45) and with an epilogue located in 1952, as the only surviving *huido*, Juan (played by the director, Sancho Gracia), is released from Franco's prison.

Huidos offers another dignified view of the *maquis*, and one based on a real story, which, like *Luna de lobos*, illustrates the solitude of the fighters. Like its predecessor too, this next 'democratic' film shows the repression and ultimate defeat of those left in the mountains, as well as the plight of those who were neither fighters nor winners or losers of the Civil War but were made to suffer through their (willing or unwilling) association with them (Figure 4.2). The title, *Huidos*, signals the fact that the film concentrates on those forced to flee as Franco's army conquered Spain, and not on those choosing to resume the struggle after fighting fascism in Europe. As with the remaining films on the topic, however, women's roles are quite eloquent in this film, including the fate of a little girl, symbol of hope, who dies in her father's arms. She is the innocent victim of the shootout that ensues when her father, Marcial (Fernando Valverde), attempts to rescue her from the religious institution to which she had been taken with her mother and in which the latter had died after being raped by the *señorito* ('landlord') before her daughter's eyes.

Figure 4.2 Huidos/Runaways (1993). Of the men at the beginning of the film, only Juan survives, after spending time in jail

In spite of the sadness and anger that these events represent, the film offers a dim glimmer of optimism at the end, with one couple reuniting in 1952, after the main protagonist, Juan, spends five years in jail. Although all his companions have died, for Juan their defeat is a victory of sorts, as he indicates that 'we will win even if we lose' ('ganaremos aunque perdamos'). Such a perspective is obviously inspired by the hindsight provided by the film's production taking place after nearly two democratic decades. Juan further qualifies this statement when he presciently announces the fin-de-siecle 'memory boom': 'no creo que para conquistar el futuro haya que olvidar el pasado',[2] which for him means that he will never forget the fight and destiny of his colleagues.

A similar timeframe is taken by the film that closes the twentieth century, Antoni Ribas' *Terra de canons*, scheduled to be released in 1994 but only completed in 1998. Ribas' film is particularly relevant to the Catalan struggle, and he frames his film from the struggles in Civil War Tarragona to Franco's visit to Barcelona on account of the celebration of the Eucharistic Congress in 1952. *Terra de canons*, which is dedicated to the *maquis'* struggle, follows the life of a civilian associated with them, Contxita (Cristina Pineda), from the Civil War, when she falls in love with anarchist fighter Lluís (Mario Guariso), who disappears from her life unaware that he has fathered a daughter, Flora. The film next moves to 1943, when Contxita marries a local landowner, Eduard de Sicart (Lorenzo Quinn), whose father, Señor de Sicart (Anthony Quinn), is well known as a Catalan nationalist. Eduard adopts Contxita's daughter. Unbeknown to Contxita, Eduard is aiding the *maquis*, one of whom is her former lover, Lluís, who plan to assassinate the dictator on the occasion of his visit to Barcelona's Eucharistic Congress. At the film's end, however, Contxita witnesses the cold-blooded murder first of Llúis and then of her husband, remaining alone to bring up her daughter, who marries in the film's epilogue, set in 1964.

Like many of the films studied thus far, Ribas' *Terra de canons* associates a woman with the land, attributing to Contxita a sense of continuity but distancing her from the on-going fight to which he dedicates his film.[3] Interestingly, however, to be able to shoot *Terra de canons*, Ribas confronted the Catalan government ('Generalitat') that denied him sponsorship, staging a three-month sit-in in the square where the autonomous government is located, Plaza Sant Jaume. Eventually, and with help from Anthony Quinn, the film was shot and released a few years later, closing the fictional productions on *maquis* of the twentieth century.

The production that inaugurates the twenty-first century, Armendáriz' *Silencio roto*, charts the rise and demise of the guerrilla movement, although tracing a shorter period, 1944 to 1948, which makes the film travel between hope and despair. The main protagonist of this film, Lucía (Lucía Jiménez), is closely associated with the *maquis* and suffers directly the effects of a repression that is presented as a clash of freedom versus oppression. Lucía, the character from whose perspective we view all events in the film, soon becomes a point of support for the fighters in the mountains.

Armendáriz represents the repression of the *maquis* during the 1940s through the conflicts of a woman who supports them, Lucía, who shares the role of *enlace* with a boy, Juan (Andoni Erburu), and a teacher, Don Octavio (Álvaro de Luna). Armendáriz thus reconstructs the history of anti-Francoist resistance through the memories of the civilians supporting them.[4] Through these characters, Armendáriz portrays the *maquis'* guerrilla war against Franco's regime as an integral part of the struggle against fascism taking place in the rest of the world. The resistance is also represented as a direct continuation of the Spanish Civil War, as Teresa (Mercedes Sampietro) indicates: 'Hay guerras y guerras ... Y algunas, como ésta, no terminan nunca' (Armendáriz 2001: 24).[5] The assumption that the first decade of the *posguerra* could be integrated into the *guerra* is not restricted to this film, as the regime extended the Civil War's outcome and the division of the country between winners and losers right until its very end.[6]

The time span covered in the film is indicated by means of intertitles, placing the dates on the same frame of a mountain, following two black dissolves. These temporal transitions are emphasized by seasonal changes that are highly significant to the film's narrative. The transition between the three segments of *Silencio roto* effectively traces the position of the *maquis* and the regime at different times of the struggle, from the increasing hope of 1944 to the utter despondency of 1948, the year that the film ends. The two dissolves that embed the film's chronological shifts become ominous, even though they take place over two embraces, the first between Lucía and her aunt, Teresa, and the second between Lucía and her boyfriend, Manuel (Juan Diego Botto). For Armendáriz, the embraces indicate the end of a particular time, marked initially by women's solidarity in suffering and, thereafter, by Lucía urging Manuel to take care of himself. Both black dissolves designate that these moments, as Armendáriz remarks, are loaded with 'presagios atemorizadores' ('threatening omens'):

> El cierre a negro tiene, para mí, el sentido de expresar que ese tiempo llega a su fin. La primera fase es la del otoño, que acaba cuando Teresa abraza a Lucía y le dice: 'Siempre nos toca sufrir a nosotras'. La segunda es la del verano, que termina cuando Lucía abraza a Manuel y le dice: 'Cuídate mucho'. Las dos escenas transcurren en un interior oscuro que es prácticamente el mismo, y ambas recogen los dos abrazos más simbólicos de la película, dos situaciones que apuntan hacia cambios inmediatos cargados de presagios atemorizadores. (Armendáriz 2001: 150)[7]

The mood in *Silencio roto* changes on the two occasions referred to above to signify the different approaches and the shifting historical outlook during the 1940s. Autumn, as Armendáriz remarks, is the time of 'resistencia y espera' ('resistance and wait'), whereas the summer of hope follows upon the international developments vis-à-vis fascism in World War II. Ultimately, however, the film ends in winter, a time suitable to hiding and to the passivity adopted by Lola (María Botto), an attitude which would become more widespread during the Spanish *posguerra*: 'Sí, el otoño se corresponde con un tiempo de resistencia y de espera, el verano con la euforia que produce la salida a la luz y el invierno con el repliegue y la derrota. De esta manera, el otoño y el invierno acogen momentos de clandestinidad y ocultación, mientras que la luz del verano propicia la salida de los guerrilleros y su bajada al pueblo' (Armendáriz 2001: 150).[8]

As Armendáriz notes, a cinematic photography suggesting summer light helps to communicate to the audience the sense of coming out into the open when the *maquis* descend from the mountains to the village in which the action is located. With the anticipation that the imminent defeat of the Axis powers in World War II would mean the end of Francoism, the *maquis* enter the local village and occupy it, restoring the Republic momentarily and raising its flags. Soon, however, they abandon it on the arrival of the Civil Guard, while those left behind endure the repression for aiding the fighters.[9] As an informer walks among the villagers, pointing at those to be singled out for punishment, we realize that these local people, of whose innocence we have been made aware, will become the indirect victims of the *maquis'* Pyrrhic victory. As this scene is presented from the point of view of the villagers, we infer that they are the willing or unwilling fatalities of the fight that they support, which is increasingly seen to be doomed (Figure 4.3).[10] The film thus posits that, at this point, the guerrillas were embarking on a path of self-annihilation which contributed to their undoing, even if their tragic abandonment by international antifascist forces was a major contributor to their demise.

It is, therefore, clear in *Silencio roto* not just that the fighting men fall victims to the atmosphere of revenge that the aftermath of the Civil War signified. Manuel's sister, Lola, one of the most outspoken supporters of the guerrillas at the beginning of the film, is shown to be utterly defeated and bent on her own survival after all those close to her have disappeared. In fact, the film goes so far as to imply that Lola might have become an informer, revealing the hiding place of the teacher, Don Octavio, and therefore contributing to his death and to that of Lucía's aunt, Teresa. Octavio is arrested in the house of Teresa, who is his lover and protector, and is taken to the *Cuartelillo* ('Civil Guard barracks') alongside Teresa and Lucía. On arrival,

Figure 4.3 Montxo Armendáriz, *Silencio roto/Broken Silence* (2001). Villagers are rounded up after the *maquis* have gone

Octavio attempts to run away, probably in order to escape torture, and is shot in the back in full view of the two women.

At this point in the film, Manuel, who has also been taken prisoner by the Civil Guard, joins Teresa and Lucía, and shares a few moments with them before being taken out to be shot with Teresa. While both Manuel and Teresa face death, Lucía endures a punishment reserved for her by the *Teniente* of the Civil Guard (Joseba Apaolaza), who orders her to remain behind when her lover and aunt are taken out 'for a walk' ('de paseo'). Shifting from a first-person to a third-person cinematic narrative, the camera takes sides with Lucía by means of point-of-view shots that switch between what she sees and close-ups of her face, showing the way in which she internalizes the pain that audiences are made to share. Likewise, viewers partake of Lucía's humiliation, having to stand, waiting for the shots that will end the lives of those dear to her. As we hear those shots, we notice her contained expression and a small movement of shock that rewards the *Teniente*. For the audience, however, the understatement of her silence is an effective appeal for solidarity in the endorsement of what Lucía stands for, and disgust for her unwarranted torment and the unjustified deaths of Manuel and Teresa. At the end of the sequence, as throughout the rest of the film, the use of Lucía as the point of identification for spectators renders her dignity the most compelling condemnation of the *Teniente*'s murders, as well as his voyeuristic contemplation of her suffering.

This end could thus be said to embody the wishes of the local teacher, Don Hilario, in *Silencio roto* to 'maintain hope' and use the imagination as the only means to escape and survive in the face of untold suffering and adversity. By contrast, however, in *Silencio roto*, audiences remain unsettled by the fact that, as Lucía reminds Hilario, hope might be built on deceit: '¿La ilusión en qué? Eso es un engaño y usted lo sabe.'[11] Hilario, however, counters Lucía's despondency by alluding to the important role played by the faked letters from a lost son that he writes for Genaro. At the end of the film, Lucía and the boy, Juan, agree to continue writing these letters, thus perpetuating this gesture.

Throughout *Silencio roto*, we are stunned by the brutality of the summary execution of a Civil Guard caught by the guerrillas, which we see from Lucía's shocked perspective. Nevertheless, Armendáriz tries to demystify the guerrillas on a personal level through our identification with Lucía's suffering. We are also given to understand that, in militaristic style, any suggestion of dissidence or abandonment within the ranks of the *maquis* would be punished internally with death, as happens to Manuel's father, Matías (Helio Pedregal). Significantly, however, Manuel, one of the main protagonists and the object of Lucía's love, condones such attitudes. It is this same nonchalant commitment to fighting for a 'good cause' in spite of the odds against him that dooms him to his final end. With a faint smile clouded by the signs of the physical torture that he has endured, Manuel dedicates his last look to Lucía. He sketches the smile which Lucía had urged him to keep throughout his life as he exits the Civil Guard's quarters to be shot with Lucía's aunt, Teresa. Manuel leaves behind his lover, Lucía, and their baby daughter, whose photograph is deposited on his unmarked grave outside the cemetery in the next scene.

The faint illusion to which Lucía clings is, at the film's end, signalled by the rainbow which is briefly reflected on the bus's window as she leaves the village, in a circular movement that takes the film back to its beginning. This takes place as the repeated shot of the mountains fills the screen once more, this time to announce the final credits (Figure 4.4).[12] If the film's start had signalled the breach of the silence of the mountains, this end places the film firmly in its social context.[13] As an epilogue to the story, a stanza from a poem by Bertolt Brecht is inscribed on the window next to Lucía's face, in

Figure 4.4 Montxo Armendáriz, *Silencio roto/Broken Silence* (2001). View of the mountains which stand in for the *maquis* at several points in the film

the direction of her distant stare towards the mountains that have become a synecdoche of the *maquis*. These lyrics sum up the sadness and the ray of hope embedded throughout the film's narrative: 'En los tiempos sombríos,/¿se cantará también?/También se cantará/ sobre los tiempos sombríos.'[14]

The year in which *Silencio roto* begins is a year that saw the *maquis* increase their activities and is the same year in which Guillermo del Toro's *El laberinto del fauno* is set, 1944. From the very onset of *El laberinto del fauno*, 11-year-old Ofelia (Ivana Baquero) joins forces with her stepfather's housekeeper, Mercedes (Maribel Verdú), who is an *enlace* for the local *maquis*. Mercedes becomes the film's second protagonist, sharing with Ofelia the heroism of resisting in the face of the direct and daily tyranny that she encounters.[15]

The Spain of the Civil War's aftermath is represented at a microcosmic level in *El laberinto del fauno* by the mill compound ruled by Ofelia's evil stepfather, Captain Vidal of Franco's Civil Guard (Sergi López). Throughout the film, Ofelia faces up to Vidal's lethal world with the same courage and determination with which she tackles the three tasks set to her by the faun. Ofelia has to fulfil these three tasks in order to recover a link with a past from which, we are told at the beginning of the film, she has been severed to the point of having lost all memory of it. Memory and its recuperation are therefore crucial to a film that can be firmly located within the Spanish 'memory boom' in its quest to reconstruct the lost memories of the vanquished.

El laberinto del fauno had broad critical and audience appeal, especially because of its use of original, colourful and exciting special effects, evocative of the dark inner world of fairy tales. It is a world whose tonalities – red, yellow and, above all, dark blues – are intimately associated with the maternal and the feminine, and are also reminiscent of the colours of the Republican flag, red, yellow and purple. Although there is an apparently seamless merger of reality and fiction in *El laberinto del fauno*, the film does not project the timelessness inherent in fairy-tale narratives. Instead, from its very beginning it is firmly situated in a particular time and place which, as the intertitle indicates, is 1944 Spain, in the midst of the gloomy socio-political landscape created in the aftermath of Francisco Franco's victory.

Within this world, del Toro casts a resourceful girl as the main character through whom we view the events and thus acts as the vehicle through whom to convey values such as courage and individual freedom. Supported by Vidal's housekeeper, Mercedes, Ofelia actively opposes the despotism incarnated by Vidal from the very first scenes of the film, which associates Ofelia's personal resistance with that of the *maquis* in the mountains. Since Mercedes is the point of contact of the guerrilla fighters it is, ironically, her friendship with Ofelia that will play a part in the girl's undoing, which further relates Ofelia's fate to that of anti-Francoist resistance fighters. *El laberinto del fauno* thus grounds Ofelia's plight firmly within one of the darkest and most silenced chapters in the history of twentieth-century resistance to fascism: the desperate fight of the Spanish *maquis* during the 1940s.

The struggle against oppression that Ofelia candidly embodies aligns her with the anti-Francoist fighters with whom she is repeatedly linked sequentially throughout the film. This association is reinforced by the juxtaposition of scenes from the film's beginning, when Ofelia is presented as Princess Moanna and, immediately after the opening credits, as an orphan travelling with her pregnant mother, Carmen (Ariadna Gil), to meet her stepfather. In fact, her initial visit to the fantasy world takes place on the same night that Vidal butchers two poachers that his men have surprised, which likens

Ofelia's escape to the fantasy world to a rejection of his cruel world. Even more salient in this regard is the crosscutting of the scene in which Ofelia meets a giant toad which lives under a desiccated tree with another scene in which Vidal and his men ride up the mountain in pursuit of the *maquis*.

As in *Silencio roto*, the movement between hope and despair is pointed out in *Laberinto del fauno* by the weather, with rain invading the screen in most scenes after the establishing sequence. The rain is used as a pathetic fallacy more effectively in, for example, the scene in which the guerrilla El Tarta is about to be tortured and the door closes on an isolated Mercedes whose figure is sharply drawn in the blue of the evening light and in the middle of the rain. This serves to accentuate the anguish of those resisting Vidal's ruthless repression and, by implication, the distress of the audience.

Although the script of *El laberinto del fauno* contains unequivocal references to the abandonment of the *maquis* by international forces, most of the scripted words did not make it to the final version of the film. This can be seen early on, when Mercedes takes supplies and letters to the *maquis*' camp. There, El Tarta (Iván Massague) stutters when he reads news about D-day: 'T-t-tropas norteamericanas, británicas y c-canadienses han desembarcado en una pequeña playa al norte de Francia.'[16] While this is the end of the segment in the film, the actual script continues when another *maquis*, Trigo (Chani Martin), grabs the cutting impatiently from El Tarta and finishes the news. On completion of the item, Mercedes' brother, Pedro (Roger Casamajor), shows his delight that the Allies 'will liberate Spain', while the wounded man referred to as Francés (Gonzalo Uriarte) remarks that they are expendable for the Allies and are, therefore, 'solos': 'No les importamos. A ver si te enteras de una puta vez, Pedro: estamos solos.'[17] Even though the editing of this segment from the film could simply be due to the pressure to cut some scenes, it can also be attributed to its targeting a mainstream audience that might not like to be overtly censured. Perhaps not coincidentally, the section deleted refers to the Allies' decision not to support the Spanish guerrillas, as they feared that they were too closely aligned with Soviet communism.

The resonance of Ofelia's struggle in the fantasy world with the real universe in which she lives comes to a climax at the film's end. There, Ofelia, running away from her stepfather, meets the faun of the film's title (Doug Jones) at the edge of the labyrinth. As Ofelia holds her half-brother close to her chest, the faun, showing her a dagger that shines bright in the blue of the night, asks her to fulfil her third and last task: to shed 'the blood of an innocent'.[18] Ofelia, clasping her baby brother, refuses the knife that the faun holds out to her – a decision that produces an immediate change of scene. This is effected by means of a shot/reverse-shot in which the menacing figure of Ofelia's evil stepfather, Captain Vidal, appears behind the girl. The change of places between the faun and Vidal corresponds to a change of weapons, with Vidal's gun replacing the faun's knife. It is this gun which brings about Ofelia's nemesis when Vidal shoots the girl at point-blank range, after demanding and taking his son forcefully from her. Ofelia's dripping blood then starts to slip through her fingers, falling over the labyrinth's edge and punctuating the blue and dark tones of the scene.[19] In an ironic twist, Ofelia's 'innocent' blood enables her and, by implication, the audience's atonement and ultimate redemption from a world in which all fantasies have been violently superseded. Ofelia's end, like the trials that she faces during *El laberinto del fauno*, thus mirror and are mirrored by those of the anti-Franco resistance with whom her struggle is connected throughout the film.

Ofelia's death and her final resurrection in a different universe bring home some of the terrible truths to which the film has exposed its audiences, highlighting the dimensions of the oppressive climate of revenge that dominated 1940s Spain. The Spain in which Ofelia lives is a fascist universe where neither innocence nor age prevents people from paying the ultimate price. In Ofelia's case, her main crime is to protect her only friend, Mercedes, with her own silence. Ofelia finally abandons this environment, accessing her fantasy world through the accomplishment of the three tasks given to her by the faun at the beginning of the film.

The personal trials of Ofelia correspond closely to those of the guerrillas up to the very last scene, when Ofelia's tragedy takes place. At this point, Mercedes and the *maquis* arrive too late to save the girl, although they manage to rescue her half-brother from his father, Vidal. This 'victory' is significantly placed at the end of *El laberinto del fauno*, suggesting a degree of hope for the future which, as audiences know, is historically fallacious. The *maquis* reach the labyrinth next to which Ofelia has fallen after being shot by Vidal, just in time for Mercedes to hold the girl while the camera captures Ofelia's last moments, returning full circle to the very beginning of the film. We recognize this move not just by the setting, but also, and perhaps more importantly, by the diegetic sound of Ofelia's syncopated pant, which increases in intensity as she draws her last breath. As Mercedes holds the dying girl, we start to hear the murmuring lullaby that she had sung for Ofelia previously in the film, and the melancholic tune accentuates the overall sadness of the scene. The song acquires a privileged character in the mise-en-scène, expressing not just emotions, but bringing to the foreground the way both characters complement one another and their intimate relationship. The sense of grief that the music and Ofelia's breath creates is further punctuated by the darkness of the blue palette of colours used. In the midst of this dim environment, it is easy to discern Ofelia's white sleeping robe under her coat, which stands out to ratify the girl's innocence and, implicitly, that of the resistance fighters whose fate Ofelia has joined.

The lullaby that had linked Mercedes and Ofelia earlier in the film resonates as both a solace and a point of entry into the lost world of Ofelia's dreams, where she reaches her 'home' and where her memory is finally restored. We are led into that universe through Ofelia's own eyes, in a circular moment that takes Ofelia to her kingdom, where she recovers both her parents and her lost universe, leaving behind some minor traces of her existence, as a husky voice-over informs us.[20] Suitably, we are told, the sign of Ofelia's existence, the remembrance of her life on this earth, is a small, white flower which blossoms from the desiccated tree inside which Ofelia had confronted the toad (Figure 4.5). This flower, the disembodied male voice concludes, can only be seen by those who try to see beyond the superficial veneer of things. Del Toro's finale thus skilfully draws his audience to become part of a collective that will seek, view and appreciate all the 'white flowers' of a barren universe. Thus, the film invites viewers to look for and treasure Ofelia's memories through the living mementoes that she left on the landscape, once more linking the girl with the defeated *maquis*.

Ofelia's blood becomes the redemptive life-source of a newly born human being whose future, like that of twenty-first-century Spain, will be marked by forgetting her half-brother's origin as the offspring of fascism. Ofelia can be considered the surrogate mother of a child whose memories of an oppressive past need to be transcended in

Figure 4.5 Guillermo del Toro, *El laberinto del fauno/Pan's Labyrinth* (2006). A white flower is used as *memento mori* for Ofelia and the Spanish *maquis*

order to forge a renewed future in a different universe. At the film's end, Ofelia opens up again the dialectics between remembering and (voluntary or forced) forgetting that inform the film's narrative. In many ways, therefore, *El laberinto del fauno* attests to the relationship between memory and a society's interpretation of its past and, through it, its future.[21] Memory and oblivion are presented as intricate elements in the process of constructing a past that can help a society to live in the present, very much as twentieth-century democratic Spain did.

With their direct references to historical memory, the last scenes of *El laberinto del fauno* suggest that the deaths that take place in the film, including those of Doctor Ferreiro (Álex Angulo), Ofelia, Vidal and Carmen, have not been in vain. Indeed, their demise could be said to be essential for social renewal, as only a child who is denied memory of his heritage can be the harbinger of that new future. It is highly significant that the heroism that brings about a more hopeful future is embodied by those who would not normally be regarded as likely and willing heroes: a housekeeper, Mercedes, a bookish girl, Ofelia, and an unassuming physician, Doctor Ferreiro. These three characters are linked to the active resistance fighters whose plight informs the film's narrative from its very beginning but who are not central to the story.

As resolute as Lucía in *Silencio roto* is Mercedes in *El laberinto del fauno*, although she is more vigorous in her ultimate challenge to Vidal. Making use of the kitchen knife that she kept and that we knew would play a part in the film after a few close-ups earlier on, Mercedes unties herself and stabs Vidal as he talks about the means of torture that he is about to use on her. Interestingly, Mercedes first shocks him by stabbing him in the back, subsequently splitting his mouth open. She thus literally silences him before running away to the hills, pursued by mounted Civil Guards and meeting a timely rescue by the *maquis*, led by her brother, Pedro.

Mercedes' deployment as a point of identification for the audience serves to filter our view of the *maquis*, accentuating the humanity of their fight. This dimension is furthered by her association with Ofelia, to whom she offers support from the moment that the girl arrives until her untimely death. Indeed, Mercedes' dual relationship, which is established at various points of the film, is finally heightened when she embraces the dying Ofelia and sings the lullaby that punctuates their connection at different times in the film. With Mercedes' affecting murmur as diegetic sound, the camera enters Ofelia's field of vision and, through the girl's own eyes, we are led into the otherworldly universe in which her blood and suffering literally disappear.

The end of *El laberinto del fauno*, therefore, conveys the ambiguity of a momentary triumph of sorts for the guerrillas and for Ofelia, which is corroborated by having the film finish with the culmination of Ofelia's fantasy: a resuscitation in her lost kingdom introduced by an unusual yellow dissolve and set in brightly golden, triumphant colours.

El laberinto del fauno shares with the first and second segments of *Silencio roto* the upbeat note that the hope for international intervention offered for the resistance during the early 1940s, which is mentioned explicitly on two occasions: the intertitle that begins the film and the scene (mentioned above) in which the *maquis* comment on the news. The sense of failure is also remarked on by Doctor Ferreiro's scepticism prior to that scene. In spite of offering medical support and, eventually, his own life, to support the *maquis*, the doctor clearly tells them that, should they triumph against Vidal, another like him would surely replace him. However, the fact that *El laberinto del fauno* ends precisely after Pedro shoots Vidal and the guerrillas encircle his corpse implies a possible victory over the dictator for an audience ignorant of history. Also significant is the fact that the Manichaean presentation of good and evil in del Toro's film avoids any suggestions of wrongdoing on the part of the guerrillas, with even Vidal's execution being justified in the eyes of the audience by his cruelty and his murder of Ofelia. Ultimately, audiences remain ignorant about the possible significance of this victory or of the silence with which Mercedes counters Vidal's appeal to let his son know about his bravery in death. In fact, this is Vidal's only human moment in the film, which is shattered when Mercedes informs him that his son will not know who his father was. By erasing Vidal's name Mercedes is also hiding from sight that part of the country's history which, as events have demonstrated, still require time for the healing processes to be completed.

The reconstruction of the past achieved in these films associates civilian resistance with the struggle of the guerrillas in the mountains. More importantly, the films take an active stance in the struggle to remember them. Whereas Francoism stigmatized the guerrillas, classing them as bandits, the democratic Spain that emerged from the dictatorship strove to distance itself from its own past and effectively buried the *maquis* in oblivion. In the twenty-first century, their memory, fuelled by the very few mementoes that they left and the words of aging survivors, is being reconstructed in films and in documentaries.[22] A similar effort can be appreciated in a handful of twenty-first-century films in which the *maquis* are only subsidiary to the main plot, including Garci's *You Are the One*, Suárez' *El portero/The Goalkeeper* and Chávarri's *El año del diluvio*.

Garci's *You Are the One* features a feminine world in which the main agents are the males absent from the screen, and to whom the lives of the women are attached. Set in 'España, años 40', it casts an upper-class woman, Julia (Lydia Bosch), who mourns the death of her artist boyfriend. Her loneliness is shared by Pilara (Ana Fernández), the wife of a *maquis*, making both women of different social classes 'equal' in their solitude and their yearning for the men in their lives. Julia is a young wealthy woman who goes to her country house in an Asturian village after she learns of the death of the man she loved, a painter who was against the regime. In the house, which is in the care of Tía Gala (Julia Gutiérrez Caba), Julia remembers her childhood, and meets Gala's daughter-in-law, Pilara, and Pilara's son, Juanito (Manuel Lozano), who miss the man who was their son, husband and father respectively, a *maquis* who has been absent for three years. It is in this situation of being alone that acts as a leveller, endearing Julia to the others. These are women whose lives are centred on their men, and whose solidarity stems from their abandonment. As in the anti-Francoist films mentioned above, *You Are the One* stresses the innocence of these civilians who suffer both at the hands of a regime that oppresses them and from the men who fight it, on account of their absence.

If the references to the *maquis* are oblique in *You Are the One*, the opposite is the case in Suárez' *El portero*, where an intertitle that appears in front of a rural landscape at the beginning informs us that the narrative takes place in Asturias in 1948 in the middle of the *maquis*' struggle: 'España 1948 mientras los maquis prosiguen desde las montannas su lucha contra Franco, un hombre llega en su camioneta a un pueblo asturiano.'[23] Although the film's tone borders on a type of parody reminiscent of Luis García Berlanga's *La vaquilla/ The Heifer* (1985), *El portero* attempts to humanize the fighters and the Civil Guards who pursue them. The film also deals candidly with the local priest, a character who adds humour to the situation, far removed from those described by the friar Fray Gumersindo de Estella as siding with the oligarchy and showing little compassion for victims, whom they saw as enemies of the Church in Spain.[24]

El portero is clearly an example of the contemporary wish to find a 'third way' to address the Spanish conflict, bypassing the duality of left and right, vanquished and winners, and even good and evil. It does so by focusing on people who might have been caught in the fight but who were not militants, and thus will always be identified by the audience as essentially innocent. This 'innocence', however, is extended to those who traditionally defended Francoism literally and 'spiritually': the Civil Guard and the Church. This, in many ways, is a distortion of the 'three Spains' suggested by Paul Preston (1998), but one that has appeal for those wishing to move forward from the rifts that the Civil War and, more especially, the long repression that followed it, caused. Wishing to transcend the duality of victims and perpetrators of crimes can, however, entail another form of oblivion, as well as a disregard for the causes that made many Spaniards into an 'opposition' that they did not choose for themselves.

As an adaptation, *El portero* effects some important changes to the short story on which it is based. Some of these alterations are obviously due to the need to expand the narrative or to the use of a different medium which relies on visual clues and needs to appeal to that sense. Nevertheless, other changes are significant for what they suggest about the intended audience and the wider politics of cinema. In this context, it is important to note how *El portero* alters substantially the appearance, age and condition of the two main protagonists, dramatizing significantly the life of the woman who is called Isabel in the book and Manuela (Maribel Verdú) in the film. Whereas in the film the two main protagonists are evenly matched in terms of age and physical appearance, in the book Ramiro Forteza (Carmelo Gómez), 'the king of penalties', is described as an aged man who looks older than his true forties ('un cuarentón avejentado' [Hidalgo 2003: 99]). More radical, however, is the modification of Isabel, who in the book is only 'around nineteen' and who appears to be more mature in the film (Hidalgo 2003: 100). Also important for Manuela's characterization is that of the child she looks after, who in the book is a mentally disabled brother, Javier, and in the film is Tito (Adrián Ramírez), a mixed-race son born from the gang rape committed on Manuela by the Moorish troops of Franco. Both in book and film, Manuela looks after this child, making ends meet by sewing and mending clothes, which is what she offers to do for Ramiro when she sees the holes in his jumper.[25]

The story charts the arrival of Ramiro in Manuela's village, where he hopes to make some money by gambling on people to score penalties. As the film starts, we meet him travelling in a van, transporting a wounded *maquis*, Nardo (Eduard Fernández), in the back, and being intercepted by the local Civil Guard, who warn him that 'there are *maquis* in the area'. Ramiro then sets up his 'stall' and 'rudimentary, wooden goal posts' in a green paddock, waiting for the locals to challenge him. When nobody takes any interest in him, the local priest, Don Constantino (Roberto Álvarez), suggests that he will encourage people to take part in the challenge provided Ramiro helps him bury a man and confesses his sins. It is at this point that we notice the film's humorous tone, whose main exponents are the priest and the lieutenant of the guards, Sargento Andrade (Antonio Resines).[26] Spurred on by the priest, who acts as referee, some local men start shooting at the goal but are interrupted by a 'partida de maquis', who threaten Ramiro with the 'confiscation' of his booty and valuables. Ramiro suggests that they gamble them by trying to score penalties, which the men accept. As the game progresses, a group of Civil Guards appear and the *maquis*, in turn, challenge the guards to score more penalties than them and let them go if they lose.[27] While the boy acts as referee, Manuela keeps guard over the weapons, left in a pile on the ground.

In *El portero* Manuela has considerably more substance than in the short story on which it is based, and this is not just because of the brevity of her appearance in the latter. Active in her opposition, Manuela is in the film not only an *enlace*, who helps her brother, the wounded *maquis*, she has also hatched plans to leave the village and does so at the end of the film, with Tito and Ramiro Forteza. More dramatic in the film than in the short story is the moment when Manuela indicates her reluctance to being touched by men, which triggers her confession about her son being the fruit of a collective rape. By comparison with the earlier films, Ramiro's acceptance of Manuela's 'pollution' echoes *Pim, pam, pum ... ¡fuego!*, although here the mixed-race child represents a more optimistic and tolerant future.

A less caricatured presentation of the *maquis*' fight is given in another film to whose plot they are marginal: Jaime Chávarri's adaptation of the novel by Eduardo Mendoza, *El año del diluvio* (2004 and 1992 for the novel). Here, what Mendoza refers to as an 'anachronistic' love story between a nun and a landowner in 1950s rural Catalonia is set against the backdrop of the desperate struggle of a group of *maquis*, whose leader ends up being an unlikely benefactor of the asylum finally built by the film's main protagonist, Sor Consuelo (Fanny Ardant).

As with many post-1960 films on the *maquis*, Chávarri uses a woman as a point of identification for the audience even if, as he suggests, Constanza Briones/Sor Consuelo is a rather unlikely protagonist for a twenty-first-century narrative. Even less ordinary is the character with whom she falls in love, Augusto Aixelá (Dario Grandinetti), a wealthy middle-aged seducer who is the target of the *maquis* for his association with the Falange during and after the Civil War. As the plot develops, however, Augusto becomes an increasingly ambiguous character to the point that, at the film's end, we remain unsure whether he did or did not fall in love with the insistent nun who repeatedly visited him, trying to canvass his support for her plan to transform the old hospital into a residential home for the elderly. Ironically, in the book on which the film is based, Augusto spends his last days in that very home, which had been built with the funds provided anonymously by the *maquis*, Balaguer (Ginés García Millán), while Augusto Aixelá claimed to have been its benefactor.

Although there is a degree of ambiguity vis-à-vis the film's presentation of Augusto Aixelá and even of the Civil Guard Cabo Lastre (Francesc Orella), whose 'ubiquity' at times borders on parody, there is no possible ambiguity in the book's and film's presentation of the regime's ruthlessness with the *maquis*. The scenes in which Sor Consuelo, after helping the wounded Balaguer, witnesses their summary execution leave no doubt as to what it meant to be in the opposition. From the gardener Bartolo (Eloy Azorín), who appears to be mentally disabled, to the wounded man, Balaguer, all are killed on the spot. Lastre retrieves a plain-dressed Sor Consuelo from the line formed by the survivors waiting to be shot only after recognizing her. Also, as Mendoza indicates in the book's introduction, the fact that one of them had given the fighting men away after having been tortured and having had his ears cut off is validated by his research into actual events.

It is significant that, when backgrounding the *maquis*, the earlier films cast them mostly in contemporary black-and-white detective stories about low-life criminals, while most modern films opt for dramas or melodramas. These romantic films are, however, different from the earlier ones in that the woman's plight is not, or not only, to be equated with a reductive view of volatile femininity which would extend to embrace the understanding of society in general. The approach towards gender of directors like Trueba or Chávarri showcases the changes taking place in Spain from the 1970s and, especially, from the 1990s onwards. Their perspective is also, and perhaps more importantly, representative of a way of looking at history that distances itself from the earlier ones, humanizing both women and *maquis*. While aiming to give a sense of immediacy about the Civil War and its aftermath, these productions acknowledge explicitly the comfortable distance afforded by the solidity of Spain's democracy. They are films which, like the novels on which they are based, enable their authors to cast an individualized look at the twentieth century from the vantage point given by more than half a century since the events described in them. Unlike their predecessors, these directors obviously attempt to eschew Manichaean views, while showing that there is no unambiguous way to address the legacy of the Spanish dictatorship.

The film closing the first decade of the twenty-first century stands out from the rest by introducing a *maquis* in an uncommon setting, which does not fit in with any of the traditional cinematic genres. Lluís Galter's *Caracremada* is a highly personal take on the *maquis'* fight that is also highly unusual for being the first biopic devoted exclusively to one historical character, Ramón Vila Capdevila (Lluís Soler), also known as *Caracremada* (a nickname meaning 'Burnface'). Vila's eventful life provides ample material for a fiction film, and this film offers a comprehensive summary of the ideas explored in this book, as it merges effectively fiction and documentary, as well as the personal and the political in its portrait of Vila. Born in 1918, the anarchist Ramón Vila is often referred to as the 'last *maquis*', although this title was also given to others (see p. 179, note 1). As with the characters of Francoist films, Vila was, in fact, a *maquis* who returned from France after fighting in both the Spanish Civil War and World War II. As a young man, Vila joined the anarchist union, CNT (Confederación Nacional de Trabajadores), and fought in the Civil War before going into exile in 1939. In France, he ran away from the infamous concentration camp of Argelès-sur-Mer in the south of the country to join the French Resistance, returning to Spain thereafter for several 'destabilizing actions'. After many of those 'actions', Vila was finally caught and shot in Manresa in 1963, when he was trying to blow up some electric pylons. He was left to bleed in the night until he died.

Galter's film offers a view of this historical *maquis*, Vila, in what is a largely silent film that concentrates on the solitude of the fight. Lengthy takes of landscapes intermingle with close-ups of tools, and, especially, hands and boots (Figures 4.6 and 4.7). We learn about Vila precisely through those silences, which show a character opting to fight as a way of life in spite of knowing well that his 'war' was already lost and abandoned first by the Communist Party of Spain in 1948 and, eventually, by the anarchist CNT in 1951. The style of the film emphasizes and celebrates this idealism, which we attribute to the real-life man on whom the character is based.

Like many of the films on Spanish *maquis* looked at in this book, including some of those made under Franco's rule, Galter's can be considered a celebration and a memorializing effort, along the lines of the monument inaugurated in 2001 in Santa Cruz de Moya. These

Figure 4.6 *Caracremada/Burnface* (2010). Solitary landscape as setting for the struggle

Figure 4.7 *Caracremada/Burnface* (2010). Last shot of Ramón Vila Capdevila's shoes as his corpse is loaded onto a cart by the Civil Guards

efforts articulate the present with the past, through memories of those long forgotten by the official historical narrative that dominated Spain. They also provide sites for remembering, understanding, mourning and honouring their struggle, keeping their memory, and the basic humanity that informed their cause, alive and relevant.

Altogether, most of the films studied in this chapter relate the *maquis* to the women who supported them, offering an alternative notion of womanhood that, to some degree, also stands in for the body politic. Whether active *enlaces*, as Mercedes or Lucía, or accepted as part and parcel of a 'violated' past, as in *El portero*, these women are, nevertheless, central to the films, as well as to the society represented in them. These twenty-first-century films invoke notions of memory and social identity that reveal some marked differences from earlier productions, showing the *maquis* as markedly distant from the society that is targeted as audience but as part and parcel of the past that constructed that present. While the older films avoid explicitly mentioning these men and women as opponents of the regime, twenty-first-century films treat them as participants in a shared past to which women's experiences are central, even when they appear to be marginal to the fight. These films thus trace the legitimization of a certain view of the past, highlighting alternative manners in which the present and the past merge, pointing towards a historical time for which the Civil War and its aftermath are paradoxically both more distant and closer to their viewers. This is a past that can be observed from a semi-detached viewpoint and can be treated from a tempered position that enables it to be parodied. It is also a past looked at from a desire to dissolve its entrenched antagonisms and through a sentimentality that is, nevertheless, devoid of nostalgia.

The films on *maquis* released in democratic Spain pay homage to those whose resistance to fascism was traditionally ignored or forced into the background. The viewers' empathy with their main characters enables the directors to vindicate the dislocated memories of their real-life inspirations: the *maquis* and the *campesinos*, intellectuals or ordinary people who were oppressed, tortured and murdered for offering support to others. Also, by connecting the experiences of spectators and characters, the films can make audiences accessory to the resistance itself. Above all, the use of characters that include *maquis*, as well as children, young women, doctors or teachers, enables the directors to conciliate both militant and pacifist views of the Spanish conflict, highlighting the humanity of the struggle. The dignified attitude of these characters, who ultimately display courage when circumstances require them to, makes them unsung heroes of the Civil War's aftermath.

In spite of the constraints imposed by fitting into the parameters of a normal-length fiction feature, these films recreate *maquis'* lives in ways that are relevant to their memorialization. As the fighting men interviewed by Vidal Castaño indicate, it is, nonetheless, surprising for them to view their deeds on screen, and they often fail to identify themselves with the characters representing them:

> El vaivén de planos y contraplanos, de imágenes superpuestas y de recreaciones de la 'realidad' les parecen [a los guerrilleros entrevistados por Vidal Castaño 2004] bastante irreales, les llevan a decir que las cosas no podrían nunca ocurrir como se muestra en la pantalla de cine. Es imposible dice *Grande* que se hicieran contactos en un bar, en clara alusión a la figura del maestro que aparece en la cinta *Silencio roto*. (Vidal Castaño 2004: 91)[28]

By and large, nonetheless, Spanish *maquis* have appreciated the efforts made in films and documentaries to represent their lives or the difficulties they and their supporters had to face.[29] Outnumbering the actual fighters, *enlaces* were often relatives or friends of the *maquis* and became targets of savage torture, punishment and death.[30] In fact, not just those identified as *enlaces* were cruelly dealt with by the regime: girlfriends, relatives and even acquaintances of insurgent fighters were routinely detained, raped, tortured and murdered as a means to root out the guerrillas.[31] These characters, therefore, represent the many silent people on whose information and supplies the guerrillas depended for their survival.[32] Moreover, their characterization renders them the main points of access to the history of the guerrilla struggle in twentieth-century Spain, enabling the directors to focus the struggle mostly on the plight of the civilian population.

By deploying civilian characters as points of identification for the audience, directors reconstruct a collective memory that is based on the social attitudes and lives of people who have not been traditionally thought to be historical protagonists or war heroes. These cinematic men and women embody a notion of humanity that celebrates solidarity, as well as unarmed resistance to despotism. In fact, it is their very ordinariness and their choice to become unlikely heroes only when forced by circumstances around them that make them effective points of identification. Their representation enters into a dialogue with the historical characters on whom they are based, and are made relevant in terms of resistance and opposition to injustice in general terms. Consequently, these characterizations both reflect on and contribute to the process of inventing, forging or forgetting elements of individual, social and cultural identity. These films illustrate the difficulty of separating collective and individual memories, and the important role played by women in twenty-first-century Spanish history, as well as the cultural remembrance and reconstruction of those events.

5
Documenting 'Historical Memory' (1985–2008)

From the last years of the twentieth century and, more especially, since the beginning of the twenty-first, Spanish audiences have grown increasingly acquainted with the testimonial accounts of victims of the Civil War and its aftermath, many of which have aired on regional or national television. These productions, which started to be released as the generation who took a direct part in the conflict was fast disappearing, fill some of the fissures in our knowledge, especially regarding personal experiences which had been ignored or silenced. The accounts remain necessarily fragmented partly because of the limitations inherent in personal memory and oral testimony.[1] Also, in spite of the genre's claims to truth and objectivity, the documentary format imposes certain constraints, including the tension between a recreation of lives of individuals with whom the audience can identify and the representation of their experiences as sources of dramatic entertainment.

Besides the testimonies of surviving fighters, documentaries about the Spanish *maquis* make up their historical characters from interviews conducted with those who knew them and the visual evidence left behind, which in this particular case is quite scarce. This is not only because the *maquis* lived underground lives and avoided keeping written or visual records of their deeds. Also, for different reasons, much personal, historical and archival documentation was consistently purged in Spain throughout the best part of the twentieth century, up to and including the 1990s.[2] This chapter will show how, in spite of these shortcomings, documentaries can bring audiences closer to understanding the guerrilla struggle through the lens of their personal experiences and the perspective given by those who were close to them. These accounts, moreover, allow us to elucidate the attitudes of the largely forgotten segment of the civilian population associated with them: the relatives and *enlaces* on whom much of this book focuses.

Overall, the titles and content of documentaries produced in Spain from the 1970s onwards illustrate the staggering dimensions of Francoist repression, as well as the overwhelming sense of loss. This sense of loss is, furthermore, tinged at times with guilt for the historical oblivion to which these people were confined, firstly by Francoism and, subsequently, by the democratic Spain that followed it. Although there are a number of earlier exceptions, by and large documentaries have been visible products of the 'memory boom' which they have both spurred on and illustrated.[3] The quantity of productions has grown exponentially since the mid-1990s, often urged by the impending disappearance of the main witnesses and of those who knew them directly.

Without a single exception, the documentaries that focus on *maquis* released after Franco's death set out to honour and vindicate their protagonists, many of them legendary at the time of their production. They also centre and rely on the testimony of the civilian men and women who supported them, often classing them as guerrilla fighters themselves, in spite of the fact that they had never held a weapon. *Maquis* and *enlaces* are thus interrogated in a belated attempt to counter the misrepresentation to which they had been subjected under Francoism's classification of bandits and 'internal aliens'.

While some documentaries trace single lives mostly through interviews with acquaintances, friends and relatives, others address broadly the fate of groups. Nevertheless, the continuous presence of some 'stars' among the surviving *maquis* makes them comparable figures to those addressed in fictional productions. Among the most often cast historical protagonists, veterans Eduardo Pons Prades and José Murillo stand out. Also, the presence of women, as *enlaces*, relatives or as part of the guerrilla band itself, has been highlighted in many productions, with surviving *maquis*, *Sole* and *Celia*, appearing in a good number of documentaries. In fact, the couple formed by Remedios Montero and Florián García, known as *Celia* and *Grande*, whose eventful lives certainly provide ample raw material for any production, has become 'stellar'.[4]

This chapter will explore the ways in which documentaries make use of the testimonies of the survivors, *enlaces* and relatives to negotiate the gap between individual and collective memory. It will thus take into account the documentaries' close relationship with the memory associations that have been formed in Spain with the objective of recovering the voices of war victims, finding the corpses of those summarily executed and vindicating their lives and deeds. In order to evaluate the topic, I will use mostly references to twenty-first-century productions of two documentaries that single out one individual – Daniel Álvarez and Iñaki Pinedo's *Girón: El hombre que murió dos veces/Girón: The Man Who Died Twice* (2004) and César Fernández' *La guerra de Severo/Severo's War* (2008) – and two that address the guerrillas in collective terms – Javier Corcuera's *La guerrilla de la memoria/The Guerrilla of Memory* (2002) and Manuel Gutiérrez Aragón's *Los del monte/The Men from the Mountains* (2006). The context of these documentaries is partly provided from details drawn from one of the earliest productions made during the first democratic years, namely an episode dedicated to *La guerrilla* in Eugenio Monesma's nine-episode series for television *España: Historia inmediata/Spain: Immediate History*, which was first aired in 1985. Lastly, an unusual cinematic release directed by Carles Balagué, *La Casita Blanca: La ciudad oculta/The Little White House: The Hidden City* (2002), will be investigated on account of its inclusion of a complete re-enactment, alongside the standard interviews and archival footage.

Altogether, the documentaries studied in this chapter demonstrate the claim made by director Gutiérrez Aragón in his own work on *Los del monte* regarding the everlasting presence of the guerrillas in the mountainous landscape that harboured them. With reference to the land in which he was born, Cantabria, Gutiérrez Aragón invokes the local feelings suggested by the scenery associated with the *maquis*' fight in people's imagination. As his own documentary shows, besides the historical traces that appear in books, films and other media, the *maquis* are a 'memoria viva' ('living memory'), surviving in the landscape, local lore and other 'sites of memory'.

The efforts to recover the memories of the Spanish guerrilla fighters in documentaries need to be contextualized not only within the aforementioned 'memory boom', but also with different approaches to the study of documentary and testimony.[5] From the end of World War II and, more especially from the 1970s onwards, scholars have incorporated the study of personal memoirs and oral testimonies into the writing of history. It is an approach that has meant the inclusion of personal experiences in historical narratives, adding new dimensions to the inherently complex process of interpreting past events. This is precisely the perspective that has been largely adopted by those directing, producing and scriptwriting documentaries about the Spanish Civil War and its aftermath, although it is not, in itself, devoid of contradictions. Firstly, these productions have to address the biases and limitations inherent in personal recollection of what often were highly traumatic events. Secondly, many documentaries have been screened with the lofty aim of achieving some sort of moral or even juridical reparation for the victims. This might be achieved by an overwrought focus on victimization, which may be reached, as Ángel Loureiro remarks, 'at the expense of a rigorous examination of the past' (Loureiro 2008: 227).[6]

An emphasis on victimization and the desire for the implementation of reparative justice foregrounds the relationship between the personal and the political that is at the core of these documentaries and has become central to contemporary debates about the interpretation of Spain's recent past. This is an emphasis that is apparent both in fiction and in non-fiction productions, and is quite prominent in television documentaries.[7] These productions can thus be situated, according to John Corner's classification, at the crossroads between 'drama' and 'journalism'.[8]

While the use of personal testimonies can force audiences to empathize with the plight of the victims in documentaries, the deployment of basic cinematic techniques can also manipulate wilfully their response.[9] Nevertheless, an unquestioning identification of viewers with victims does not necessarily presuppose a strictly Manichaean view of the events presented. However, it can entail the disregard of motifs or impose a certain relationship between cause and effect. An obvious example of this technique is given in one of the first documentaries dedicated to the *maquis* soon after the *Transición*, *La guerrilla*, which is a one-hour episode of Monesma's series *España: Historia inmediata* (1985) on *La guerrilla*.

The opening scene of Monesma's *La guerrilla* offers the testimony of a man identified by an intertitle as Pedro Vicente, member of the Communist Party of Spain (PCE). Vicente informs the audience that he became a *maquis* because he did not accept the end of a struggle whose origins were a military coup against the majority of Spaniards who had elected the Popular Front in 1936. As soon as those words, assumed to be honest and truthful, are heard, a cut directs viewers to the (in)famous end-of-war report that celebrated the demise of the 'Red Army' on 1 April 1939: 'En el día de hoy, cautivo y derrotado, el ejército rojo ha sido vencido. La guerra ha terminado.'[10] The next scene, also introduced by a cut, shows archival images of Civil Guards surrounding a derelict country house from where a man comes out with his hands up high, only to be immediately shot. This makes apparent where the director's sympathies lie, and what the audience's response to such a blatant wrong should be, inflecting the documentary's narrative with the unquestioning aim of moral or restorative justice. The sequence and the fast action, with cuts between the three different segments, associate the events and stress the point of view from which we are to see the testimonies that unfold thereafter.

In spite of the genre's claims to truth and objectivity, the documentary format relies on and shares many of the tactics used in fiction films to bring audiences to an understanding of their subject matter, often inviting empathy or sympathy by means of direct or indirect appeal to the viewers' feelings. In the particular case of the Spanish *maquis*, most documentaries rely necessarily on interviews because of their limited means to stage re-enactments of events and the scarcity of visual material to illustrate their narrative.[11] They therefore cast 'characters' with 'speaking parts' out of ordinary people, whose commentaries often appear as unquestionably true, and whose words, anger or sadness can be deployed so as to manipulate the audience's response.[12]

From its origin, film in general, and not just documentary, was seen in terms of its relationship with reality, either departing from it or trying to imitate or recreate it. Among the early film theorists, Ricciotto Canudo thought in 1911 that film was an art, the seventh art, and should not imitate reality (2002). By contrast, Sergei Eisenstein thought that film was closer to theatrical performance in its relationship to the real world. Dziga Vertov and, later, John Grierson also believed that the notion of reality should be preserved, whereas for Luis Buñuel the world of dreams should be invoked openly by the cinema.[13] Among these critics, the most influential writer on documentary was Grierson, who outlined in 1932 the 'First

Principles of Documentary', highlighting the genre's 'sense of social responsibility':

> This sense of social responsibility makes our realist documentary a troubled and difficult art, and particularly in a time like ours ... But realist documentary, with its streets and cities and slums and markets and exchanges and factories, has given itself the job of making poetry where no poet has gone before it, and where no ends, sufficient for the purposes of art, are easily observed. It requires not only taste but also inspiration, which is to say a very laborious, deep-seeing, deep-sympathizing creative effort indeed. (Grierson 2002: 43)

After Grierson, André Bazin exposed his famous ideas as regards the 'aesthetic of reality' embedded in neorealism and in Orson Welles' idiosyncratic use of deep focus in *Citizen Kane*.[14] Bazin believed that it was a wish to recreate an image of the world that gave rise to the emergence of cinema so that, starting with the films made by the Lumière brothers, the realist strand informs the development of film history, and not just in its documentary form.

While cinematic documentary has changed since these theorists outlined its parameters, it has also become increasingly frequent in television, where it is often sponsored by public bodies and showcased for educational purposes. In all cases, however, documentary faces the paradoxes inherent in the use and interpretation of oral history and personal memories in the construction of a coherent narrative.[15]

The incorporation of oral history within the historical paradigm was traditionally disregarded by the established schools of thought until the 1970s. The gradual acceptance of the validity of oral sources follows the seminal work of, among others, Luisa Passerini (1979) and Alessandro Portelli (1991), who accorded oral history the same importance as archival material, and argued for its importance for the reconstruction of historical experience.[16] These efforts, which derived from the changes initiated by developments in social and popular history after World War II, widened the horizons of historiography considerably. They did so by adding alternative practices and new spheres of reality, such as domestic life and the everyday practices of people traditionally subordinated and absent from historical narratives, including women, minorities and the working classes. In fact, oral narrative, as Raymond Williams observes, was accessible to the working classes, who, when trying to write, found it easier to do so in autobiographical form that followed patterns established by trials or religious confessions:

> Very few if any of us could write at all if certain forms were not available ... Instead, they wrote marvellous autobiographies. Why? Because the form coming down through the religious tradition was of a witness confessing the story of his life, or there was the defence speech at a trial when a man tells the judge who he is and what he had done, or of course other kinds of speech. These oral forms were more accessible forms centred on 'I', on the single person. (Williams 1980: 25)

The spontaneity, use of plain language and lack of technical skills on the part of the writer or the interviewee also add to the autobiographical genre's sense of reality and truthfulness, very much like court testimonies. As John Beverley remarks, this contributes to the 'truth effect' of the literary genre which arose from those accounts, *testimonio*: '[The] assumed lack of writing ability or skill on the part of the narrator of the *testimonio*, even in those cases where it is written instead of narrated orally, also contributes to the "truth effect" the form generates' (Beverley 1989: 15).[17]

The work of early social and oral historians thus highlighted some shortcomings of traditional historiography, while using the potential inconsistencies of oral sources as essential parameters for clarifying the immanence and, at times, the contingency of existing relationships of power. In this way, the political aims and objectives of historical writing have been brought to the fore. Although, as Passerini observes, 'the tendency to transform the writing of history into a form of populism' should be avoided, historians nowadays are urged to consider 'that the raw material of oral history ... is pre-eminently an expression and representation of culture, and therefore includes not only literal narrations but also the dimensions of memory, ideology and subconscious desires' (Passerini 1979: 84).

It is not, therefore, the use of oral sources that comes into question when assessing documentaries, but their potential misuse, especially when they disingenuously claim to be offering nothing but 'the truth'. This is not to say that the deployment of oral testimonies as potential sources for historical, ethical or even judicial redress for the victims of the Francoist repression could or should be dismissed. But it is to acknowledge that many documentaries seek a response on the part of the viewer by deploying cinematic techniques of identification with and distancing from their subject matter that may not be always obvious to them. The fact that these documentaries target those who were silenced for decades can also mean not just the inevitable partiality afforded by temporal and emotional distance but also an absence of alternative views. Thus, as Loureiro censures, many documentaries that have been produced by and aired on Spanish television offer 'highly streamlined versions of the past', aimed at provoking an emotional and uncritical identification with the victims, while raising 'no genuine questions':

> One would expect the more recent documentaries to show something of the sophistication attained by contemporary documentary film-making. However, their directors are content to remain on the surface of things, engaging in the facile presentation of suffering without making any effort to raise genuine questions or to engage in a probing examination of the past. The aim is merely to win over the audience through a pathetic rhetoric based on the surviving relatives' pain and a highly streamlined version of the past. (Loureiro 2008: 233)

According to this view, documentaries presenting the *maquis'* struggle from the point of view of the fighters themselves can arguably diminish their value as historical documents. Victimization, melodrama and sentimentality would contribute to that bias, forcing empathy at the expense of analysis. The dangers inherent in these attempts are part and parcel of the compilation of oral stories, as Jordanova remarks:

> One potential danger associated with oral history ... is that of overidentification with those being interviewed, a point that links in with issues in other historical fields – the cult of authenticity and romanticisation ... A person speaking to a historian of their own experience generates an especially direct kind of evidence, which is all the more valued if it comes from those who were not previously considered significant historical actors. And if such

testimony contains, as it often does, accounts of suffering and deprivation, of heroism and stoicism, then our romantic sensibilities are readily engaged ... Such emotional investments have their generative side, but they can also reinforce simple moral polarities, which are necessarily, given what we know of the human condition, strategic fictions. (Jordanova 2000: 53)

Emotional identification *per se*, however, does not necessarily entail manipulation, even when 'sentimentality' can mean simplification or the absence of 'genuine questions'. Also, the putative dangers of 'overidentification' can be tempered by the director's admission of his or her own point of view, and their integration of alternative views or a questioning of the content or structures of their productions. Nevertheless, it is worth remembering that the directors and scriptwriters of the type of documentaries looked at in this chapter present a particular viewpoint not only because it is, to them, a 'legitimate' one that airs a forgotten struggle against fascism and oppression. They also wish to counter the fact that such views were excluded from official narratives for the greater part of the twentieth century.[18] Therefore, it is necessary to have these documentaries to balance the biased representation of history given within Spain from the 1930s onwards. It is, furthermore, a way of making relevant to the present the experiences of large segments of the population that the dictatorship obliterated in every possible way. These documentaries, and the testimonies informing them, seek to contribute actively to the incorporation of *maquis* into a history from which they were either wilfully deleted or in which they had their portrait severely distorted. In this way, they participate in the 'retrieval of time' that, according to Thomas Austin, is the most salient characteristic of the 'documentary project':

If, in the face of proliferating formats, hybridization and the interpenetration of modes of fiction and non-fiction, one can talk with any authority about a shared documentary project, it might be tempting to characterize it as concerned with the retrieval of time: re/calling the past into the present, and preserving something of the past or present for future contemplation. (Austin 2008: 51)

Like fiction films, observational documentaries generally employ an impersonal narration that does not explicitly address the viewer.

In the majority of the documentaries concerning Spanish *maquis*, interviews are normally held in the interviewees' own houses, displaying their social background in what are normally seen to be small, modest and neatly arranged lounges, where they sit wearing casual clothes. This setting of a traditional working-class background is clearly conveyed in Corcuera's *La guerrilla de la memoria*, which, at the beginning of the film, tracks José Murillo walking to his flat, where he opens the door and we enter alongside him. In this way, the film acquiesces with what Grierson called a 'sense of social responsibility' associated with documentary making (Grierson 2002: 43).

La guerrilla de la memoria starts with a reading of the end-of-war memorandum, after which the credits are given and we follow Murillo on a bus and then to his home, thus highlighting his 'ordinariness'. His home, which offers a setting for the film's beginning, is likewise shown to be clean and modest, and this provides the background for his admission that the Civil War started for him precisely that 1st of April, when Franco proclaimed its end. Murillo, who, like the remaining 'characters' in this documentary, is unidentified until the final credits, was 15 years old at the time, in 1939. The life story of this *maquis*, known as *Comandante Ríos*, provides the context for other interviewees that follow, who include Esperanza Martínez, *Sole*, who was a member of the Agrupación Guerrillera de Levante y Aragón, AGLA ('Guerrilla Association of Levante and Aragon'), and Remedios Montero, *Celia*, also identified in the credits alongside her husband, Florián García, *Grande*, as activists of AGLA. Other people interviewed are *maquis* Francisco Martinez, *Quico*, Manuel Zapico, *Asturiano*, and Eduardo Pons, *Floreado Brasino*, as well as *enlaces*, including Ángela Losada and Benjamin Rubio, and relatives, such as the elderly Emilia Girón, sister of one of the most famous fighters from León.

The 'sense of social responsibility' that informs *La guerrilla de la memoria* is also apparent in a documentary that concentrates on an individual and idiosyncratic *maquis*, Adolfo Lucas Reguilón García, known as *Severo*. César Fernández' *La guerra de Severo*, released in 2008, starts with the ubiquitous end-of-war declaration over which a male voice-over sums up briefly the feature's focus. We hear the voice while a dissolve of an image of the imperial eagle adopted by Franco gives way to a superimposed photograph of the dictator's face at the time, the 1940s. After informing us of the brief occupation of a small village in the province of Madrid, Alameda del Valle, which was 'declared' Republican by a group of guerrilla fighters in 1946, we hear the adopted and real name of Adolfo Reguilón, *Severo*, which is a shortened form of his longer pen name, *Severo Eubel de la Paz*.[19] Unusual as a guerrilla fighter and a human being, *Severo* is singled out on account of the idiosyncratic type of fight that he led, which was paradoxically 'peaceful', and in which he went so far as to sign a non-aggression pact with the Civil Guard. The initial voice-over is punctuated by non-diegetic orchestral music that associates the narrative with a thriller or action film, leading to a further dissolve, this time to the 'tricolour' Republican flag (purple, red and yellow), over which the film's credits appear. Altogether, therefore, this introduction conveys what Bill Nichols labels the 'voice of documentary', which 'refers to a given film's situated, embodied expression as it is conveyed by spoken words and silences, intertitles, music, composition, editing, tone or perspective with a primary emphasis on the effect of this symbolic form of action on the viewer' (Nichols 2008: 36).[20]

In line with documentary conventions, *La guerra de Severo* contains black-and-white footage, mostly photographs of the time and shots of relevant archival documents, as well as characters with 'speaking parts'. Among these characters, several *maquis*, family members and neighbours of the villages where *Severo* lived and worked appear repeatedly. Added to them, historian Benito Díaz and a local chronicler ('cronista'), Suso Fernández, contribute what is normally referred to as 'the voice of the expert'.

After this introduction and the opening credits, the next scenes of *La guerra de Severo* transport viewers to the twenty-first century, from which we travel back and forth several times. The storytelling is set out chronologically, indicated by intertitles on a black screen, or pinpointing the different historical crossroads throughout, using black-and-white photographs over which the same landscape appears in colour. Old newspapers or maps are also used to indicate location and to signal time.[21] We thus begin to reconstruct *Severo*'s life story through first the voice-over and then the physical presence of Suso Fernández, a *cronista* ('local historian') from the city of Foz, where *Severo* spent ten years working as a well-liked teacher, under the name Don Bernardo, living with his wife, Isabel Villalba, and another guerrilla fighter, Teodoro del Real Yáñez, known there as his brother-in-law, *Paco Cobo*. Black-and-white footage of the village at the time, maps and a photo of *Severo* in a suit and wearing glasses, add information to this narrative (Figure 5.1).[22] This establishes the setting and characters through which audiences meet *Severo*, presenting him as a 'normal' human being, as far as possible removed from any notion of 'banditry' that might have been attached to his image.

The reconstruction of *Severo*'s personality is complemented by further interviews with people who knew him and his 'family', including his landlord, Javier Mecía, and two pupils (Elvira Macía and Alonso García), who corroborate the essential goodness of his character. While Javier Mecía informs us that *Severo* rented a house owned by extreme right-wing people, which helped his anonymity, another person interviewed, María Gómez, identified simply as 'Vecina de Foz', framed within her modest but neat lounge, clarifies that they were not just right-wing but belonged to the Falange ('falangistas todos') (Figure 5.2). Within this setting, the voice of the *cronista* over another black-and-white photograph of *Severo* corroborates that he aroused no suspicion because his attitude was nothing short of 'exemplary'.

Figure 5.1   La guerra de Severo/Severo's War (2008). Contemporary photograph of Severo as respectable teacher 'Don Bernardo'

Figure 5.2 La guerra de Severo/Severo's War (2008). Interviewee María Gómez at home, foregrounding the working-class arrangement and implicit honesty of the speaker

It is interesting to note Fernández' use of location for these interviews, which is meant to reinforce the 'characterization' of each of these 'speaking parts'. While the local historian, Suso Fernández, is situated in the town of Foz, leaning on the railings of the Maritime Walk, from which he talks to the camera directly, the landlord, Javier Mecía, is introduced in front of the house *Severo* rented, meeting and shaking hands with Fernández before entering it to sit and converse with the director, directing his view away from the camera (Figure 5.3). Fernández here explicitly acknowledges his presence as the interviewer as he walks from behind the camera to meet Mecía, even if we do not see him again when conducting other interviews or hear him asking the questions that lead to the documentary's narrative. In this way, each character is given a 'territory' and a position of authority vis-à-vis their testimonies, reinforcing the feeling of truth and authenticity in their assertions. The setting is fundamental to our understanding of the subject and can also be considered a character, contributing directly to the narrative. It also serves to locate the

Figure 5.3 La guerra de Severo/Severo's War (2008). Still of Severo's house at the time of the documentary. Director César Fernández meets the owner

speakers' position towards and knowledge of their subject matter, as well as their relation to the production and the audience.

As mentioned above, transitions which take us from the present of the documentary to the time when the events described took place are often effected in *La guerra de Severo* through dissolves from a black-and-white photograph to the shooting in colour of the very same location (Figures 5.4 and 5.3). This type of identification is used with the house *Severo* and his family occupied, as well as with the landscape surrounding Foz, which further stresses the authenticity of the footage, even though most of the settings will have inevitably changed over time. The sense of time, which the black-and-white conveys, also intensifies the notion that the repressive past is monochrome, adding a sense of nostalgia, emptiness, oppression and uniformity.

After the local historian spells out before the camera *Severo*'s achievements as teacher and promoter of cultural events, one of his pupils, Alonso García, occupying the same position as the local historian in Foz' Paseo Marítimo, indicates that 'one bad day', in 1956, the authorities caught up with our protagonist. Ironically, *Severo*'s

Figure 5.4 La guerra de Severo/*Severo's War* (2008). Old photograph of Severo's house

identification resulted from the fact that his colleague, *Paco Cobo*, had fallen in love with a local woman, Elvira Macía, and the local priest requested his birth certificate from his home town in order for them to be married. Several members of *Severo*'s family are then showcased alongside historians and guerrilla fighters, including Eduardo Pons Prades and Eulalio Barroso, *Carrete*, to tell us that *Severo* was convicted of 'rebelión militar' and condemned to death. A male voice-over, reading a letter by *Severo*, and thus taking on his role, indicates in the first person that he has 'aceptado lo inevitable', that is to say, his own death. The documentary then, as it were, goes back in time and starts to trace *Severo*'s life, from 1911, when he was born, the son of a *campesino*, Benito Díaz, in Villa del Prado, Madrid. Benito, we are informed, was killed by the Civil Guard in an 'arbitrary manner' in 1920, when *Severo* was only nine years of age. Following his father's death, *Severo* studied to be a teacher and married his lifelong companion, Isabel Villalba, becoming a successful 'socialist' teacher in Navamorcuende (Toledo) before joining the Republican militia during the Civil War.

At the end of the Spanish Civil War, *Severo*, having been, to use the idiom of the time, 'significado', was arrested in Alicante and, according to his sister, Tinita Reguilón, taken to the concentration camp of Albatera (Alicante). From there, *Severo* was transferred to several jails in Spain, until he was condemned to die, a sentence which was commuted. Following his release, *Severo* worked in a private academy, teaching typing and shorthand, but his life was hampered by his criminal record. Thus, in 1946 *Severo* joined the guerrilla fight for the 'reconquista' of Spain, modelling himself, according to his son Lucas, on Lenin, Gandhi and Jesus Christ, even though he was an atheist. It is in a pacifist vein that in 1945 *Severo* wrote to the Civil Guard in Arenas de San Pedro (Ávila), urging them to accept his proposed 'peace treaty' with the guerrillas.

Throughout this documentary, then, the guerrillas' background is provided by cartographic material, archival documents, the work of 'authorities', such as the historian Benito Díaz, and the testimonies of contemporaries who knew *Severo* or witnessed relevant events. These include *maquis*, such as Barroso, Pons Prades, Donato García, *Arruza*, and Gregorio Sierra, *Hierro*, and other people with knowledge of the time and environment. For example, the then PCE leader, Sixto Agudo, indicates that the fact that *Severo* did not adhere to the PCE's guidelines, being considered egocentric and potentially dangerous at the time, is precisely what attracts us to his figure in our days. Surreal deeds, like their 'restoration of the Republic' in the Madrid village of Alameda del Valle, are equally attractive on account of being as daring and grandiose as they were useless. *Severo*'s pacifism, which made the famous doctor Gregorio Marañón intercede on his behalf to save him from the death penalty, augments the magnetism of his figure.[23] Fortunately for *Severo* too, after spending 16 years in jail, he was released in 1972, in time to enjoy first the *Transición* and, subsequently, a democratic Spain to which he contributed during the last two decades of his life. *Severo*'s wife, Isabel, died one year before him, in 1993, and a shot of their shared tombstone with the label Familia Regulón Villalba closes Fernández' documentary.

Besides his fleeting appearance as 'interviewer' early in the documentary, Fernández conforms to the widespread convention of having directors absent from the scenes that they create, conveying the effect that the documentary may be, in fact, unmediated representation of reality. *La guerra de Severo* uses unquestionably standard documentary conventions, such as old maps and photographs, the male voice-of-God narration, display of archival photographs and recitation of facts. What Fernández records, however, is not just oral history but testimonies of people who act as witnesses, with the result that the audience are given the position of potential judges. This agrees with the definition of *testimonio* given by Beverley, and the genre's concern with giving a voice to the subaltern, implicating readers by putting them in a position 'akin to that of a jury in a courtroom':

> In oral history it is the intentionality of the *recorder* – usually a social scientist – that is dominant, and the resulting text is in some sense 'data'. In *testimonio*, by contrast, it is the intentionality of the *narrator* that is paramount. The situation of narration in *testimonio* has to involve an urgency to communicate, a problem of repression, poverty, subalternity, imprisonment, struggle for survival, and so on, implicated in the act of narrator itself. The position of the reader of *testimonio* is akin to that of a jury member in a courtroom. (Beverley 1989: 14)

Documentary conventions thus include personal research, as well as the commentaries of experts and, rarely, an alternative point of view, often used as reinforcement of the main argument. An alternative point of view happens, for example, in *La guerrilla*, which is the fifth episode of the television series *España: Historia inmediata*, when a Civil Guard renders the *maquis* an indirect homage by reflecting on their 'honest' face-to-face fight, which he compares negatively to the terrorism of the Basque terrorist organization, ETA, during the last part of the twentieth century.[24] In this documentary, moreover, guerrilla Murillo pays homage to the doctors, peasants and women who could not leave like them and who supported them at high cost, thus deserving to be honoured ('ellos merecen ser honrados').

Another documentary that conforms to most of the parameters of the genre and the 'documentary project' is Daniel Álvarez and Iñaki Pinedo's *Girón: El hombre que murió dos veces* (2004).[25] This production, moreover, also uses some devices that documentaries borrow from detective films in order to create interest in the audience. As in Fernández' *La guerra de Severo*, Álvarez and Pinedo's *Girón* includes archival footage, interviews with experts or relatives and voice-over information.[26] Girón himself is initially described as the man who 'died twice', and, like *Severo*, is introduced through the testimony of several people, who, without mentioning his name, comment on his intelligence and the fact that he was not a party follower, although he was a member of the socialist union UGT ('Unión General de Trabajadores').[27] As with *Severo*, the departure point of this documentary is to establish the innocence and rightfulness of the character to be developed through a conjunction of images and commentaries. Thus, this opening is followed by a cut to a tombstone, the inscription of which singles Girón out as the main member of his family, 'Familia Manuel Girón Bazán'. The tomb is located in the mining town of Ponferrada, León, traditionally a left-wing area of Spain, where Girón is thus laid to rest and honoured as head of his 'family'. A disembodied male voice-over informs us that Girón fought for 15 years, with the background non-diegetic tune of another famous Civil War song, 'Si me quieres escribir' ('If you want to write to me'). This is superimposed on a landscape with gorges and cascades, which convey an idea of cleanliness and purity. The impression thus created is furthered when, in the next sequence, we see a rural village and hear the diegetic sound of cowbells that contextualize the voice-over narration of Girón's birth and upbringing. He was born, we are told, in Salas de los Barrios (León), and after signing up for the socialist *Unión General de Trabajadores*, he joined the militia against Franco's regime in 1936, aged 26. His sister, Emilia, frail and elderly at the time the documentary was shot, informs us of some events in his life, and the deep humanity of her brother's personality, while sitting on a chair in a prototypical neatly arranged, modest 'salón' (lounge). Emilia also attests to the suffering that her family underwent on account of their ideas and their unflinching support of their 'bandit' relative, including her own contribution, when she boldly identified the corpse of one of his colleagues as her brother's, leading to his being proclaimed 'dead'.

Throughout this documentary, besides Emilia Girón's, we are given the voices of the *enlaces* who worked on behalf of the guerrillas in the Bierzo area of León: Ángel Losada, Laudelino Vidal, Francisco Nieto, Matilde Franco and José Valle. They tell us that, on account of Girón's activities as a union member, he fled to the mountains when the area fell to the Nationalist Army in 1937. After that, Girón became legendary largely because of his extraordinary ability to survive, which he owed greatly to the support around him. Although the group to which

Girón eventually belonged, the *Federación de Guerrillas de León–Galicia* ('Federated Guerrillas of León and Galicia), was dissolved five years after it was formed, in 1947, Girón remained fighting, while many of his colleagues went into exile. He was joined by a small group of *maquis* that included his partner, Alida González, who was the widow of another *maquis*. Subsequent investigations have revealed that the group was infiltrated by an informer who betrayed them, something that had been previously assumed to have resulted from González' confession after she was arrested and questioned.

As with the remaining examples cited in this chapter, *Girón: El hombre que murió dos veces* forges a notion of reality through personal experiences in an attempt to give a voice to those consigned to oblivion. At the same time, like the rest of the documentaries mentioned here, this production foregrounds the problems attached to a medium that relies heavily on attracting public attention through an identification with people largely presented as victims, which can lead to partiality and easy emotionality. Nevertheless, in spite of possible claims of truth or manipulation, these documentaries present 'partial truths', in line with Linda Williams' argument that:

> Truth is not 'guaranteed' and cannot be transparently reflected by a mirror with a memory, yet some kinds of partial and contingent truths are nevertheless the always receding goal of the documentary tradition. Instead of careening between idealistic faith in documentary truth and cynical recourse to fiction, we do better to define documentary not as an essence of truth but as a set of strategies designed to choose from among a horizon of relative and contingent truths. (Williams 1998: 386)

More unusual regarding both the documentary format and its subject matter is Carles Balagué's *La Casita Blanca*, which, with the city of Barcelona as protagonist, re-enacts one of the most famous raids during the Franco regime, led by legendary anarchist *maquis* Josep Lluís i Facerías. Mixing interviews, documentary footage and a rehearsal of the robbery on a high-class *meublé* ('brothel'), this documentary, as its director remarks, offers a different viewpoint from the official narrative of the times, a 'historia de la ciudad, la que aparece en los libros y la que formaba parte de la tradición oral. Una historia que no se debe seguir disfrazando' (Qtd Ramos 2002: n.p.).[28]

Dramatizations of events often appearing in documentaries such as Balagué's *La Casita Blanca* are normally associated with fiction films and can undermine a documentary's claim to realism. However, they can also function as overt admissions of the fact that handling a camera entails the unavoidable deployment of a point of view, even if disguising it as a third-person or 'eye of God' perspective. This documentary thus shows, as its subtitle – *La ciudad oculta* – spells out, 'the hidden' Barcelona, exposing the double standards of a high bourgeoisie that had largely supported Franco's uprising in 1936 or adapted efficiently to it in order to gain benefits. *Estraperlo* ('black market'), poverty, rationing and underground political activity converge in this representation of this most famous 'casa de citas' ('brothel'), in which a famous Catalan businessman, Antonio Masana, was killed by Facerías (played by Roger Casamajor in the film). The documentary is unique in its focus on a city, and also in references to Catalan collaborationism, a taboo subject for a long time, even if some of its 'facts', especially whether Masana was found with his under-age niece, have been hotly disputed.[29] Stressing the duplicity of the Catalan high bourgeoisie, the film thus draws an alternative history of the city between the years of 1947, when Eva Perón visited Spain, and 1952, when the Eucharistic Congress was celebrated there. Along the way, Balagué retraces the steps of one of the most famous Catalan urban fighters, Facerías.

Balagué's documentary came out at the onset of the twenty-first century, a time which witnessed an increase in the production of documentaries, especially those reassessing Spain's past. This coincidence is not merely circumstantial, as it reflects a social tendency to look into social and historical events from the perspective of 'witnesses' who may have been disregarded in other formats. These documentaries thus take on a surrogate role for the justice that was never fulfilled, and offer a form of reparation for the victims of Francoism. The complicity that these documentaries achieve from audiences converges with one of the aims of *testimonio*, which, as Beverley notes, is designed to engage the readers' 'sense of ethics and justice': 'The complicity a *testimonio* establishes with its readers involves their identification – by engaging their sense of ethics and justice – with a popular cause normally distant, not to say alien, from their immediate experience' (Beverley 1989: 19).

The documentaries studied in this chapter both invite and offer an alternative to the juridical processes that many believe should never have been forgone, as shown not only by the 2007 Law of Historical Memory but also by the legal efforts to bypass the Amnesty Law of 1977 led by Judge Baltasar Garzón in 2008. As with Holocaust victims, these documentaries have allowed many survivors of the Spanish oppression and resistance to come to terms with their past. These productions afford a means to 'work through' the individual and social traumas of Spanish history, offering a salutary outlet for the voicing of events that many rightly wish not to be forgotten or consigned to history books; they seek to make these men and women part and parcel of the 'memoria viva' of their country. To quote Dori Laub, 'What ultimately matters in all processes of witnessing, spasmodic and continuous, conscious and unconscious, is not simply the information, the establishment of the facts, but the experience itself of *living through* testimony, of giving testimony' (Laub 1995: 70).[30] In this, it could be said that the Spanish processes echo those of Holocaust history, both in their desire to draw lessons from the past and in the need to resist the desire to establish what Jordanova calls 'moral polarities':

> The notion of 'lessons from history' is so glibly invoked [in Holocaust history] that the difficulties behind it are often missed. These are extraordinarily difficult questions, and people easily misunderstand each other because feelings about them run so high. The result is a desire for simple answers and for clear moral polarities ... At the heart of these difficulties lie guilt and shame. The need to find culprits for terrible deeds is deep rooted: it is emotionally satisfying to have hate-figures. (Jordanova 2000: 167)

The individualized or 'collective' documentaries looked at in this chapter can be seen to fulfil clearly different, though often complementary, functions. Not only do they offer what Bill Nichols labels as 'views of the world' (1991: xi) but they also stand at the intersection between the individual and the collective memory that Maurice Halbwachs defined (Halbwachs 1992: 51).[31] Like the *testimonios* alluded to by Beverley, the documentaries that focus on the Spanish *maquis* have the aim of giving a voice to people who had been silent.[32] Very much as with testimony, these documentaries negotiate the interaction between fiction and history, serving to make what Beverley calls a 'reality effect' (Beverley 1989: 22). The convergence of the political with the social is summed up by the centrality of these living rooms to which we have gained access when talking to the *maquis* or to the relatives. This homely environment provides the bridge between history and memory that testimony affords.[33] Similarly, the witnesses called to 'testify' about these men and women have attested to the latter's honesty and selflessness, constructing people with human flaws as a new type of war hero in line with our times.

The documentaries produced at the onset of the twenty-first century strive to present militant views that are paradoxically in line with some pacifist and conciliatory trends that we associate with the Republic's best traits. It should not come as a surprise to find that they are contemporary with the idea of the 'third' Spain that Paul Preston proposed when he singled out people, mostly Republicans, who strove to conciliate the duality of the war's split. These documentaries construct people who are either peaceful or drawn to use violence due to the circumstances in which they lived. Furthermore, the modesty of their lives thereafter effects a rapprochement between the past and the present. In this way, their testimonies provide a tool for the personal and social healing necessary after the traumatic events that dominated Spain from 1936 until the death of the dictator in 1975. Looking at this 'ordinary' history, as Eric Hobsbawm reminds us, is a way to highlight an aspect of the past that was ignored, this time wilfully.[34]

Conclusion

Just as the healing of personal trauma depends on facing up to what actually happened and on revisioning the past in a new light, so it is with groups of people, with nations. (Lerner 1997: 204)

One of the main issues surrounding the remembrance of traumatic events such as the Spanish Civil War and the long repression that followed it is how to make sense of the past and commemorate its victims while cementing social solidarity and healing personal and social wounds. The balance between forgetting and remembering is a delicate one, and societies need to tread carefully when trying to address past grievances, especially in the case of internal conflicts. Nonetheless, besides the need to administer justice for all, remembrance can also facilitate the processes of social cohesion and individual healing, while resisting the reification of a hierarchy of victimization. As John Brewer observes, 'Society needs to find ways in which victimhood can be honoured as an experience in public ways (in acts of remembrance and commemoration, sites of memorial, recovered memory projects, truth recovery projects and the like)' (Brewer 2006: 223). Many of the films studied in this book illustrate the extent to which cultural products can contribute to social reconciliation or simply engage in the debate about a conflictive situation.

After 1939, the victors of the Spanish Civil War controlled the interpretation and transmission of the country's history, including their version of the Civil War's origins and denouement, enforcing their one-sided story. This left the rest of the country, which was lumped together as 'defeated', without a voice with which to articulate theirs, as shown by the films studied in Chapter 2 of this book. The 'losers' were prevented from having their version of events listened to, and were forced to participate in events that celebrated the victors. Aided by their strict control of education and censorship, Francoist supporters had four decades to present these views in the public arena. Thereafter, because of the conditions undergone during Spain's particular transition to democracy, the victims of the Francoist repression did not have any public hearing of their plight, as illustrated in cinematic productions from the 1970s onwards. Even though this gap obeys in part the circumstances and peculiarities of its time and place, it also coincides with the temporal distance needed to assimilate social and personal traumas and constitute 'holes of memory'. As Ferdinand Mount observes, it is not unusual to find these 'great silences' throughout substantive periods of time at the end of an autocratic and repressive period and before its historical, juridical or social apprehension.[1]

Following traumatic events, societies often relegate willingly or unconsciously from public memory situations or attitudes that can rehearse the past or reactivate violence in the form of retaliation.[2] Nevertheless, communities need to find ways of remembering the victims in order to ensure that a historical episode is effectively and affectively closed and that society can embark on the construction of a collective future. Obviously, there is a need to do so in a way that contributes to peaceful coexistence and encourages the participation of the majority in community building. This is often achieved individually and collectively through a process of 'selective memorializing', as Gerda Lerner has noted, which can be rather precarious in the case of internal conflicts and civil wars.[3]

Inspired by the study of Holocaust victims, twentieth-century scholars have shown the ways in which individual and collective traumas tend to resurface many years after they took place. In fact, revisiting past traumas often requires the intervention of new generations whose affective links to the events are not direct but mediated through familial or social memories, as has happened in Spain from the 1990s. The Spanish 'hole of memory' fits quite precisely within what Dori Laub calls the 'belatedness' experienced by Holocaust trauma victims in dealing with their situation. With reference to the aging survivors when they recorded their own stories late in their lives, Laub remarks that:

> It is not by chance that these testimonies ... become receivable only *today*, it is not by chance that it is only now, *belatedly*, that

the event begins to be historically grasped and seen. I wish to emphasize this *historical gap* which the event created in the collective witnessing. This emphasis does not invalidate in any way the power and the value of the individual testimonies, but it underscores the fact that these testimonies were not transmittable, and integratable, at the time. (Laub 1995: 69)[4]

Survivors of the Spanish conflict began to tell their stories in public late in their lives, and many of these have found an outlet in books, fiction films and documentaries. The articulation of these testimonies was made the more urgent as the direct participants were reaching the end of their lives, and they would take with them not only memories of suffering but also knowledge about some events or the whereabouts of anonymous graves. This effort to recover those memories was largely spurred on by the second generation of those taking part in the struggle, seeking to understand what happened or find the corpses of lost relations. The spearhead of that movement was the work of Emilio Silva and Santiago Macías, who eventually founded the *Asociación para la Recuperación de la Memoria Histórica* ('Association for the Recovery of Historical Memory') in 2001, which led other 'memory associations' in the search and archaeological digs for the remains of many summarily executed during the 1930s and 1940s. At the same time, the efforts to honour these people also gathered momentum, and there has been a plethora of public events held in their memory, especially since the mid-1990s.

As with Holocaust victims, the process of healing, at both individual and collective levels in Spain, has been largely contingent on being able to articulate a narrative about the long-silenced past.[5] The celebrations, monuments, films and documentaries produced in Spain since the 1990s have contributed to this narrative, providing a forum in which to express grievances or debate about this past. This exposure, according to Laub, is a necessary step to work through individual trauma:

> The 'not telling' of the story serves as a perpetuation of its tyranny. The events become more and more distorted in their silent retention and pervasively invade and contaminate the survivor's daily life. The longer the story remains untold, the more distorted it becomes in the survivor's conception of it, so much so that the survivor doubts the reality of the actual events. (Laub 1995: 64)

Like individuals, societies need to acknowledge and come to terms with the past, while showing the rule of law operating at all levels so as to project a fairer future for all. When trying to overcome internal conflicts, however, seeking redress for past injustices can destabilize a fragile compromise for peace, and it can become practically impossible to revisit human rights violations immediately after they have taken place, even when those may be classed as 'massive'.[6]

It is worth noting in this context the parallel development of the individual and social dimensions of trauma, which is one of the aspects neatly articulated through the medium of film. Although intimately related, collective trauma is not simply the sum of individual traumas, even if both may coexist and result from the same socio-political causes. A community, as Kai Erikson proposes, can be traumatized in ways that go beyond the individual traumas suffered by its members:

> [O]ne can speak of traumatized communities as something distinct from assemblies of traumatized persons. Sometimes the tissues of community can be damaged in much the same way as the tissues of mind and body ... but even when that does not happen, traumatic wounds inflicted on individuals can combine to create a mood, an ethos – a group culture, almost – that is different from (and more than) the sum of the private wounds that make it up. Trauma, that is, has a social dimension. (Erikson 1995: 185)

In other words, traumatized communities can endure long-lasting consequences that include the breach of social trust and ties of solidarity.

Erikson's definition of collective trauma partly explains some of the reasons for the Spanish 'collective amnesia' following the end of the dictatorship, which could be seen, in many ways, as a type of collective numbness. This caused and was caused by the erosion of all-important social connectors, which is of particular importance for a community that relies for its wellbeing on familial and group ties and activities. By and large, Spain became a society whose 'basic tissues' were severely damaged and the repair of its social connectors became pretty much impossible for the generation that suffered the trauma.[7] Francoist Spain lived a collective trauma that started to be understood and treated following the 1990s 'memory boom', when it became clear that those wounds were still open, and how much the past haunted the living.[8] While the earlier productions studied in this book contributed to cementing division through the humiliation and alienation of the Civil War's losers, those released after the death of the dictator have sought to engage actively in that healing process.

The Francoist long-lasting repression effectively rendered the category of vanquished or losers a rather nebulous one, lumping together many different classes of people within it. The incalculable suffering of civilians, which can be glimpsed through some of the films looked at in this book, shows that it became practically impossible to segregate the categories of mainstream civilians, Civil War losers or resistance fighters.[9] That the repression embraced many people, notwithstanding their innocence, is acknowledged by the cinematic use of women and children as protagonists in fiction films or when documentaries class unarmed and peaceful civilians as *maquis*. It is also suggested, for example, when characters, such as Doctor Ferreiro in *El laberinto del fauno*, become victims or unlikely heroes simply on account of fulfilling their professional duty or because of their refusal to comply with the regime's impositions. The relationship between passive and active resistance is thus, in many ways, rendered meaningless by these characters. This was clearly the historical case of those on whom these characters are modelled, as the Franco regime retroactively classed as opposition to it those who did not support the regime even if this meant they had simply supported a legitimately elected government.

The Francoist repression, therefore, caused deep fissures in social trust that rendered people unable (or unwilling) to face up to the past, rendering the process of healing a rather protracted one, still to take place in the twenty-first century. This study has argued that films and documentaries can play an important role in the processes involved in healing collective traumas by giving a voice with which to articulate individual and social trauma. These cultural products can help people 'work through' personal and public memories in order to assimilate the past as part and parcel of the present and in order to be able to construct a collective future. The memories embodied in films can make the past relevant to the present, appealing to people's emotional identification and drawing in the audience, effectively linking the present back to a severed past. Films, documentaries and celebrations 'perform' memory, rendering the past alive and meaningful for future generations in ways that concur with Peter Glazer's study of commemorative events as performances of memory. These events, as Glazer proposes, seek to engage the audience through what he terms 'radical nostalgia' in order to incorporate those who might otherwise remain detached (Glazer 2005: 172).[10]

Films like *Pim, pam, pum ...*, *Los días del pasado*, *Silencio roto* or *El laberinto del fauno* may be classed alongside events held in the public arena as 'atonement strategies'; that is to say, as vehicles to deal with past traumas.[11] To address a past of conflict, there is a need to deploy what John Brewer calls 're-memorialising strategies', which include 'museums, exhibitions, memorials that celebrate peace ... Centres for Remembrance or Reconciliation (buildings, places, heritage centres, even forests or parks devoted to peace)' (Brewer 2006: 219). Like these 'strategies', films can be effective means to work through social reconciliation, using the cultural arena to address injustices whenever these may not be faced openly for fear of igniting the divisions that led to the social break.[12]

My book has treated films as memorializing strategies, as well as 'agents of social life' where individual experiences may be integrated.[13] This treatment provides some interesting insights into the films that were made during the Spanish 'times of silence' (1939–95), further illuminating the contrast between these and those produced up to and including 2010. This book considers films as potential sites of memory in the context of contemporary commemorations and monuments erected to honour the struggle against the Francoist repression within Spain. Like commemorations, films and monuments are 'lieux de mémoire' which enter into a dialogue with the ways the past informs social relations in the present. Films are particularly important in making Spanish *maquis* a living memory on account of their immediacy. In this sense, they can be considered social 'rituals', in that, as Mary Douglas notes, they provide a 'frame' within which to treat their memory, making it relevant to the present.[14]

The memorializing effort needed for communities to work through the effects of trauma can thus involve films as sites for the articulation of individual or collective acts of remembrance. The significance attached to films as 'events', I have suggested, is of paramount importance to the process both of healing and of honouring victims, as well as pointing forward to a shared future. They offer, to borrow Laub's words, a way to 'repossess' the life stories of those whose testimonies were only heard long after they took place.[15] Films, in other words, make those events part of everybody's life story and are a 'form of action' that can facilitate understanding and become integral to a society's wellbeing.[16] They are part of the processes of creating a collective memory, both in the meaning attributed to the term by Maurice Halbwachs (1992), and in that given by the Spanish memory associations' invocation of 'historical memory', as highlighted in Chapter 1 of this book. In the present case, it means the long-overdue recognition of the resistance of the Spanish *maquis* and their civilian supporters as part of the resistance against the various forms in which totalitarianism, repression and intolerance populate the world.

Notes

Introduction: The Legacy of the Spanish Civil War and Cinematic Melodrama

1. The nineteenth century was a time of considerable political upheaval in Spain. The short-lived First Spanish Republic (1873–74) followed the abdication of King Amadeo I. This Republic was replaced by the Bourbon Restoration under Alfonso XII. Following elections in 1931, when Republican candidates won the majority of the votes, the king went into exile and the Second Spanish Republic was proclaimed. New elections were held in 1936.
2. Vicente Sánchez-Biosca (2006) charts the development of the associative movement around the recovery of 'historical memory' from the 1970s to 2006 and the political 'abuses' embedded in the process.
3. This is the case in spite of the fact that, unlike its opponents, the Republic strove to impose its legality and curb any criminal offences soon after the coup had taken place. On this topic, see Graham (2005: 26–33).
4. In the elections of 1936, the Popular Front (*Frente Popular*), a coalition of republican, socialist and communist parties, won a narrow victory (34.3 per cent) over the right-wing alliance of the National Front (*Frente Nacional*) (33.2 per cent). Catalan parties mostly adhered to the Popular Front, whereas Basques went largely on their own, gaining 5.4 per cent with other centrist parties. Seventy-one per cent of the 13 million voters took part in the elections.
5. 'To the people ... who from 1 October 1934 and before 18 July 1936 contributed to creating or aggravating the subversion of which Spain was a victim, and of all those who, since the mentioned dates, have opposed or oppose the *Movimiento* with concrete deeds or through passivity.' *Movimiento Nacional* was the label given to the fascist party, Falange, post-1945. The Law of Political Responsibilities was partly reformed on 19 February 1942 when the special *Tribunales Regionales* ('Regional Tribunals'), which had been in charge of judging these cases, were replaced by the *Audiencias Provinciales* ('Provincial Courts'). The law itself, however, remained in place until 10 November 1966, with the special jurisdiction allocated to the *Audiencias* removed in 1945. The law targeted 'those who contributed with grave acts or omissions to forge the red subversion', outlawing 'all parties, political and social groups which, since the call to suffrage of 16 February 1936 have been part of the Popular Front, as well as the groups and parties allied or adhered to this front, separatist organizations and all those which opposed the triumph of the *Movimiento Nacional*, including the Masonic Lodges'. (Author's translation.)

6. The acronym CEDA stands for *Confederación Española de Derechas Autónomas* ('Confederation of the Autonomous Right').
7. Falange was founded by José Antonio Primo de Rivera in 1933, along the lines of Italian fascism. In 1937, Franco decreed the unification of Falange with the traditionalist Carlists into FET y de las JONS (*Falange Española Traditionalista y de las Juntas de Ofensiva Nacional Sindicalista*). From 1945 onwards, it became known as *Movimiento Nacional* ('National Movement').
8. The PSOE, led by Felipe González, then renounced Marxism and positioned itself closer to the centre of the political spectrum, along the lines of social-democrat parties elsewhere in Europe.
9. ETA stands for *Euzkadi Ta Askatasuna*, which means 'Basque Homeland and Freedom'.
10. Judge Baltasar Garzón, who became internationally known when he issued an international warrant for the arrest of Chilean dictator Augusto Pinochet in 1998, was indicted in 2010 for investigating atrocities committed during and after the Spanish Civil War. Garzón was charged with knowingly acting without jurisdiction by launching an investigation in 2008 into executions and disappearances of civilians during and after the Civil War by forces loyal to Franco. The indictment argued that those were crimes covered by the 1977 Amnesty Law, and do not constitute Crimes Against Humanity as defined by the UN.
11. On this cultural movement, see especially Cervera (2002).
12. For four decades, as Richards puts it, 'Defeat in the Civil War meant the denial of even the most basic vestiges of dignity to much of the population' (Richards 1998: 142).
13. This has created what Vicente Sánchez-Biosca believes to be one of the most significant 'cultural industries' of the twenty-first century (Sánchez-Biosca 2008: 40).
14. Known as the 'Ley de Memoria Histórica', this law's complete title reads as follows: 'La Ley por la que se reconocen y amplían derechos y se establecen medidas en favor de quienes padecieron persecución o violencia durante la Guerra Civil y la Dictadura' ('Law which recognizes and rewards the rights of those who suffered prosecution or violence during the Civil War and the Dictatorship and establishes measures in their favour'). It was passed by the Spanish Congress on 31 October 2007.
15. Regarding national formation, Ernest Renan famously observed that 'suffering in common unifies more than joy does' (1990: 19).
16. In Román Gubern's words: 'El cine de adoctrinamiento explícito ... no pretendió que el expectador olvidara, antes lo contrario, pues su misión consistía precisamente en hacerle recordar la guerra civil, legitimando ante él la insurrección armada franquista contra un régimen constitucional' ('The cinema of explicit indoctrination ... did not seek forgiveness from spectators. On the contrary, because its mission consisted precisely in reminding people of the Civil War, thus legitimizing the armed Francoist insurrection against a legitimately constituted regime' [Gubern 1986: 82]). In a chapter dedicated to 'El cine de Cruzada', Gubern studies seven films, produced

between 1939 and 1942, after which time there would be no films about the Civil War until 1947 (Gubern 1986: 81–103).
17. Richards remarks how within this paradigm: 'The "purity" of society depended on women: the devil, evil and sin were revealed in men when women failed to conform' (Richards 1998: 55).
18. 'Women who had defended the Republic suffered a double tragedy at the end of the war: the disappearance of a short-lived democracy in which many had invested their hopes for social equality, and the destruction of further economic, social, and political advancement for women' (Mangini 1995: 57).
19. Richards quotes extensively from Franco's speeches to show that, for the dictator, there could be 'no redemption without blood' (Richards 1998: 14). The particular quotation chosen above is taken from Franco's address to Asturian coal miners in 1946.
20. As Marsha Kinder puts it, 'Girard suggests violence is a performative language that speaks through an elaborate series of conventions that are codified by the social order it seeks to uphold' (Kinder 1993: 139–41).
21. '[The] violence directed against the surrogate victim might well be radically generative in that, by putting an end to the vicious and destructive cycle of violence, it simultaneously initiates another and constructive cycle, that of the sacrificial rite – which protects the community from that same violence and allows culture to flourish' (Girard 1989: 93).
22. Kinder's words read as follows: 'Thus, this oppositional system of violent representation developed against a double hegemony: domestically, it had to be distinguished from the conventions of the Counter-Reformation (particularly as remolded by the fascist aesthetic), where violence was eroticized as ritual sacrifice; globally and commercially, it had to be distinguished from Hollywood's valorization of violence as a dramatic agent of moral change' (Kinder 1993: 138).
23. 'Many women's testimonies describe helping husbands or brothers to escape from their villages. For example, María Castanera was accused of aiding her brothers; she was detained, then released, and later found in a ditch near the highway with a bullet through her neck and her hands cut off. Some women who were charged were pathetically innocent; their crimes were as heinous as having sewn a Republican flag. Teachers, almost invariably sympathetic to the Republic, were imprisoned for activities that were deemed for men only, such as carrying a gun or wearing overalls. Others went to jail for having participated in a leftist organization, working in the rear guard to win the war and to achieve the revolution they saw as necessary to create social justice in Spain' (Mangini 1995: 100).
24. Elsaesser, as Mulvey remarks, 'showed how the specific motifs associated with a genre carry aesthetic imperatives and ideological constraints that both determine and are realized within narrative space and *mise-en-scène*' (Mulvey 1992: 54).
25. Singer interprets Elsaesser's views in these terms: 'By demonizing venal, abusive aristocrats, melodramas reflected the revolutionary shift in political

and ideological power ... This formulation is complicated somewhat by the fact that the bourgeoisie traditionally has disdained melodrama as a product of lowbrow vulgarity. It would be more apt to say instead that melodrama manifested the powerful new populist consciousness. Melodrama was a cultural expression of the populist ideology of liberal democracy, even if the bourgeois champions of that ideology did not have populist aesthetic sensibilities' (Singer 2001: 132).

26. See, for example, the articles selected by Christine Gledhill in *Home Is Where the Heart Is* (Gledhill 1987).
27. Mulvey further proposes that: 'Enigmas and secrets generate the image of closed hidden spaces which generate in turn the divided topography of inside and outside. If a certain image of femininity is associated with mystery, its attendant connotations of a phantasmagoric division between an inside and an outside effects the iconography of the female body' (Mulvey 1992: 58).
28. 'We can observe, for example, the prevalence and influence of melodrama in all films produced in Spain about the conflict, as much during the Francoist stage as when democracy was established. Even in the so-called "cine de cruzada", of marked propagandistic intention and where adventures and epic deeds are frequently depicted, we find melodrama in the essential elements of the plot. This occurs again in productions during the 1960s and 1970s, increasing even more in films shot after Franco's death ... Because, in our opinion, the subgenre made up from films about the Civil War will never belong to war cinema but will make bellicose scenes a complement to a melodramatic plot. In this way, this cinema is more closely related to drama as much through characters as through stories and the way to tell them, even if it presents a singularity caused by the nature of the conflict and its effects on the civilian population.' Unless otherwise noted, all translations from Spanish films and critical works are the author's.
29. The timeframe used in this book takes into account Aguilar's classification of the different epochs of Spanish cinema, which he divides as follows: 1896–1930; 1930–39; 1940–50; 1952–62; 1962–69; 1970–82; 1982–96; 1996–2007 (Aguilar 2007: 22–9). Of relevance to my study are the five last listed, although there were no productions in 1960–69 or 1980–87.
30. For the translation of titles and other details about the films, I have relied heavily on Bernard Bentley's comprehensive *A Companion to Spanish Cinema* (2008). The dates used are, by and large, those from the Internet Movie Database (IMDb).

1 Memory, History and 'Historical Memory' of the Spanish *Maquis*

1. The Italian invasion of Ethiopia in 1935, one year before the Spanish Civil War, was another warning that was ignored. One of the main reasons for

this policy of 'appeasement' was the recent legacy of devastation caused by World War I and the fear of escalating the antagonism with Germany and Italy into another world war.
2. The bombing of the Basque towns of Guernica and Durango took place on 26 April 1937 and was immortalized by Pablo Picasso's painting, today kept at the Reina Sofía Museum in Madrid. The aerial attack, which targeted the civilian population, caused widespread destruction and casualties.
3. The International Brigades were disbanded by the Republican government of Juan Negrín, who announced the decision to the League of Nations on 21 September 1938. Negrín was trying to ensure that there would be international pressure for the withdrawal of support for Franco's forces by Italy and Germany, and an end to the arms embargo dictated by France and Great Britain.
4. In theory, the main purpose of the Non-Intervention Committee (1936–39) was to prevent personnel and supplies reaching the two warring parties of the Spanish Civil War. It was set up as a result of the Non-Intervention Agreement, which had been proposed in August 1936 as a joint diplomatic initiative by the governments of Léon Blum in France and Neville Chamberlain in Great Britain. The policy was aimed at mediating between the support received by Franco from Germany and Italy and the Soviet support of the Republic. The Committee first met in London on 9 September 1936 and was attended by representatives of all European countries, except Switzerland, while their second meeting, on 14 September was attended by representatives of Belgium, Britain, Czechoslovakia, France, Germany, Italy, Russia and Sweden.
5. 'The Republic's defeat was facilitated by the failure of the democracies of France and Britain to come to its aid. British Conservatives, in particular, had been hostile towards the Republic because they saw it as a communist Trojan Horse ... Millions of Spaniards paid for the Allies' mistake with incalculable suffering' (Balfour 2000: 264).
6. For a comprehensive account of this historical period and the eventualities leading to the Allies' decision, see Preston (1990).
7. Some similarities between Armendáriz' film and Guillermo del Toro's *El laberinto del fauno* can be accounted for partly by the commitment of both directors and also by the fact that both films shared a director of cinematography, Guillermo Navarro, and had similar production teams, as Quim Casas notes, including cinematographer Guillermo Navarro and the production team Tequila Gang (Casas 2007: 56–7).
8. 'In his zeal to create an atmosphere suitable to realism and true to the testimonies [of the surviving *maquis*], Armendáriz installed his team in some country houses in the area where they would shoot (the Navarra Pyrenees) for around two weeks. His purpose while he completed rehearsals was to simulate cohabitation and to recreate a climate of isolation and concentration that he considered necessary for the actors' performances.'
9. As *maquis Grande* (Florián García) remarks: 'Pienso que todo lo que se hable de la guerrilla, es favorable aunque tenga muchos defectos. Porque,

por ejemplo, la película no refleja en absoluto cómo era nuestra vida allí. Porque tienes a esa chica que va en bicicleta y que pasa por delante de la Guardia Civil de día, en pleno día ... Y luego después, que el punto de apoyo es aquel bar ... aquello es un desastre. Todos los puntos de apoyo nuestros estaban separados, luego además había siempre unas consignas, unas estafetas que, antes de entrar en el punto de apoyo, mirabas a ver cómo estaba y tal, todas esas cosas' ('I think that all that may be spoken about the guerrillas is favourable, even if it is not strictly factual. Because, for example, the film [*Silencio roto*] does not reflect at all how our life there was. You have that girl who cycles past the Civil Guard in broad daylight ... And afterwards, the meeting point is that bar ... That's a disaster! All our points of support were separated and, on top of that, there were always passwords and couriers that you'd check before those meetings to make sure it was safe') (Qtd Vidal Castaño 2004: 141).
10. This evanescence is bluntly exposed in Manuel Gutiérrez Aragón's *El corazón del bosque/The Heart of the Forest* (1979) and Julio Sánchez Valdés' adaptation of Julio Llamazares' novel *Luna de lobos/Wolves' Moon* (1987 and 1985 respectively), as will be seen in Chapters 3 and 4.
11. Vitini's life is the subject of Andrés Trapiello's book, *La noche de los cuatro caminos: Una historia del Maquis, Madrid, 1945* (2001). Trapiello uses abundant documentary material and interviews for this fictional reconstruction of the events.
12. Vitini's brother, Luis, also a *maquis*, had already been caught and executed by firing squad the previous year, 1944, in Barcelona.
13. Serrano (2002) offers some comprehensive summaries of the developments in each of these and other geographical areas. See especially, for the period 1939–44, Extremadura, La Mancha and Andalucia (82–92); León-Galicia (92–107); Santander and Asturias (107–12). For the important period of 1945–47, Serrano studies Galicia-León (149–52); Asturias (163–71); Centre (171–82); Andalucia (182–90), and Levante and Aragón (190–7).
14. Regarding *Silencio roto*, Sánchez-Biosca indicates that 'Armendáriz supo dotar al paisaje agreste de un protagonismo especial y dio al silencio un intenso papel dramático, la latencia de una espera rota por periódicas explosiones' ('Armendáriz managed to make the rugged landscape a special protagonist and gave silence an intense dramatic role, an expectant wait broken by periodic explosions'). Sánchez-Biosca, however, criticizes the film's conventions, which, he believes, result in 'una historia de amor fuertemente codificada en las convenciones fílmicas ... un montaje dramatizado por métodos enfáticos hasta la asfixia ... el uso de una música de sabor a menudo crepuscular e incluso melodramático que realza artificiosamente los hitos del drama conduciendo sin ambigüedad algunas [sic] los afectos que el espectador está llamado a sentir en cada momento' ('a love story strongly codified by cinematic conventions ... a montage dramatized by emphatic means that suffocate viewers ... the use of music reeking of sunset and so melodramatic that it stresses artificially the main points in the drama, directing in each moment the affections that the spectator is supposed to feel') (Sánchez-Biosca 2008: 45).

15. The struggle of *huidos* during the Civil War has often been disregarded, as noted by Álvaro Jaspe in relation to Galician dissidence (2009). Discounting *huidos* as largely spontaneous fighters, Vidal Sales locates the beginning of the guerrilla movement after the end of the Civil War, even though it was not organized as such until 1944: '[E]l movimiento guerrillero no empezó en 1944 – hacia el fin del conflicto mundial, como generalmente se cree –, sino en 1939, y anteriormente en las regiones en las que triunfó la rebelión militar' ('The guerrilla movement did not start as is commonly accepted in 1944 – towards the end of the world conflict – but in 1939, and prior to that date in those regions in which the military uprising triumphed') (Vidal Sales 2006: 18).
16. In a book on the *maquis* published in 1940s Spain, *La ofensiva mundial del comunismo contra España*, Gonzalo Rodríguez del Castillo remarks that: 'En el otoño de 1944, los grupos comunistas del Mediterráneo francés consideraron llegado el momento de decidir la invasión armada de España. El Partido Comunista de Francia proporciona armas, utillaje y municiones. El objetivo supremo es crear un frente más o menos estabilizado en España que obligase a intervenir a los ejércitos aliados. Y por descontado, ocupación o conquista de una capital de provincia en la que se constituiría un Gobierno provisional, para ser inmediatamente reconocido por las potencias occidentales.' ('In the autumn of 1944, the communist groups of the French Mediterranean considered that the time for an armed invasion of Spain had arrived. The Communist Party of France provided weapons, artefacts and ammunition. The main objective was to create a more or less stable front in Spain which would force the intervention of the Allied army. And, it goes without saying, the occupation or conquest of one important city where a provisional government could be constituted so that it would be immediately recognized by the Western powers') (Qtd Vidal Sales 2006: 45).
17. This *Agrupación de Guerrilleros* would later be named *Ejército Republicano de Liberación* (Vidal Sales 2006: 32, 49).
18. 'Rightly speaking, the guerrillas were a resistance movement from its origin, as Manuel says at the beginning of the film. That initial phase is the one symbolized by the first segment of the film, a stage that extends to the summer of 1944, when it can be seen – after the fall of Paris in May that year – that the Allies are going to win World War II. The Spanish guerrilla fighters who have collaborated with the French Resistance and who have weapons use them then to initiate the invasion that takes place through the Aran Valley ... That momentum climaxes from 1944 to 1945, the time in which the *maquis* are more active ... until ... it starts to become clear that the World War II victors will ally themselves with Franco and will not help the guerrillas. Then, the Civil Guard and the army start pounding the supporters indiscriminately, leading to the demise of the movement.'
19. Rationing ended only in 1952. The effects and extent of the black market or *estraperlo* will be explained in Chapter 3 in relation to Pedro Olea's *Pim, pam, pum ... ¡Fuego!* (1975).

Notes to Chapter 1 173

20. The Fortunoff Video Archive for Holocaust Testimonies, hosted at Yale, was founded in 1981, from a project started under the direction of Laurel Vlock, and a survivor of the Holocaust, the psychiatrist Dori Laub, in 1979.
21. In Sayer's words, 'memory is the dimension in which, above all, [the] fixation of identity in an imago takes place; the self is always recollected, forever being put together (again), re-membered, after the fact. What Baudelaire calls "the memorizing faculty" is pivotal to maintenance of identity' (2004: 76).
22. *Les lieux de mémoire* is a three-volume collection edited by Nora, Lawrence D. Kritzman and Arthur Goldhammer, published between 1984 and 1992. The volumes outline French sites and concepts of national memory, dealing with 'Conflicts and Divisions', 'Traditions' and 'Symbols'.
23. Nora adds that: '*Lieux de mémoire* are complex things. At once natural and artificial, simple and ambiguous, concrete and abstract, they are *lieux* – places, sites, causes – in three senses: material, symbolic, and functional ... These three aspects of embodied memory – the material, the symbolic, and the functional – always coexist' (Nora 1989: 14).
24. On the relationship between history and memory, Nora remarks that: 'Memory and history, far from being synonymous, are thus in many respects opposed. Memory is life, always embodied in living societies and as such in permanent evolution, subject to the dialectic of remembering and forgetting, unconscious of the distortions to which it is subject, vulnerable in various ways to appropriation and manipulation ... Memory is always a phenomenon of the present, a bond tying us to the eternal present; history is a representation of the past' (Nora 1989: 8).
25. Alison Ribeiro de Menezes censures Richards' approach as one that seals the past, 'treating it like something complete and finished' ('como algo ya complete y acabado'), which she believes to be adequate for a 'pure historian' ('historiador puro'). Instead, Ribero de Menezes sees memory as 'algo interactivo' ('something interactive') (De Menezes 2009: 9).
26. Normally, the term 'memory' is used for its 'presentist' connotations, as Geoffrey Cubitt observes: 'the study of memory is the study of the means by which a conscious sense of the past, as something meaningfully connected to the present, is sustained and developed within human individuals and human cultures' (Cubitt 2007: 9).
27. As Andreas Huyssen remarks, 'the past is not simply there in memory, but it must be articulated to become memory' (Huyssen 1995: 2–3).
28. Kritzman concludes that: 'The recollection of the French past ... is the result of a cataloguing of the memory places produced over time which depict the "imaginary communities" binding national memory' (Kritzman 1996: ix).
29. 'The focus on memorialization, however, suggests an inherent tension between memory as mutable, transitory, fleeting, and fragile and memory as permanent and uncontested' (Mookherjee 2007: 284).
30. 'Secondary memory is no longer presentation at all; it is re-presentation' (Ricoeur 2004: 35).

174 *Notes to Chapter 2*

31. 'Postmemory is a powerful form of memory precisely because its connection to its object or source is mediated not through recollection but through representation, projection, and creation – often based on silence rather than speech, on the invisible rather than the visible. That is not, of course, to say that survivor memory itself is unmediated, but that it is more directly – chronologically – connected to the past' (Hirsch 1997: 9).
32. 'Modernity makes possible and necessary a new form of public cultural memory. This new form of memory, which I call prosthetic memory, emerges at the interface between a person and a historical narrative about the past, at an experiential site such as a movie theater or museum. In this moment of contact, an experience occurs through which the person sutures himself or herself into a larger history ... In the process that I am describing, the person does not simply apprehend a historical narrative but takes on more personal, deeply felt memory of a past event through which he or she did not live. The resulting prosthetic memory has the ability to shape that person's subjectivity and politics' (Landsberg 2004: 2).
33. 'Working-through requires the recognition that we are involved in transferential relations to the past in ways that vary according to the subject-positions we find ourselves in, rework, and invent ... In addition, working-through relies on a certain use of memory and judgment – a use that involves the critique of ideology' (LaCapra 1994: 64).
34. Cathy Caruth provides what has become a classic definition of trauma when she suggests that: 'In its general definition, trauma is described as the response to an unexpected or overwhelming violent event or events that are not fully grasped as they occur, but return later in repeated flashbacks, nightmares or other repetitive phenomena. Traumatic experience, beyond the psychological dimension of suffering it involves, suggests a certain paradox: that the most direct seeing of a violent event may occur as an absolute inability to know it; that immediacy, paradoxically, may take the form of belatedness. The repetitions of the traumatic event – which remain unavailable to consciousness but intrude repeatedly on sight – thus suggest a larger relation to the event that extends beyond what can be known and what is inextricably tied up with the belatedness and incomprehensibility that remain at the heart of this repetitive seeing' (Caruth 1996: 91–2).
35. Connerton posits that: 'control of a society's memory largely conditions the hierarchy of power ... the control and ownership of information being a crucial political issue' (Connerton 1989: 1).
36. Collective memory is used here in the meaning given to the term by Maurice Halbwachs (1992), as the memory which is constructed, transmitted and disseminated by a social group or subgroup. The concept is further delineated by Paul Connerton in *How Societies Remember* (1989) and is explained in more detail in Chapter 1 of this book, pp. 26–42.

2 Francoism's *Bandoleros* (1954–1964)

1. 'The people and facts appearing in this film are not all imaginary. Most of the time they are fragments of our history, still not remote, although

fortunately overcome. All wars leave behind the leprosy of banditry as a bitter sediment. Division among brothers, spurred on by illegitimate passions and interests, leads inexorably to ruin and to death.'
2. As Michael Richards observes, the notion of a 'guerra fratricida (a war between brothers)', remained intact in democratic Spain, situating 'the location of responsibility ... deliberately unspecified', and therefore leaving 'a great deal buried' (2006: 88).
3. For an outline of the rights and situation of women, see Geraldine Scanlon's classic study, *La polémica feminista en la España contemporánea* (1976) and Chapter 1 of Mary Nash's book, *Defying Male Civilization: Women in the Spanish Civil War* (1995: 6–42).
4. 'First, within traditional humanist discourse, melodrama is usually a pejorative term for a low form of entertainment drama, characterized by Manichaean morality, one-dimensional characters, histrionic posturing, musical intervals, and emotional manipulation' (Kinder 1993: 54).
5. The acronym FET y de las JONS stands for the convoluted term *Falange Española Traditionalista y de las Juntas de Ofensiva Nacional Sindicalista*, which was the result of the amalgamation of the fascist party, Falange, and the Traditionalist Carlists. The Carlists were originally a dynastic faction arising from the succession conflicts of the eighteenth century and evolving into a conservative party with a strong base in Navarra and the Basque Country. On Carlism and its influence and part in the Spanish Civil War, see especially Blinkhorn (1975).
6. These words were uttered during the Conversaciones de Salamanca (14–19 May 1955), which had been organized by the Student Union (SEU), led by the then student Basilio Martín Patino: 'El cine español es políticamente ineficaz, socialmente falso, intelectualmente ínfimo, estéticamente nulo e industrialmente raquítico' ('Spanish cinema is politically ineffective, socially false, intellectually worthless, aesthetically non-existent, and industrially crippled'). (See Caparrós Lera 1999: 88 and Kinder 1993: 27).
7. Heredero notes that besides the 'older' generation of directors (which included Sáenz de Heredia, Orduña, Lazaga, Ruiz-Castillo and Rafael Gil) the 1950s witnessed the arrival of directors who dedicated themselves mostly to comedy and who included León Klimovsky, who came to Spain from Argentina after the fall of Juan Domingo Perón (Heredero 1993: 21).
8. 'By displacing all political issues onto the family, this melodramatic system implies that if an individual peasant family can preserve its traditional values, then the state, no matter how severe its socioeconomic problems, will survive. Thus, the moral restoration of the patriarchal family ... becomes the primary "popular objective"' (Kinder 1993: 42).
9. The Spanish Film Institute – *Instituto de Investigaciones y Experiencias Cinematográficas* ('Institute of Cinematic Investigations and Experiences') – was created on 26 February 1947 and was subsequently named Official School of Cinematography ('Escuela Oficial de Cinematografía' or EOC). When it was founded, it was the first time that cinema was taught at tertiary level in Spain, and it was attended by students who would become famous directors thereafter, including Bardem and Berlanga (Caparrós Lera 1999: 85).

10. The use of the medieval title Caudillo by Franco was a reflection of the atavistic ideals unleashed by the conservative National–Catholic coalition that brought him to power. He was also referred to with the hyperbolic title of *Generalísimo*.
11. Kinder associates *Raza* with *Surcos* in their deployment of the patriarchal family as model of the state: 'What *Surcos* seems to offer as the primary seme of Spanishness is ... a rigid moral adherence to the feudal patriarchal family in the face of historical change. This same seme was dominant ... in Franco's *Raza* (1941), which officially sanctioned the fusion of the compatible discourses of fascism and melodrama' (Kinder 1993: 45).
12. Heredero observes that 'Los orígenes [de las películas sobre la guerra civil] deben buscarse en el "cine de cruzada", que había fundamentado y sublimado en la pantalla las razones de la sublevación militar contra la legalidad republicana durante el período 1939–1942; es decir, desde el final de la contienda hasta el cambio de rumbo de la Segunda Guerra Mundial' ('The origins [of films about the Civil War] must be sought in the "cine de cruzada", which provided bases for and sublimated on the screen the reasons for the military rebellion against the Republican legality during the period 1939–42; that is to say, from the end of the conflict until the change of direction in World War II') (Heredero 1993: 203).
13. Gubern posits that with the change from 'nacionalsocialismo a nacionalcatolicismo ... comenzaron a adquirir creciente protagonismo los sacerdotes, en detrimento de los militares y los falangistas' ('National Socialism to National Catholicism ... priests started to gain greater prominence to the detriment of military personnel and Falangists') (Gubern 1986: 113).
14. Heredero sees *Balarrasa* as 'expresión paradigmática de la simbiosis entre la militancia ideologica y la militancia religiosa' ('paradigmatic expression of the symbiosis between ideological and religious militancy') (Heredero 1993: 204).
15. As Heredero notes, the film 'propone, en el fondo, una metáfora política de la familia desunida por el odio ideológico: lectura recurrente del franquismo para enmascarar el verdadero conflicto histórico' ('proposes, in the end, a political metaphor of a family split by ideological hate: Francoism's recurring reading designed to mask the true historical conflict') (Heredero 1993: 212).
16. 'An appeal for the submission of the defeated who persevered in their fight for democracy, showing, instead, the peaceful integration into civil and professional life of those among the defeated who were docile'.
17. *Dos caminos* was released in 1954, the year after Franco and US President Dwight Eisenhower signed the military agreement that would allow the USA to have military bases in Spain, which led to its acceptance into the United Nations. The film was showcased at the first Semana Internacional de Cine in San Sebastián in 1953, causing friction with the French delegation, which threatened to abandon the event because of its twisted representation of the combat of Spanish Republicans in France (Heredero 1993: 158).

18. Gubern sees *El santuario no se rinde* as a film bridging the divide beween the 'crusade cinema' and the reconciliatory note of 1950s films (Gubern 1986: 112).
19. In November 1950, the UN rejected the 1946 resolution, marking the beginning of the end of Spain's isolation.
20. This plan was engineered by men occupying ministerial positions since 1957, many of whom were members of the Opus Dei. The plan contemplated the economic opening of the country to investment and tourism, making the national currency, the peseta, convertible, an increase in interest rates and a tax reform designed to reduce the national deficit and increase revenue. The measures of the plan included the devaluation of the currency and the freezing of salaries, which stimulated the migration of workers to Europe, especially to Germany, Switzerland, France and Great Britain during the following decade.
21. Douglas goes on to remark that: 'Just as it is true that everything symbolizes the body, so it is equally true ... that the body symbolizes everything else' (Douglas 1989: 122).
22. Heredero studies this film alongside others which deal with variants of Andalusian banditry (Heredero 1993: 260–5).
23. Lazaga also directed one of the most important films made about the Civil War, *La fiel infantería/The Proud Infantry* (1959), as well as *El frente infinito/The Infinite Front* (1956), which was based on a novel by Rafael García Serrano, a Falangist and former combatant. In fact, Lazaga is, according to Gubern, the Spanish director who made the greatest number of films dealing with the Civil War during the 1950s (Gubern 1986: 120).
24. M. Cinta Ramblado Minero sees Lazaga's film as an unquestionably pro-Franco film whose main aim is 'to vilify the enemy', in this case the dissidents or *maquis* (Ramblado Minero 2009: 188). Ramblado Minero compares this film with two later productions, which will be studied in Chapter 3, Pedro Olea's *Pim, pam, pum ... ¡Fuego!/One, Two, Three ... Fire!* (1975) and Mario Camus' *Los días del pasado/The Days of the Past* (1978).
25. Heredero notes how this approach 'refuerza la querida tesis franquista que contempla a Espana como una familia dividida por el odio extranjero' ('reinforces the appreciated Francoist thesis that contemplates Spain as a family divided by foreign hate') (Heredero 1993: 207).
26. Two brothers who follow different paths is also the theme of Julio Salvador's *Lo que nunca muere/That Which Never Dies* (1955), while in Rafael Gil's *Murió hace quince años/He Died Fifteen Years Ago* (1954) a member of the Communist Party returns to Spain to kill his own father.
27. On the peculiarities of the Spanish representation of woman as 'angel in the home', see Aldaraca (1991).
28. As Gubern remarks, this was 'una réplica franquista a esta consigna, en el bien entendido que su llamada a la reconciliación significaba una reconciliación a favor de los vencedores, que reiteraba así la necesidad de reconciliar políticamente a la familia española desunida por la guerra, según la alegoría de *Raza*, o lo que era lo mismo, pidiendo la sumisión al

orden franquista, que había superado felizmente la autarquía y el cerco internacional' ('a Francoist response to this call, in the well-understood meaning that their appeal to reconciliation signified a reconciliation in favour of the winners, which thus reiterated the need to reconcile politically the Spanish family divided by the Civil War, according to *Raza*'s allegory or, in other words, asking for total submission to the fascist regime which had thus happily overcome autarky and the international siege') (Gubern 1986: 121).

29. 'How could a terrorist talk directly with an urban lady? They changed everything because they could not tolerate the rapprochement between them. They gave us back the dialogues rewritten so that many expressions were replaced by stupidities.' Heredero mentions the lack of 'didacticism' in a film that, he considers, offers a 'more oblique' version of events which met the constraints of the existing censorship (Heredero 1993: 205).
30. Richards quotes from speeches delivered between 1938 and 1940.
31. Alexandre remarks on the 'intellectual communication' that arises between the *maquis* and the woman, whose life he saves by coming out of the train coach (Alexandre 1991: 24).
32. Paloma Aguilar observes the recurrence of the word 'peace' in books of the era, suggesting the obsession with war on the part of society: 'Only a nation traumatized by war could be so devoted to peace ... This is the only possible explanation for the huge number of books that appeared during the Franco period containing the word "peace" in their title' (Aguilar 2002: 135).
33. Romero voices these ideas through López, who remarks that: 'El pueblo no sabía lo que quería cuando votaba. Se movía por impresiones y por emociones' ('People did not know what they wanted when they voted. They were moved by impressions and emotions') (Romero 1979: 71).
34. 'Pure, integral fascists ... the only people willing to fight then, who were the Falangist lads'.
35. On the casting of Cooper, Gubern comments on the actor's 'porte, gestos y tics de cow-boy' ('deportment, gestures and tics of a cowboy') (Gubern 1986: 105).
36. This is very much in line with the failed family invoked by Nieves Conde in his famous *Balarrasa/Reckless* (1951), as seen above.
37. The script of *Los atracadores* was written by director Rovira Beleta and Manuel María Saló Vilanova.
38. On this film, see Sánchez Barba (2007: 373–81).
39. Sánchez Agustí comments on these young men and the actors cast in these roles as follows: 'El trío de descarriados sociales en *Los atracadores* halló óptimos intérpretes en Pierre Brisce (El Señorito que estudia para abogado, odia a su padre porque es famoso y tiene amante), Manuel Gil (chico Ramón, futbolista de tercera división y rebelde sin causa) y Julián Mateos (Compadre Cachas cinófogo de *thrillers*)' ('The trio of social misfits ... was superbly acted by Pierre Brisce (the *señorito* who studies

to become a lawyer and hates his father because he is famous and has a lover), Manuel Gil (the lad, Ramón, a third-division footballer and rebel without a cause) and Julián Mateos (*Compadre Cachas*, fan of thrillers))' (Sánchez Agustí 2006: 251).

40. '*Los atracadores* was reconstructed from the original novel with several changes in the final outcome … It is a neorealist film which was questioned in France and amputated in the German Berlinale on account of the cruelty of its final scene: a garrotte execution, a high-resolution copy of the capital punishment used since Ferdinand VII. It was "ordinary" for normal criminals, "vile" for infamous crimes and "noble" if it was devised for a person of blue blood. The difference … consisted in the way the condemned were led to the scaffold.'

41. The film's original title, *La senda roja*/*The Red Path*, was rather more eloquent in its association with the guerrillas. Eulàlia Iglesias notes the unusual fact that the raiders command a good degree of sympathy 'between the lines' (Iglesias 2007: 154).

42. *El mensaje* was first performed in Bilbao's Teatro Arriaga in 1955 and subsequently in Barcelona in 1959.

3 From *Apertura* to Democracy (1970–1980)

1. The title of the 'last *maquis*' is a disputed one. Those who consider the late 1940s the waning of the rural guerrillas that originated in the Civil War see Francisco Bedoya, who died in 1957, and his legendary companion, Juanín (Juan Fernández Ayala), as the last fighters. José Castro Veiga, *O Piloto*, shot in 1965 in his native Galicia, in Chantada, is also given the title 'último guerrillero', although in *Fuxidos de sona*, journalist Carlos G. Reigosa suggests that *O Piloto* was not a guerrilla fighter but simply a *fuxido*, or 'waiting man' ('un hombre que esperaba') (Qtd Albo 2005: n.p.). As far as urban guerrillas go, the anarchist Quico Sabaté, who centred his activities mostly in urban Barcelona, is also referred to as 'el último guerrillero', in spite of the fact that Ramón Vila Capdevila, known as *Caraquemada*, died three years later. Sabaté was shot dead in January 1960 with four of his companions in Sant Celoni, between Barcelona and Girona, while Vila was shot in 1963 in Manresa, as described in Chapter 4.

2. Román Gubern sees the cinematic crisis of the last years of the dictatorship to have been partly social and partly commercial (Gubern 1986: 346). On this topic, see also Chapter 11 of José María Caparrós Lera's book, *Historia crítica del cine español*, entitled 'La crisis del sistema' (Caparrós Lera 1999: 145–50).

3. The Ministry of Information and Tourism, then in charge of cinema, closed the Dirección General de Cinematografía y Teatro, which was headed by José María García Escudero, in 1967, creating a new department, Dirección General de Cultura y Espectáculos, directed by Carlos Robles Piquer, brother-in-law of the then-minister, Manuel Fraga Iribarne (Caparrós Lera 1999: 145).

4. This is the case in spite of the constraints imposed by the existing censorship, which remained in full force in the country for two years after Franco's demise. Casimiro Torreiro observes that a good number of films criticized the regime in an 'elliptic' and 'metaphorical' manner in order to avoid censorship. These films, conceived during the last years of the dictatorship, connected with a wider public in what Torreiro describes as a 'honeymoon' lasting until 1978 (Torreiro 2000b: 352). John Hopewell's *Out of the Past: Spanish Cinema after Franco* (1986) offers a comprehensive study of films released during the Transition years.
5. Lazaga himself directed a number of these films, including the eloquently titled *La ciudad no es para mi/The City Isn't For Me* (1965), with Martínez Soria in the role of a country bumpkin confronting snobbish relatives ashamed of his backward manners. In fact, this production was the highest grossing film of the 1960s, and is one of the types of films often resuscitated in the 'Cine de Barrio' programmes on Spanish national television, long scheduled for Saturday afternoons.
6. Torreiro's assessment is worth quoting at length: 'La comedia hispana en todas sus variantes, incluida la musical ... [era] fuertemente conservadora y respetuosa del orden instituido, con frecuencia exponente de la reivindicación reaccionaria de la superioridad de los valores de la cultura campesina frente al tumulto y la perversión de lo urbano ... agresivamente machista y reforzadora de los tópicos tradicionales, basó gran parte de su funcionamiento en generosas alusiones sexuales y recurrió con frecuencia a la satirización ... de algunos de los nuevos elementos del paisaje consumista español ... Y también a la violenta caricatura de la mujer y la ilustración de la implícita superioridad masculina' ('Spanish comedy, in all its variants, including musicals ... [was] strongly conservative and respectful of the existing order, frequently exposing the reactionary vindication of the superiority of values associated with rural culture against the hustle and bustle and perversion of everything urban ... It was aggressively sexist and a reinforcement of traditional stereotypes, and based by and large its appeal on generous sexual innuendo, often resorting to satire ... of some of the new elements of the consumerist Spanish landscape ... It also included a violent caricature of women with its implicit illustration of masculine superiority.' Torreiro singles out Lazaga's *No desearás a la mujer del prójimo/You Shall Not Covet Your Neighbour's Wife* (1968) as an example of these features, as well as of the consecration of familial life and prolific procreation (Torreiro 2000a: 333).
7. There were adaptations of literary works of authors whose work had been sidelined by the regime on account of their social liberalism, such as, for example, Angelino Fons' version of Benito Pérez Galdós' classic novel *Fortunata y Jacinta/Fortunata and Jacinta* (1970).
8. The Carlist wars, which took place between 1833 and 1876, were originally succession conflicts, endorsing the pretender to the throne, Infante Carlos. The Carlists, however, were traditionalists who eventually defined themselves against liberals and Republicans, and took an active role in the

Spanish Civil War under the rebel army of Franco. On Carlism's role in the Civil War, see especially Blinkhorn (1975).
9. Antonio Brevers' *Juanín y Bedoya: Los últimos guerrilleros* (2007) offers a thorough investigation of the lives and deeds of these two men.
10. Officially, the government declared its *Apertura* from 1962 to 1969 in an attempt to 'open up' the country to investment and tourism while maintaining a tight grip on the political life and human rights of its people, who were increasingly mobilizing against the regime. The *Apertura* encountered opposition from the regime's right, with the likes of extreme-right lawyer Blas Piñar condemning it (see Torreiro 2000b: 343).
11. In the script, this is made quite explicit with the guideline that: 'Ambition has started to corrode the spirit of the villagers' (Lazaga 1979: 65).
12. In fact, this is the title of the film in the Catalogue of the Biblioteca Nacional, with *El ladrido* in brackets.
13. The film was released in the USA in 1977 with the title *Impossible Love*.
14. The script indicates that he is 'accused of being a traitor to King Carlos' and thus not a Carlist but a follower of Isabel II, whom he considers the 'reina legítima' ('legitimate queen') (Velasco and Gil Paradela 1974: 3).
15. Anarchist pamphlets with the slogans 'El anarquismo lucha por la libertad y la tierra para todos' (Anarchism struggles for freedom and land for all) and 'Viva la anarquía' (Long live anarchy!) fall on his corpse before the film's credits appear (Velasco and Gil Paradela 1974: 5).
16. The actress Sara Lezana was one of the writer Romero's lovers, as journalist Jesús María Amilibia explains in his book, significantly entitled *Emilio Romero. El gallo del franquismo* ('Francoism's Rooster') (Amilibia 2005). Sánchez Agustí (personal communication) suggests that Romero simply put Lezana in the film because she was his lover at the time.
17. 'I want to close the list of this house's victims. My child will not be born in Casa Manchada.'
18. 'This film is not based on real events. Its characters are imaginary products of their author. Any resemblance between them and living or dead people is a mere coincidence.'
19. This term was used by Kinder in 'The Children of Franco in the New Spanish Cinema' (1983) to refer to directors, such as Erice or Carlos Saura, who grew up during the Civil War's immediate aftermath.
20. 'Sometimes I think that for those who have lived in their childhood that emptiness which, in so many basic aspects, was inherited by those of us born immediately after a civil war like ours, the older generation were frequently just that: an emptiness, an absence … what reveals that absence is something deeply mutilated that lives in them forever.'
21. Salvador Puig Antich was infamously garrotted in March 1974 and five young men, two from ETA and three from the communist FRAP (*Frente Revolucionario Antifascista y Patriótico*), were executed in September 1975, just two months before the dictator died.
22. As Gubern affirms: 'Con gran sensibilidad poética y exquisito sentido plástico, Erice y su operador Luis Cuadrado han sabido expresar la soledad

de los personajes con grandes planos generales que los insertan empequeñecidos en el paisaje, mientras que su aislamiento y su soledad es tratada con primeros planos y planos medios que en los interiores aparecen bañados a veces con una luz que evoca a Vermeer' ('With great poetic sensibility and an exquisite plastic sense, Erice and his cameraman, Luis Cuadrado, have been able to express the solitude of the characters with long shots which, belittling them, inserts them into the landscape, while their isolation and solitude are treated with close-ups and mid-close-ups within interior settings tainted with a light that evokes Vermeer') (Gubern 1986: 166).

23. Richards explains *estraperlo* as follows: 'In Madrid, class divisions in the consumption of basic necessities were evident. The condition of the lower classes was rapidly deteriorating by the end of 1939. There was an abundance of bread, cakes, and buns, at a price ... but the virtually inedible bread was difficult to obtain at official prices. Flour sold officially at 1.25 pesetas but was actually traded at 12 pesetas per kilo. Black-market bread normally also sold at 12 pesetas per kilo. A casual labourer, in an urban centre, was due 9.4 pesetas per day, but there was no effective mechanism for enforcing the regulations' (Richards 1998: 143).

24. 'The authorities ... would set a price ... Very quickly, as the collusion of state authorities became entrenched, official prices became virtually meaningless. An illicit market developed, which dwarfed "official" transactions.' (Richards 1998: 135).

25. This cold, which has become one of the most prevalent signifiers of the *posguerra*, is foremost in one of the most representative films of the era, Mario Camus' *La colmena*/*The Beehive* (1982), based on the novel by Nobel Prize winner Camilo José Cela (1951).

26. 'Look his foreigner's name/inscribed here on my skin/If you find him, sailor/Tell him that I die for him.' The song 'Tatuaje' was written by Rafael de León, Xandro Valerio and Manuel Quiroga, and was sung by, among others, the famous Conchita Piquer.

27. Martín Patino's film was released five years later, in 1976, one year after Franco's death.

28. As Vázquez Montalbán indicates: 'los años cuarenta (época que engloba realmente unos quince años, 1939–1954), en que la cultura canora está muy condicionada por la etapa autárquica de la organización político-económico-social de España. Esta etapa se caracteriza por el intento de creación de una *canción nacional*, melódica y temáticamente condicionada por una determinada idea de la peculiaridad española. Es una canción andalucista en la imaginería, la melodía y la pronunciación, vinculada a una España agrícola y provinciana' ('the 1940s (which really encompass 1939–54), are years in which the singing culture is conditioned by the autarky of the socio-economic and political organization of Spain. It is a time characterized for the attempt to create a *canción nacional* ['national song'], melodious and thematically conditioned for a determined notion of Spanish characteristics. It is a type of song that is Andalusian in its

imagery, melody and pronunciation, and is linked to an agrarian and provincial Spain') (Vázquez Montalbán 2000: xv).
29. The Spanish Communist Party decided to forgo armed struggle in favour of infiltrating the trade unions and other legal bodies in 1948 and it ordered the dismantling of its own guerrillas completely in 1952.
30. 'There is nothing left to do. They were hunting us like rabbits.'
31. As Vázquez Montalbán argues, 'La *canción nacional* ... no puede evitar cierto numero de contrasentidos el inmoralismo evidente en la mayor parte de personajes femeninos y una tristeza de fondo que se correspondía al temple a satisfacer de un pueblo que había pasado por la experiencia de una guerra' ('The *canción nacional* ... cannot avoid a certain number of contradictions, including the immorality evident in most of its feminine characters and a background of sadness which corresponded to the mood of a people who had experienced a war') (Vázquez Montalbán 2000: xvi).
32. Julio is described in the script as self-sufficient ('suficiencia'), with a superior tone ('tono superior'), fatuous ('habitual fatuidad') and persuasive ('persuasivo') (Azcona and Olea 1974: 39, 43 and 45). These features are incarnated to near perfection by the charismatic anti-Francoist actor, director and writer Fernando Fernán Gómez.
33. On arriving back in her room, Paca puts water into a washing bowl, an act that suggests her need to erase the feeling of dirt from Julio's physical invasion.
34. 'One afternoon, he departed in an unknown direction ..., leaving behind a lover's kiss that I asked of him.'
35. Torreiro locates Olea's film at the onset of the 'cine reformista del tardofranquismo' (Torreiro 2000b: 386).
36. Many of these films were clearly obscure for audiences and this, according to Caparrós Lera, accentuated the cinematic crisis to which I have alluded at the onset of this chapter (Caparrós Lera 1999: 174–5).
37. For Ángel Loureiro this is the most important feature of the *Transición*: 'The constant strikes and popular demonstrations that caused a stream of steady concessions by Franco's heirs were precisely one of the transition's most notable features' (Loureiro 2008: 235).
38. Even giving assistance to certain films was a type of resistance, and directors and audiences shared a complicity in their opposition to the regime's curtailing of basic freedoms (see Torreiro 2000b: 354).
39. 'A new personal memory which was shared collectively'. The success of *Asignatura pendiente* was preceded by the other films, which were largely addressed to more restricted audiences (Gallego 2008: 692).
40. As late as 1974, the right-wing leader Blas Piñar insisted that the Civil War was still being fought, as Gallego quotes, 'Por eso, la guerra no ha terminado porque está planteada en todos los campos, en todos los países ... La Guerra de España, siendo netamente española, incide, penetra sin posibilidades de esquivo ni evasión en cada hombre de nuestra época ... Desdichados, pues, los perezosos o egoístas que creyeron en la paz y en la reconciliación' ('The war has not ended because it is based in all areas

and in all countries ... The Spanish Civil War, being clearly Spanish, influences and penetrates without the possibility of evading it, each man of our era ... Unhappy be, therefore, the lazy and selfish men who believed in peace and reconciliation' (Qtd Gallego 2008: 199). The original appeared in an article published in the right-wing newspaper *Arriba* on 3 December 1974 entitled 'La sociedad política'.

41. These protests, which had gathered momentum from the late 1960s among workers and students, were spurred from 1973 onwards by the first economic crisis that the regime had witnessed since its *Plan de Estabilización* of 1959, when the creation of OPEC led to an increase in the price of oil, triggering an international recession. On this plan see p. 177, note 20.

42. 'In modern times, perhaps the leading case of transitional amnesty is post-Franco Spain. After Fascist rule, Spain eschewed successor trials altogether ... throughout the Americas in the 1980s, the spirit of amnesty blew strong' (Teitel 2000: 530).

43. Gallego shows how the right attributed the 'constitutional process' to 'the dynamic generated by the system itself', effectively rendering Francoism responsible for the advent of democracy in Spain (Gallego 2008: 23). Throughout his scrupulous investigation, Gallego cites a plethora of examples about the political processes and the attitudes of its different actors as, for example, Carlos E. Rodríguez' declaration in the right-wing newspaper *Arriba* only a few months after the death of the dictator, stating that 'En la España de 1936 no había libertad ni funcionaba la democracia. El Estado del 18 de Julio nació legitimado por la necesidad de crear el orden que hiciera posible a todos los españoles el ejercicio de libertades reales de manera que pudieran organizar el aparato formal de una democracia' ('In 1936 Spain there was neither liberty nor democracy. The state of 18 July [date of Franco's coup] was born out of the legal need to create the order necessary for all Spaniards to be able to exercise their freedom so that they could organize the formal apparatus required for a democracy') (Gallego 2008: 21).

44. The film *Los días del pasado* is based on the novel by Óscar Muniz, published in 1969.

45. Sánchez Noriega corroborates that the plot is narrated from Juana's point of view, for not only is she in all but five scenes, but she witnesses or takes part imaginatively in the rest so that spectators only know what she does (Sánchez Noriega 1998: 269).

46. Alongside other prominent artists and intellectuals, including film director Carlos Saura, Gades vindicated a type of flamenco that was, paradoxically, 'new' and 'traditional'. Among other things, they contested the sanitized view of flamenco developed as a tourist attraction and foregrounded the social and political aspects of the *cante jondo* ('deep song').

47. On Flores' trajectory as Marisol in 1960s Spain, see Nuria Triana Toribio's study in *Spanish National Cinema*, where she locates the actor within both the 'continuity and the desire for change' of the time (Triana Toribio 2003: 84–95).

48. 'The sands of the sea, the drops of rain, the days of the past, who will be able to recount them?' These words come from Ecclesiasticus or the Wisdom of Jesus the Son of Sirach 1:2. Significantly, Camus changed 'eternity' to 'past' in the expression 'the days of the past'. For Sánchez Noriega, the words simply suggest the inevitability of time passing: 'The impossibility of counting the grains of sand, the drops of rain or the days of the past is a metaphor about the passing of time and the unstoppable advent of events' (Sánchez Noriega 1998: 273).
49. These scenes, which echo *El espíritu de la colmena*, are clearly reminiscent of the Lumière brothers' famous 'L'Arrivée d'un train à La Ciotat' (1895), where the train is a symbol of progress, linking the village with the unseen world elsewhere.
50. The film's music score was by Antón García Abril, who also worked with Camus on his most famous film, *Los santos inocentes/The Holy Innocents* (1984), based on Miguel Delibes' book of the same title (1981).
51. As Sánchez Noriega remarks, 'La fotografía es realista, aunque con tintes intimistas y románticos. Expresamente parece que se renuncia a subrayar la belleza del paisaje. La oscuridad está presente en todos los interiores (escuela, casa, bar del puerto), a pesar de ser de día. La lluvia y las nieblas proporcionan un ambiente de oscuridad y tristeza, al mismo tiempo que refuerzan la narración en momentos dramáticos' ('The cinematography is realist, although containing shades of intimacy and romanticism, which refuses expressly to underline the landscape's beauty. Darkness pervades all interior settings (school, house, harbour bar), in spite of it being daytime. Rain and fog create an ambiance of darkness and sadness, while reinforcing the narrative's dramatic segments') (Sánchez Noriega 1998: 270–1).
52. By contrast, the sea, normally presented cinematically as a space of freedom and open to the imagination, becomes an intractable border which sends the fighters back to the forest: 'La mar, que teóricamente debería ser un lugar liberador, aparece como el límite infranqueable que devuelve a los guerrilleros al bosque' ('The sea, which theoretically should be a liberating space, appears as an insurmountable space which returns the fighters to the woods') (Sánchez Noriega 1998: 272).
53. 'Miedo y frío son los rasgos de una sociedad ... solidaria con los guerrilleros' ('Fear and cold are the traces of a ... society that shows solidarity with the guerrillas') (Sánchez Noriega 1998: 274).
54. The song, a popular tune dating to nineteenth-century Spain, was rewritten by Irish International Brigades, who changed slightly its first line, replacing fifth for fifteen ('quinta' for 'quince'), which was the number of their Brigade in the famous Battle of the Ebro. It was later popularized by American folk-singer Pete Seeger in the 1940s and 1950s. Seeger also sang it in October 2010 at the Museum of the City of New York, in an event commemorating American volunteers of the Abraham Lincoln Brigade, where blues guitarist Guy Davis and singer-songwriter Patti Smith also participated.

55. These 'Cantabrian Wars' started in 29 BC and lasted for ten years. The Cantabrian north of Spain (today's Asturias and Santander) were the last outposts which resisted the Roman invasion. The event refers to groups of people who took refuge in the mountains, the Picos de Europa, and who were besieged until they died of starvation in 26 BC. Asturias itself was named by Augustus in 14 BC as Astúrica Augusta.
56. Juana, according to Sánchez Noriega, is here 'attempting to recover the historial memory' of the place (Sánchez Noriega 1998: 274), associating the *maquis* with it.
57. 'Those overseas will come and we will come out into the light of day. But now we are too few ... I am happy with the fact that those down there know that we are here. That we haven't surrendered. That the war is going to last longer than us.' Sánchez Noriega interprets this scene, suggesting that they knew that time would prove them right: 'Hicieron la guerra en alpargatas y siguieron en ella durante largos años porque siempre pensaron que el tiempo les daría la razón y la victoria' ('They fought the war with peasant shoes and they continued thereafter because they always thought that time would prove them right and make them victorious') (Sánchez Noriega 1998: 275).
58. 'Religious and political unity of Spain'. The Catholic Queen and King of Spain, Isabella and Ferdinand, united Spain through their marriage and the conquest of Granada, which was the last Muslim enclave, in 1492. They were often invoked during the Franco regime as the clearest embodiments of the sense of Spanishness that the regime promoted.
59. The symbol of the dog barking in the night is used by Federico García Lorca in his plays *House of Bernarda Alba* and *Yerma*, as well as by Erice in his second film, *El sur/The South* (1983), to signal the death of Agustín (Omero Antonutti) at the beginning of the film. The mythological reference is that of Cerberus, the three-headed dog who guarded the entrance to Hades, in the underworld.
60. 'The starting point of the script he [Gutiérrez Aragón] wrote with the producer, Luis Megino, was their childhood memories of the anti-Francoist resistance fighters, who were feared, admired and magnified by the mountain people, remaining imprinted in a child's memory as heroes not so much of a guerrilla struggle as of timeless deeds.'
61. 'Gutiérrez Aragón remarks upon the mythical character of a *maquis* who has been abandoned by History [because] the enemy now is not the repressive force of Franco's regime but a Communist Party for whom the fighters are no longer useful.' A later film to present this situation is Sánchez Valdés' adaptation of Llamazares' novel *Luna de lobos* (1987), which will be studied below. Molina Foix sees *Luna de lobos* as a 'realist' film by comparison with Gutiérrez Aragón's (Molina Foix 2003: 68).
62. Red and black were also the colours of the anarchist union CNT (*Confederación Nacional de Trabajadores*) and of the Falange.
63. These are, according to Molina Foix, familiar motifs used throughout Gutiérrez Aragón's productions (Molina Foix 2003: 71). Molina Foix

analyses Gutiérrez Aragón's film in relation to Juan Benet's novel *Del pozo y del Numa* (1978) and thus entitles the chapter dedicated to this film 'Los dos Numas: *El corazón del bosque* (1978)' (Molina Foix 2003: 64–72).
64. For Molina Foix, the bird of prey appearing at the beginning and end of the film is 'como el ángel del la historia o el único corazón vivo en el bosque' ('like the angel of history or the sole surviving heart in the forest') (Molina Foix 2003: 72). An imperial eagle was at the centre of Franco's Nationalist flag.
65. This 'double amnesty', Stephanie Golob argues, symbolized 'the guilt of both sides in the past civil conflict' (Golob 2008: 127). One of the main studies of transitional justice is Ruti Teitel's, where she argues that: 'Transitional amnesties have their greatest legitimacy when they result from democratic processes, such as direct referenda … Ultimately, amnesties and punishment are but two sides of the same coin: legal rites that visibly and forcefully demonstrate the change in sovereignty that makes for political transition' (Teitel 2000: 59). Teitel makes specific reference to Latin America and Spain, where the amnesty of those who had committed massive human rights violations was not put to the vote.

4 Democratic *Maquis* (1987–2010)

1. During this Socialist era the *Academia de las Artes y las Ciencias Cinematográficas de España*, which awards the yearly Goya prizes to national and international films, and the *Instituto de Cinematografía y las Artes Audiovisuales* (ICAA) were created in Spain.
2. 'I don't believe that in order to conquer the future one has to forget the past.'
3. A director renowned for his efforts to screen the resistance against Francoist oppression, Ribas brought to light struggles against social privilege in his most famous production, *La ciutat cremada/The Burned City* (1976), which focuses on Barcelona's *Semana Trágica* of 1909. Barcelona's 'Tragic Week' took place between 25 July and 2 August after unionists had called for a national general strike to protest against the colonial wars in Morocco. Barcelona's workers decided to act earlier, as a protest against working conditions and, especially, the role of the Catholic Church. The events ended with scores dead, including eight policemen and approximately 150 workers. Over 1700 individuals were indicted in military courts and five were sentenced to death and executed, including the famous leader of the Modern School, Francesc Ferrer i Guardia.
4. The opinions about the film's 'social realism' are clearly divided, with, for example, Lluís Bonet Mojica writing in the newspaper *La Vanguardia* that Armendáriz steers clear of Manichaean views: 'La veracidad de *Silencio roto* se basa en el hecho de que Armendáriz orilla cualquier tentación maniquea' ('The truth value of *Silencio roto* is based on the fact that Armendáriz sidelines all Manichaean leanings') (Bonet Mojica 2001: 300). Along the same lines, Carlos Heredero sees the film's complexity

as an antidote against being simplistic or one-sided: 'La complejidad dramática que expresa esta simultaneidad vacuna a la película contra toda lectura maniquea o simplificadora, ... narra ... la historia inequívoca de una derrota ... pero lo hace de una forma no quejumbrosa ni victimista, sin reclamar conmiseración para los vencidos y sin ceder a la tentación del pesimismo desengañado' ('The dramatic complexity that this simultaneity expresses, vaccinates the film against all Manichaean or simplistic readings ... it [the film] narrates ... the unambiguous story of a defeat ... but it does so in a manner that is neither whingeing nor victimizing, without claiming pity towards the vanquished and without conceding to the temptation of a disenchanted pessimism' (Heredero 2001: 300). By contrast, Miguel Marías classifies the film as 'hagiographic' and 'unsubtle', adding that it is based on 'experiencias no vividas, muy de segunda mano' ('not on lived but on second-hand experiences') (Marías 2007: 228).

5. 'There are wars and wars ... And some, like this one, never end.' Although the Civil War officially ended on 1 April 1939, there was to be no respite in the attack on the real or invented enemies of the Nationalist state, as Franco's words, delivered the day after he had declared the Civil War finished on national radio, make patent: '¡Españoles! ¡Alerta! España está todavía en guerra contra todos los enemigos internos y externos' ('Be alert Spaniards! Spain continues at war against all internal and external enemies') (Qtd Abellá 1996: 16).

6. This can be seen when, for example, critics in the 1990s voted one of the most important Spanish movies of all time, Erice's *El espíritu de la colmena*, which is set in 1940, as one of the best 'films about the war'. *El espíritu de la colmena* comes third in the survey of critics taken by the magazine *Nickelodean*, which is cited by Javier Juan Payán in his book on the hundred best films on the Spanish Civil War (2006: 8).

7. 'For me, the black dissolve conveys the sense that time is nearing its end. The first phase is autumn, which finishes when Teresa embraces Lucía and tells her: "We women are always the ones to suffer." The second phase is summer, which ends when Lucía embraces Manuel and tells him: "Take care." Both scenes take place in dark interiors which are practically identical, and both present the two embraces symbolically in the film: two situations which point towards immediate changes that are charged with threatening omens.'

8. 'Yes, autumn corresponds with a time of resistance and wait, summer with the euphoria that produces the coming out into the light of day and winter with retreat and the defeat. In this way, autumn and winter shelter moments of underground activity and of hiding, while summer light encourages the exit of the *maquis* and their descent to the village.'

9. On one occasion, to celebrate the Republic, the *maquis* occupied a hamlet close to Potes in the Picos de Europa, near Santander. That night the Civil Guard arrived, the guerrillas left and the Civil Guard started questioning and torturing the locals (Vidal Sales 2006: 231). The occupation of

a village in the province of Madrid, Alameda del Valle, by *Severo* and his men is studied in Chapter 5.
10. As Eulàlia Iglesias observes, our interest is focused not so much on who is the *maquis* and who has been killed but on how this affects women in the village: 'Aquí no importa quién es el guerrillero muerto o cómo ha sido asesinado, importa cómo afecta esta muerte a las mujeres del pueblo. El punto de vista de *Silencio roto* se sitúa invariablemente a pie de valle, al lado de los habitantes que se ha[n] quedado en el pueblo. Vemos a los maquis cuando bajan de las montañas pero nunca se los muestra aislados de las mujeres. Los únicos momentos en que accedemos al terreno de los guerrilleros, y la cámara nos muestra su forma de vida, lo hacemos acompañando a Lucia' ('Here, it does not matter who is the dead *maquis* or how he has been killed but how that death affects women in the village. The point of view in *Silencio roto* is invariably placed in the valley, among the inhabitants who have remained in the village. We see the *maquis* when they come down from the mountains, but they are never shown isolated from the women. The only occasions when we gain access to the guerrillas' terrain and the camera shows us their way of life, is when we have accompanied Lucía') (Iglesias 2007: 158).
11. 'What hope? This is a lie and you know it.' Don Hilario had replied to Lucía's despondent '¿Y qué puedo hacer ahora?' ('What can I do now?').
12. The description of the scene in the script reads as follows: 'Lucía, a través de la vegetación, ve alejarse el pueblo. En su rostro, como si recordase algo, comienza a dibujarse una sonrisa. Tras una curva de la carretera, las casas del pueblo desaparecen y el monte llena la pantalla' ('Lucía, through the vegetation, sees the village getting further away. On her face a smile starts to appear, as though she remembers something. After a bend on the road, the houses of the village disappear and the mountain fills totally the screen') (Armendáriz 2001: 113).
13. At the onset, as Sánchez-Biosca observes, the stillness in the mountains is disrupted by the diegetic sound of shooting, which announces unambiguously the film's essence: 'La imagen se abre sobre unos hermosos parajes de las montañas navarras, dominados por la quietud y sin asomo de presencia humana; la niebla penetra en los espesos bosques. De repente, unos disparos y, sin dilación, unas ráfagas de fusil quiebran esa precaria paz. La cámara se eleva hasta filmar el cielo tamizado por la niebla y de ese entorno surge el título. Apenas puede hallarse mejor introito a los sentidos que encierra la expresión "Silencio roto"' ('The image opens up with some beautiful mountainous wild lands in Navarra, dominated by tranquillity and without a hint of human presence; the fog penetrates the deep woods. Suddenly ... a few bursts of rifle shot break that precarious peace. The camera tilts until it films a sky veiled by fog and the title surges through this environment. It could hardly be a better introduction to the meanings enclosed in the expression "Silencio roto"') (Sánchez-Biosca 2008: 42).
14. 'In sombre times/will there be songs?/There will also be songs/about the sombre times.'

15. In a significant scene, early on in the film, when Mercedes realizes that Ofelia has seen her take a parcel to the *maquis*, Ofelia tells her that she will never say anything because she does not want Mercedes to be harmed.
16. 'North American, British and C-Canadian t-troops have disembarked on a small beach in the north of France.'
17. 'We don't matter to them. You should realize once and for all, Pedro, that we are alone.'
18. The film here evokes ritual blood shedding, which, as mentioned in the Introduction to this book, has historical and religious connotations. As René Girard proposes, 'Spilt blood of any origin, unless it has been associated with a sacrificial act, is considered impure. This universal attribution of impurity to spilt blood springs directly from the definition we have just proposed: wherever violence threatens, ritual impurity is present' (Girard 1989: 34).
19. Besides the obvious religious connotations of blood, the film alludes directly to its use in the Nationalist rhetoric of Franco and his henchmen, quoted at length by Richards. To give one example, the shedding of blood in Málaga was alluded to as a holocaust for the fatherland that would facilitate the cleansing of 'red' sins and thus 'redeem' those 'sacrificed': Franco alluded to 'the holocaust of the Patria' as necessary to 'wash away' sins by means of 'a great deal of blood ... Málaga has offered her sacrifice for your redemption' (Qtd Richards 1998: 41). This quotation comes from Angel Gollonet Megías and José Morales López, *Sangre y fuego* (Granada, 1937). For further references to blood and social cleansing, see Richards (1998: 7–10, 37 and 63).
20. Mary Ann Doane (1980: 35–50) observes that disembodied voice-overs are usually exclusively male.
21. As John Bodnar remarks, 'public memory' is always intricately related to hegemonic relationships in society: 'Public memory is a body of beliefs and ideas about the past that help a public or society understand both its past and its present, and, by implication, its future ... Public memory speaks primarily about the structure of power in society because that power is always in question in a world of polarities and contradictions and because cultural understanding is always grounded in the material structure of society itself' (1993: 15).
22. Among the documentaries, it is important to note that Javier Corcuera's *La guerrilla de la memoria/The Guerrilla of Memory* (2002) was elaborated with material obtained by Armendáriz and Oria Productions in the making of *Silencio roto*. This documentary will be looked at in Chapter 5.
23. 'Spain 1948. While the *maquis* continue their fight against Franco in the mountains, a man arrives at an Asturian village in his van.' The film's screenplay was written by the director, Suárez, and the author of the short story on which the film is based was the journalist Manuel Hidalgo.
24. On this topic, see Julián Casanova's painstaking investigation in *La iglesia de Franco* (2005). Fray Gumersindo de Estella (1880–1974) was the name

adopted by Martín Zubeldía Inda, when taking vows as a Franciscan Capuchin. Born in the Navarran town of Estella, he was transferred to Zaragoza's prison to work as chaplain during the Spanish Civil War. There, he administered last rites for years to those sentenced to death by the Nationalist Army and wrote about these gruesome executions in his memoirs, *Fusilados en Zaragoza, 1936–1939. Tres años de asistencia espiritual a los reos*, in 1945 (published in 2003).
25. In the film she offers to sew the number on the back of the sports jumper, whereas in the book she mends its elbow.
26. When Ramiro Forteza confesses his sins, Don Constantino wants to know about the places in which they were committed because, he says, 'all sins are alike and I know them all. What I want to know is how the world is, because I have lived here since I left the seminary' (Hidalgo 2003: 101).
27. In the book, it is a football match.
28. 'The comings and goings of superimposed images and the recreations of "reality" seem to them quite unreal, leading them to affirm that things could never happen as they appear on the cinematic screen. It is impossible, Grande affirms, that they would make contact in a bar, a direct allusion to the figure of the teacher who appears in *Silencio roto*.'
29. Vidal Castaño concludes that this preference is underlined by their desire to point out the divergences between their vision of 'reality' and its cinematic embodiment. '[Consideran], a pesar de todo, que es mejor salir en las películas que no salir ... pero, dejando claro lo engañosas que pueden resultar esas imágenes en movimiento inspiradas en sus vidas ... Son conscientes del poder de seducción que encierran las películas' (They consider that: 'in spite of everything, it is better to be present in films than not to be present at all ... but stressing how those images inspired by their lives may lack factual accuracy') (Vidal Castaño 2004: 91).
30. Serrano estimates that around 5000 armed men and more than 20,000 *enlaces* were arrested during the 1940s (2002: 20).
31. On the repression used on these *enlaces*, Harmut Heine and José María Azuaga Rico cite the testimony of a Civil Guard, Manuel Prieto López, about shaving pubic hair of the *maquis*' wives and of a woman bleeding to death after having had her clitoris removed (Heine and Azuaga 2005: 152). This repression also included their starvation, as Michael Richards has noted (Richards 1998: 53). For a summary of women's role in the anti-Francoist resistance, see Serrano (2002: 218–27), Mangini (1995), Nash (1995) and Romeu Alfaro (2002). Armendáriz borrows Romeu's telling title (*El silencio roto: mujeres contra el franquismo*) for his film.
32. The beginning of the twenty-first century saw an increasing number of books about women in the form of literary or historical works, as well as criticism about them. Some of the most popular fiction and non-fiction books include Dulce Chacón's *La voz dormida* (2002), Ángeles Caso's *Un largo silencio* (2000), Ángeles López' *Martina, la rosa número trece* (2006) and Carlos Fonseca's *Trece rosas rojas* (2004) and *Rosario Dinamitera: Una mujer en el frente* (2006). On their writing, see Leggott (2008).

5 Documenting 'Historical Memory' (1985–2008)

1. John Beverley's now-classic definition of *testimonio* refers to a personal narrative transmitted indirectly, when an individual relates their life story to a second person who transcribes it on his or her behalf. The genre is obviously linked to courtroom testimonies, witness accounts and religious confession. Beverley's definition runs as follows: 'By *testimonio* I mean a novel or novella-length narrative in book or pamphlet (that is, printed as opposed to acoustic) form, told in the first-person by a narrator who is also the real protagonist or witness of the events he or she recounts, and whose unit of narration is usually a "life" or a significant life experience. *Testimonio* may include, but is not subsumed under, any of the following textual categories, some of which are conventionally considered literature, others not: autobiography, autobiographical novel, oral history, memoir, confession, diary, interview, eyewitness report, life history, *novella-testimonio*, nonfiction novel, or "facto-graphic literature"' (Beverley 1989: 13).
2. Although it is obvious that Francoists would censor their archival records, even in democratic times some of these were affected. One example is the treatment of homosexuality, which was treated as a crime under the Francoist 'Ley de Orden Público' ('Law of Public Order'). Once the law was removed during the Socialist years (1982–96), those documents were removed so that those affected would have no criminal record, with the consequent loss of much information.
3. These productions mostly pertain to the type of 'expository documentary', according to Bill Nichols' taxonomy (1976), which includes: expository, observational, interactive and self-reflexive documentaries.
4. Vidal Castaño notes that, while Celia and Grande have been the 'stellar couple', most surviving fighters, *enlaces* and collaborators ended up on the big and small screens by the twenty-first century (Vidal Castaño 2004: 90).
5. Writing in the first decade of the twenty-first century, John Corner observes that: 'In the past 30 years there has been a huge growth in the study and critical analysis of documentary and an increase, too, in the variety and conceptual ambition of ways of thinking about it ... From the mid-1990s, this development has been accelerated, first of all, by the phenomenon of "reality television", selectively drawing on documentary precedents, and then by the emergence ... of "feature documentary" success in the cinema' (Corner 2008: 13).
6. The whole sentence in which this idea appears reads as follows: 'In the shape it currently has, historical memory emphasizes the need to come to terms with a past purportedly neglected, and it is therefore primarily a movement geared toward a moral and political restoration, at the expense of a rigorous examination of the past' (Loureiro 2008: 227).
7. According to Loureiro, this results in 'most recent films' in an inversion of the relationship between the personal and the political, where the

latter merely serves as 'backdrop' for the former so that 'the political serves mostly as a backdrop or springboard for personal vicissitudes' (Loureiro 2008: 233).
8. For Corner, 'It is useful to see documentary positioned culturally somewhere between "news" and "drama" ... then just as aesthetics makes strong connections with drama, so cognition highlights the relationship with forms of journalism' (Corner 2008: 22).
9. As Ludmilla Jordanova remarks, the 'shift towards studying direct testimony places heavy stress on the notion of empathy with historical actors' (Jordanova 2000: 7).
10. 'Today, the red army, captive and vanquished, has been defeated. The war has ended.'
11. Although it may seem to us now to be part and parcel of the genre, the interview, in fact, was not part of the early documentaries and became more widespread from the 1970s onwards: 'Especially since the 1970s, documentary films have depended on interviews to advance their arguments and reinforce their historical armatures' (Renov 2008: 41).
12. Summarizing Nichols' classification, Corner indicates that: '"Characters" also often have speaking parts in the films, typically as interviewees, and Nichols is alert to the way in which they may be used (in a manner resembling the deployment of commentary) to provide a mode of rhetorical management for the images, one that is frequently suspect in its claims-making' (Corner 2008: 17).
13. Grierson observed that the word documentary originally meant 'travelogue' when the French first used it and included a broad range of productions: 'all films made from natural material' even if they 'represent different qualities of observation, different intentions in observation, and ... very different powers and ambitions at the stage of organizing' (Grierson 2002: 39). By contrast, in 1953, Buñuel insisted on '"The Cinema as Artistic Expression", or, more concretely, as an instrument of poetry, with all that that word can imply of the sense of liberation, of subversion of reality, of the threshold of the marvellous world of the subconscious, of nonconformity with the limited society that surrounds us' (Buñuel 2002: 45).
14. Bazin noted that: 'Thanks to the depth of focus of the lens, Orson Welles restored to reality its visible continuity' (Bazin 2002: 57).
15. Oral history, as Eric Hobsbawm observes, is a 'selective mechanism' that is always contingent on its time and place: 'But most oral history today is personal memory, which is a remarkably slippery medium for preserving facts. The point is that memory is not so much a recording as a selective mechanism ... One significant aspect of grassroots history is what ordinary people remember of big events as distinct from what their betters think they should remember, or what historians can establish as having happened; and insofar as they turn memory into myth, how such myths are formed' (Hobsbawm 1997: 273).
16. Portelli believes that the difference between what actually happened and how people make sense of and remember it is of special importance to

the historian: 'The oral sources used in this essay are not always fully reliable in point of fact. Rather than being a weakness, this is however their strength: errors, inventions, and myths lead us through and beyond facts and their meanings' (Portelli 1991: 2). For Geoffrey Cubitt, Portelli's claim that 'The discrepancy between fact and memory ... ultimately enhances the value of the oral sources as historical documents' is corroborated by the fact that 'it is this discrepancy that gives us clues to the mental strategies by which those who are caught up in history make sense of their own experience and of the political and social conflicts that have moulded it' (Cubitt 2007: 87).

17. Beverley goes on to emphasize the 'democratic and egalitarian' dimensions of testimony as follows: '*Testimonio* is a fundamentally democratic and egalitarian form of narrative in the sense that it implies that *any* life so narrated can have a kind of representational value ... Thus, one common formal variation on the classic first-person singular *testimonio* is the polyphonic *testimonio* made up of accounts by different participants in the same event' (Beverley 1989: 16; italics in the text).
18. Notwithstanding the handful of documentaries screened in the first decade after Franco's death, it is largely true that these alternative views were excluded from 1936 up to the 1990s, as suggested by the titles listed in this book's Introduction, p. 23.
19. Reguilón adopted Eubel as a name because it contains the words 'peace' (from the Greek *eu*) and 'war' (from the Latin *bellum*).
20. Nichols is one of the most important documentary scholars, with his 1983 article and 1991 book normally cited in studies of the genre.
21. The map is also used between scenes to mark historical time. As Ella Shohat and Robert Stam point out, the map is a metaphor for the film itself: 'Cinema has often used map imagery to plot the topographies touched by its adventurer heroes, implicitly celebrating its own technological superiority both to the novel's mere verbality and to the static nature of drawings and still photography. Numerous films set in Africa begin their narrative of "making sense" of an obscure continent through a map ... Cinema thus represents itself as the contemporary heir of a more ancient visual medium: cartography' (Shohat and Stam 1994: 147).
22. The sequence follows the pattern established by Corner regarding documentaries: 'The first plane is the plane of the *origination of the image* ... The second plane is the plane of the *organization of the image*. Here, the focus is on the editing together of different shots to provide various kinds of narrative and expositional continuity and then the combination of these shots with speech, including commentary, and sounds, including music' (Corner 2008: 23).
23. Marañón is one of the most important figures of twentieth-century Spain. Born in Madrid in 1887, he was a liberal physician, as well as historian and philosopher, publishing on various themes, including sexuality and endocrinology. A committed Republican during the Civil War,

Marañón tried to canvass support for the Republic overseas. He returned to Spain in 1942, and was allowed to remain in the country on account of his prominence and pacifist outlook. His return was used by the regime to showcase the softening of its right-wing extremism following the fall of the Axis powers. Marañón remained loyal to his liberal ideas and took every opportunity to sign petitions asking for the return of exiles, including the socialist leader Indalecio Prieto. Marañón died in 1960 in Madrid, where a public hospital is named after him.
24. In this documentary, the 'voice of the expert' is that of historian Hartmut Heine.
25. Here the historians interviewed or on whose work the documentary is based are Santiago Macías and Secundino Serrano. Both from León, Macías is one of the two founding members of the *Asociación para la recuperación de la memoria histórica*, and has published several books, one of them on Girón. Considered one of the authorities on the subject, Serrano has studied widely the *maquis*, especially those from the north-west of Spain.
26. 'As a mode of qualitative research, we can identify a number of research tools or *methods* available to documentary: the interview (widely used, although in different ways, across both the positivist and qualitative/interpretive paradigms of social research), narration (equivalent to the researcher's own sequencing and analysis of their results in written texts), archival footage (again by sociologists and historians) and dramatic reconstruction (perhaps more unique to documentary)' (Wayne 2008: 84).
27. In the documentary the word that historian Secundino Serrano uses to describe Girón's political outlook is 'pluralista' ('plural').
28. 'A history of the city that appeared in books and was also part of the oral tradition. A history which must not be masked any longer.'
29. The film shows Masana with his young niece in the brothel, a suggestion denied by his family, who threatened to sue Balagué for defamation.
30. In the case of Holocaust survivors, Dori Laub observes that: 'The survivors did not only need to survive so that they could tell their stories; they also needed to tell their stories in order to survive. There is, in each survivor, an imperative need to *tell* and thus to come to *know* one's story, unimpeded by ghosts from the past against which one has to protect oneself. One has to know one's buried truth in order to be able to live one's life' (Laub 1995: 63).
31. On Halbwachs, see Chapter 1, 'Memory, History and "Historical Memory" of the Spanish *Maquis*', pp. 34ff.
32. '[T]estimonio gives voice in literature to a previously "voiceless", anonymous, collective popular-democratic subject, the *pueblo* or "people," but in such a way that the intellectual or professional, usually of bourgeois or petty bourgeois background, is interpolated as being part of, and dependent on, the "people" without at the same time losing his or her identity as an intellectual' (Beverley 1989: 19).

33. As Paul Ricoeur posits, 'testimony constitutes the fundamental transitional structure between memory and history' (Ricoeur 2004: 21).
34. 'And in looking back upon the history of ordinary people, we are not merely trying to give it a retrospective political significance which it did not always have, we are trying more generally to explore an unknown dimension of the past' (Hobsbawm 1997: 270).

Conclusion

1. 'There are some events that are simply too overwhelming and terrible to confront immediately ... There is something rather impressive about these Great Silences. They seem to be observed by some mutual agreement that is itself tactic' (Mount 2009: n.p.).
2. This type of forgetting 'has been part of the nation-building project in many post violence societies in the past, such as post-Franco Spain and post-war Germany' (Brewer 2006: 217).
3. 'Civil wars and racist persecutions thrive on selective memory and collective forgetting' (Lerner 1997: 204).
4. Kelly Oliver highlights some of the paradoxes inherent in coming to terms with a type of subjection that annihilates the capacity to consider the self as a subject. Relying on the analyses of Shoshana Felman and Dori Laub, Oliver argues 'that witnessing to extreme experiences of oppression, subordination, and objectification leave[s] the victim/survivor in a paradoxical relation to witnessing. Witnessing to one's own oppression is as paradoxical as it is necessary. The heart of the paradox is that oppression and subordination are experiences that attempt to objectify the subject and mutilate or annihilate subjectivity – that is to say, one's sense of oneself, especially one's sense of oneself as an agent' (Oliver 2001: 61).
5. As Bessel A. van der Kolk and Onno van der Hart observe, 'Traumatic memories are the unassimilated scraps of overwhelming experiences, which need to be integrated with existing mental schemes, and be transformed into narrative language' (Van der Kolk and van der Hart 1995: 176).
6. In fact, as Cathy Caruth posits, 'surviving' after traumatic events can be more difficult psychologically than enduring the events themselves: 'Understood as an attempt to explain the experience of war trauma, Freud's difficult thought provides a deeply disturbing insight into the enigmatic relation between trauma and survival: the fact that, for those who undergo trauma, it is not only the moment of the event, but of the passing out of it that is traumatic; that *survival itself*, in other words, *can be a crisis*' (Caruth 1995: 9; italics in the text).
7. I borrow the term 'basic tissues' from Erikson's earlier definition of 'collective trauma': 'By *collective trauma* ... I mean a blow to the basic tissues of social life that damages the bonds attaching people together and impairs the prevailing sense of communality ... "I" continue to exist, though damaged

and maybe even permanently changed. "You" continue to exist, though distant and hard to relate to. But "we" no longer exist as a connected pair or as linked cells in a larger communal body' (Erikson 1995: 187).
8. 'Our memory repeats to us what we haven't yet come to terms with, that still haunts us' (Erikson 1995: 184).
9. Michael Richards fits this ambiguity of the category of losers within 'the representation of the war as a *guerra fratricida* (a war between brothers) where the location of responsibility was deliberately unspecified' (Richards 2006: 88).
10. Memory performances such as these, as Geoffrey Cubitt posits, can act as 'symbolic markers' of a people's collective identity with the potential to contribute to 'social cohesion': 'By constituting certain events as symbolic markers of a particular vision of collective identity, and by enlisting members of society collectively in the articulation of that vision, commemorative practices can be a force for political and social cohesion' (Cubitt 2007: 222).
11. '*Atonement strategies* ... the development of "narratives of mourning" ... help deal with the loss and grief (such as texts, images, photographs, exhibitions and story-telling that capture a society's cultural mourning), programmes to facilitate reflexivity amongst communities ... the provision of mechanisms for making public apologies' (Brewer 2006: 218).
12. Jordanova argues that: 'Memorials are built to endure but have not mainly been designed as "history"; they become so the moment they are erected ... They provide a location and object for mourning for those left behind, and are, in their own right, historical documents' (Jordanova 2000: 149).
13. I borrow the term 'agents of social life' from María Antonia Paz, who sees film in this role 'as an agent of social life through personal experiences and memories' (Paz 2003: 359).
14. 'So ritual focuses attention by framing; it enlivens the memory and links the present with the relevant past. In all this it aids perception. Or rather, it changes perception because it changes the selective principles ... ritual ... can permit knowledge of what would otherwise not be known at all. It does not merely externalize experience, bringing it out into the light of day, but it modifies experience in so expressing it' (Douglas 1989: 64).
15. 'In my experience, repossessing one's life story through giving testimony is itself a form of action, of change, which one has to actually pass through in order to continue and complete the process of survival after liberation' (Laub 1995: 70).
16. Shoshana Felman sees the value of testimony in the construction or reconstruction of a sense of identity in these terms: 'As a relation to events, testimony seems to be composed of bits and pieces of a memory that has been overwhelmed by occurrences that have not settled into understanding or remembrance, acts that cannot be construed as knowledge nor assimilated into full cognition, events in excess of our frames of reference' (Felman 1995: 16).

Bibliography

Primary sources

Films

La ciudad perdida/The Lost City (1955), Alexandre, Margarita and Rafael Torrecilla (dir.).
Girón: El hombre que murió dos veces/Girón: The Man Who Died Twice (2004), Álvarez, Daniel and Iñaki Pinedo (dir.).
Silencio roto/Broken Silence (2001), Armendáriz, Montxo (dir.).
La Casita Blanca: La ciudad oculta/The Little White House: The Hidden City (2002), Balagué, Carles (dir.).
Los días del pasado/The Days of the Past (1978), Camus, Mario (dir.).
El año del diluvio/The Year of the Deluge (2004), Chávarri, Jaime (dir.).
Metralleta Stein/Stein Machinegun (1975), de la Loma, José Antonio (dir.).
El laberinto del fauno/Pan's Labyrinth (2006), del Toro, Guillermo (dir.).
La guerra de Severo/Severo's War (2008), Fernández, César (dir.).
Caracremada/Burnface (2010), Galter, Lluís (dir.).
You Are the One (Una historia de entonces)/You Are the One (A Story of the Past) (2000), Garci, José Luis (dir.).
Huidos/Runaways (1993), Gracia, Sancho (dir.).
El corazón del bosque/The Heart of the Forest (1979), Gutiérrez Aragón, Manuel (dir.).
El cerco/The Siege (1955), Iglesias, Miguel (dir.).
Carta a una mujer/Letter to a Woman (1963), —— (dir.).
La paz empieza nunca/Peace Never Starts (1960), Klimovsky, León (dir.).
Torrepartida/Broken Tower (1956), Lazaga, Pedro (dir.).
El ladrido/The Barking (1977), —— (dir.).
Casa Manchada/Stained House (1977), Nieves Conde, José Antonio (dir.).
Pim, pam, pum ... ¡Fuego!/One, Two, Three ... Fire! (1975), Olea, Pedro (dir.).
A tiro limpio/Clean Shooting (1963), Pérez-Dolz, Francisco (dir.).
Terra de canons/Cannon Land (1999), Ribas, Antoni (dir.).
Los atracadores/The Raiders (1962), Rovira Beleta, José (dir.).
Dos caminos/Two Paths (1954), Ruiz-Castillo, Arturo (dir.).
Luna de lobos/Wolves' Moon (1987), Sánchez Valdés, Julio (dir.).
El portero/The Goalkeeper (2000), Suárez, Gonzalo (dir.).
For Whom the Bell Tolls (1943), Wood, Sam (dir.).
Behold a Pale Horse (1964), Zinnemann, Fred (dir.).

Secondary sources

Films

Les fosses del silenci/Las fosas del silencio/Silence's Graves (2004), Armengou, Montse and Ricard Belis (dir.).
Muerte de un ciclista/Death of a Cyclist (1955), Bardem, Juan Antonio (dir.).
Calle Mayor/Main Street (1956), —— (dir.).
Bienvenido Mister Marshall!/Welcome Mr Marshall! (1953), Berlanga, Luis García (dir.).
Los jueves milagro/Miracles of Thursday (1957), —— (dir.).
Plácido (1961), —— (dir.).
El verdugo/The Executioner (1963), —— (dir.).
La vaquilla/The Heifer (1985), —— (dir.).
La vieja memoria/Old Memory (1979), Camino, Jaime (dir.).
La colmena/The Beehive (1982), Camus, Mario (dir.).
Los santos inocentes/The Holy Innocents (1984), —— (dir.).
El desencanto/The Disenchantment (1976), Chávarri, Jaime (dir.).
La guerrilla de la memoria/The Guerrilla of Memory (2002), Corcuera, Javier (dir.).
Memoria recobrada/Recovered Memory (2006), Domingo, Alfonso (dir.).
El espíritu de la colmena/The Spirit of the Beehive (1973), Erice, Víctor (dir.).
El sur/The South, (1983), —— (dir.).
Fortunata y Jacinta/Fortunata and Jacinta (1970), Fons, Angelino (dir.).
Asignatura pendiente/Unfinished Business (1977), Garci, José Luis (dir.).
Murió hace quince años/He Died Fifteen Years Ago (1954), Gil, Rafael (dir.).
Los del monte/The Men from the Mountain (2006), Gutiérrez Aragón, Manuel (dir.).
El frente infinito/The Infinite Front (1956), Lazaga, Pedro (dir.).
La fiel infantería/The Proud Infantry (1959), —— (dir.).
La ciudad no es para mí/The City Isn't For Me (1965), —— (dir.).
No desearás a la mujer del prójimo/You Shall Not Covet Your Neighbour's Wife (1968), —— (dir.).
Canciones para después de una guerra/Songs for after a War (1971/76), Martín Patino, Basilio (dir.).
Las 13 rosas/Thirteen Roses (2007), Martínez Lázaro, Emilio (dir.).
El crimen de Cuenca/The Cuenca Crime (1979/81), Miró, Pilar (dir.).
España: Historia inmediata/Spain: Immediate History (1985), Monesma, Eugenio (dir.).
Las ilusiones perdidas/Lost Illusions (2005), —— (dir.).
A tiro limpio/Clean Shooting (1996), Mora, Jesús (dir.).
Balarrasa/Reckless (1951), Nieves Conde, José Antonio (dir.).
Surcos/Furrows (1951), —— (dir.).
La ciutat cremada/The Burned City (1976), Ribas, Antoni (dir.).
Rescatadas del olvido: Mujeres bajo el franquismo/Rescued from Oblivion: Women under Francoism (1991), Romeu Alfaro, Fernanda (dir.).

El santuario no se rinde/The Sanctuary Does Not Surrender (1949), Ruiz-Castillo, Arturo (dir.).
Alba de América/Dawn of America (1951), Sáenz de Heredia, José Luis (dir.).
Raza/Race (1941), —— (dir.).
Lo que nunca muere/That Which Never Dies (1955), Salvador, Julio (dir.).
Soldados de Salamina/Soldiers of Salamis (2003), Trueba, David (dir.).

Books and articles

Abellá, Rafael (1996), *La vida cotidiana en España bajo el régimen de Franco* (Madrid: Temas de Hoy).
Aguilar, Carlos (2007), *Guía del cine español* (Madrid: Cátedra).
Aguilar, Paloma (2002), *Memory and Amnesia: The Role of the Spanish Civil War in the Transition to Democracy* (New York: Berghahn).
Albo, Francisco (2005), '40 aniversario del último maquis. José Castro Veiga fue el último "fuxido" que falleció en una acción armada', *La Voz de Galicia*. http://www.foroporlamemoria.info/documentos/2005/ultimomaquis_09032005.htm.
Aldaraca, Bridget (1991), *El ángel del hogar: Galdós and the Ideology of Domesticity in Spain* (Chapel Hill: University of North Carolina Press).
Alexandre, Margarita (1991), 'Margarita Alexandre: España, Cuba, Italia', *Rosebud*, 1, 22–6.
Amilibia, Jesús María (2005), *Emilio Romero. El gallo del franquismo* (Barcelona: Temas de Hoy).
Armendáriz, Montxo (2001), *Silencio roto: Un guión de Montxo Armendáriz* (n.p.: Ocho y Medio/Oria Films/Fundación Caja Navarra).
Austin, Thomas (2008), '" ... To Leave the Confinements of His Humanness": Authorial Voice, Death and Constructions of Nature in Werner Herzog's *Grizzly Man*', in Thomas Austin and Wilma de Jong (eds), *Rethinking Documentary: New Perspectives, New Practices* (Maidenhead and New York: Open University Press/McGraw-Hill), 51–66.
Azcona, Rafael and Pedro Olea (1974), *'Pim, pam, pum ... ¡Fuego!'* (typed copy of the script: Madrid, National Library: BNE [Biblioteca Nacional de España] T/48987).
Balfour, Sebastian (2000), 'Spain from 1931 to the Present', in Raymond Carr (ed.), *Spain: A History* (Oxford University Press), 243–82.
Bazin, André (2002), 'An Aesthetic of Reality: Neo-realism (1948)', in Catherine Fowler (ed.), *The European Cinema Reader* (London: Routledge), 56–63.
Bentley, Bernard P. E. (2008), *A Companion to Spanish Cinema* (Woodbridge: Támesis).
Beverley, John (1989), 'The Margin at the Center: On *Testimonio* (Testimonial Narrative)', *Modern Fiction Studies*, 35/1, 11–28.
Blakeley, Georgina (2005), 'Digging up Spain's Past: Consequences of Truth and Reconciliation', *Democratization*, 12/1, 44–59.

Blinkhorn, Martin (1975), *Carlism and Crisis in Spain 1931–39* (Cambridge University Press).
Bodnar, John (1993), *Remaking America: Public Memory, Commemoration, and Patriotism in the Twentieth Century* (Princeton University Press).
Bonet Mojica, Lluís (2001), 'Tiempo de silencio e infamia', *La Vanguardia*, 29 April.
Brevers, Antonio (2007), *Juanín y Bedoya: Los últimos guerrilleros* (Santander: Cloux).
Brewer, John D. (2006), 'Memory, Truth and Victimhood in Post-Traumatic Societies', in Gerard Delanty and Krishan Kumar (eds), *The Sage Handbook of Nations and Nationalisms* (London: Sage), 214–24.
Buñuel, Luis (2002), 'Cinema, Instrument of Poetry (1953)', in Catherine Fowler (ed.), *European Cinema: A Reader* (London: Routledge), 45–8.
Canudo, Ricciotto (2002), 'The Birth of the Sixth Art (1911)', in Catherine Fowler (ed.), *European Cinema: A Reader* (London: Routledge), 19–24.
Caparrós Lera, José María (1999), *Historia crítica del cine español: Desde 1897 hasta hoy* (Barcelona: Ariel).
Caruth, Cathy (1995), 'Introduction', in Cathy Caruth (ed.), *Trauma: Explorations in Memory* (Baltimore and London: The Johns Hopkins University Press), 3–12.
—— (1996), *Unclaimed Experience: Trauma, Narrative, and History* (Baltimore and London: The Johns Hopkins University Press).
Casanova, Julián (2005), *La iglesia de Franco* (Barcelona: Crítica).
—— (2007), *Anarquismo y violencia política en la España del siglo XX* (Zaragoza: Institución 'Fernando el Católico' [CSIC]).
Casas, Quim (2007), 'Teoría de los opuestos', in *Montxo Armendáriz: Itinerarios* (Cáceres: Asociación Cinéfila Re Bross), 50–64.
Caso, Ángeles (2000), *Un largo silencio* (Barcelona: Planeta).
Cercas, Javier (2001), *Soldados de Salamina* (Barcelona: Tusquets).
Cercas, Javier and David Trueba (2003), *Diálogos de Salamina: un paseo por el cine y la literatura*, ed. Luis Alegre (Madrid and Barcelona: Plot Ediciones/Tusquets Editores).
Cervera, Rafa (2002), *Alaska y otras historias de la movida* (Barcelona: Plaza & Janés).
Chacón, Dulce (2002), *La voz dormida* (Barcelona: Alfaguara).
Connerton, Paul (1989), *How Societies Remember* (Cambridge University Press).
—— (2008), 'Seven Types of Forgetting', *Memory Studies*, 1/3, 59–71.
Corner, John (2008), 'Documentary Studies: Dimensions of Transition and Continuity', in Thomas Austin and Wilma de Jong (eds), *Rethinking Documentary: New Perspectives, New Practices* (Maidenhead and New York: Open University Press/McGraw-Hill), 13–28.
Cubitt, Geoffrey (2007), *History and Memory* (Manchester University Press).
De Menezes, Alison Ribeiro (2009), 'Introduction', in Alison Ribeiro de Menezes, Roberta Ann Quance and Anne L. Walsh (eds), *Guerra y memoria en la España contemporánea/War and Memory in Contemporary Spain* (Madrid: Verbum), 9–28.

Derrida, Jacques (1994), *Specters of Marx*, trans. Peggy Kamuf (New York: Routledge).
Doanne, Mary Ann (1980), 'The Voice in the Cinema: The Articulation of Body and Space', *Cinema/Sound: Yale French Studies*, 60, 35–50.
Douglas, Mary (1989), *Purity and Danger: An Analysis of the Concepts of Pollution and Taboo* (London and New York: Ark).
Elsaesser, Thomas (1987), 'Tales of Sound and Fury: Observations in the Family Melodrama', in Christine Gledhill (ed.), *Home is Where the Heart Is: Studies in Melodrama and the Woman's Film* (London: BFI), 43–69.
Erikson, Kai (1976), *Everything in Its Path* (New York: Simon and Schuster).
—— (1995), 'Notes on Trauma and Community', in Cathy Caruth (ed.), *Trauma: Explorations in Memory* (Baltimore and London: The Johns Hopkins University Press), 183–99.
Felman, Shoshana (1995), 'Education and Crisis, or the Vicissitudes of Teaching', in Cathy Caruth (ed.), *Trauma: Explorations in Memory* (Baltimore and London: The Johns Hopkins University Press), 13–60.
Fonseca, Carlos (2004), *Trece rosas rojas: La historia más conmovedora de la guerra civil* (Madrid: Temas de Hoy).
—— (2006), *Rosario Dinamitera: Una mujer en el frente* (Madrid: Temas de Hoy).
Fórmica, Mercedes (1951), *La ciudad perdida* (Barcelona: Luis de Caralt).
Gallego, Ferran (2008), *El mito de la Transición: La crisis del franquismo y los orígenes de la democracia (1973–1977)* (Barcelona: Crítica).
Gálvez Biesca, Sergio (2006), 'El proceso de la recuperación de la "memoria histórica" en España: Una aproximación a los movimientos sociales por la memoria', *International Journal of Iberian Studies*, 19/1, 25–51.
Gentile, Emilio (1996), *The Sacralization of Politics in Fascist Italy* (Cambridge, Mass.: Harvard University Press).
—— (2006), *Politics as Religion* (Princeton University Press).
Girard, René (1989), *Violence and the Sacred*, trans. Patrick Gregory (Baltimore and London: The Johns Hopkins University Press).
Glazer, Peter (2005), *Radical Nostalgia: Commemorating the Spanish Civil War in America* (University of Rochester Press).
Gledhill, Christine (ed.) (1987), *Home is Where the Heart Is: Studies in Melodrama and the Woman's Film* (London: BFI).
Golob, Stephanie R. (2008), 'Volver: The Return of/to Transitional Justice Politics in Spain', *Journal of Spanish Cultural Studies*, 9/2, 127–41.
Graham, Helen (2005), *The Spanish Civil War: A Very Short Introduction* (Oxford University Press).
Grierson, John (2002), 'First Principles of Documentary (1932)', in Catherine Fowler (ed.), *The European Cinema Reader* (London and New York: Routledge), 39–44.
Gubern, Román (1986), *1936–1938: La guerra de España en la pantalla* (Madrid: Filmoteca Española [ICAA]).
Halbwachs, Maurice (1980), *The Collective Memory*, trans. Francis J. Ditter, Jr and Vida Yazdi Ditter (New York: Harper & Row).

—— (1992), *On Collective Memory*, trans. Lewis A. Coser (University of Chicago Press).
Heine, Hartmut and José María Azuaga (2005), *La oposición al franquismo en Andalucía Oriental* (Madrid: Fundación Salvador Seguí).
Heredero, Carlos F. (1993), *Las huellas del tiempo: Cine español 1951–1961* (Valencia: Filmoteca de la Generalitat Valenciana; Filmoteca Española).
—— (1999), 'Historias del maquis en el cine. Entre el arrepentimiento y la reivindicación', *Cuadernos de la Academia*, 6, 215–32.
—— (2001), 'Entrevista a Montxo Armendáriz', in *Silencio roto: Un guión de Montxo Armendáriz* (n.p.: Ocho y Medio / Oria Films / Fundación Caja Navarra), 131–57.
Hidalgo, Manuel (2003), 'El portero', in *Cuentos pendientes* (Madrid: Páginas de Espuma), 99–107.
Hirsch, Marianne (1997), *Family Frames: Photography, Narrative and Postmemory* (Cambridge, Mass.: Harvard University Press).
Hobsbawm, Eric (1997), *On History* (London: Abacus).
Hopewell, John (1986), *Out of the Past: Spanish Cinema after Franco* (London: BFI).
Huyssen, Andreas (1995), *Twilight Memories: Marking Time in a Culture of Amnesia* (New York: Routledge).
Iglesias, Eulàlia (2007), '*Silencio roto* (2001): Las del valle y los del monte', in *Montxo Armendáriz: Itinerarios* (Cáceres: Asociación Cinéfila Re Bross), 153–9.
Jaspe, Álvaro (2009), 'The Forgotten Resistance: The Galician Rearguard 1936–45 and the Example of The Neira Group', in Alison Ribeiro de Menezes, Roberta Ann Quance and Anne L. Walsh (eds), *Guerra y memoria en la España contemporánea/War and Memory in Contemporary Spain* (Madrid: Verbum), 51–65.
Jordanova, Ludmilla (2000), *History in Practice* (London: Arnold).
Kaes, Anton (1989), *From Hitler to Heimat: The Return of History as Film* (Cambridge, Mass.: Harvard University Press).
Kallis, Aristotle (2008), *Genocide and Fascism: The Eliminationist Drive in Fascist Europe* (New York and London: Routledge).
Kinder, Marsha (1983), 'The Children of Franco in the New Spanish Cinema', *Quarterly Review of Film Studies*, 8/2, 57–76.
—— (1993), *Blood Cinema: The Reconstruction of National Identity in Spain* (Berkeley, Los Angeles and London: University of California Press).
Kolk, Bessel A. van der and Onno van der Hart (1996), 'The Intrusive Past: The Flexibility of Memory and the Engraving of Trauma', in Cathy Caruth (ed.), *Trauma: Explorations in Memory* (Baltimore and London: The Johns Hopkins University Press), 158–82.
Kritzman, Lawrence D. (1996), 'Foreword', in Pierre Nora and Lawrence Kritzman (eds), *Realms of Memory: The Construction of the French Past* (European Perspectives: A Series in Social Thought and Cultural Criticism, 1: Conflicts and Divisions) (New York: Columbia University Press), ix–xiv.
Labanyi, Jo (2000), 'History and Hauntology; or, What Does One Do with the Ghosts of the Past? Reflections on Spanish Film and Fiction of the Post-Franco

Period', in Joan Ramon Resina (ed.), *Dismembering the Dictatorship: The Politics of Memory in the Spanish Transition to Democracy* (Amsterdam/Atlanta: Rodopi), 65–82.

—— (2007), 'Memory and Modernity in Democratic Spain: The Difficulty of Coming to Terms with the Spanish Civil War', *Poetics Today*, 28/1, 89–116.

—— (2008), 'The Politics of Memory in Contemporary Spain', *Journal of Spanish Cultural Studies*, 9/2, 119–25.

LaCapra, Dominick (1994), *Representing the Holocaust: History, Theory, Trauma* (Ithaca and London: Cornell University Press).

Landsberg, Alison (2004), *Prosthetic Memory: The Transformation of American Remembrance in the Age of Mass Culture* (New York: Columbia University Press).

Laub, Dori (1995), 'Truth and Testimony: The Process and the Struggle', in Cathy Caruth (ed.), *Trauma: Explorations in Memory* (Baltimore and London: The Johns Hopkins University Press), 61–75.

Lazaga, Pedro (1979) '*Bestias humanas (El ladrido)*' (typed copy of the script: Madrid, National Library: BNE [Biblioteca Nacional de España] T/54167).

Leggott, Sarah (2008), *The Workings of Memory: Life-Writing by Women in Early Twentieth-Century Spain* (Lewisburg: Bucknell University Press).

Lerner, Gerda (1997), *Why History Matters: Life and Thought* (Oxford University Press).

Llamazares, Julio (2007), *Luna de lobos* (Barcelona: Seix Barral).

López, Ángeles (2006), *Martina, la rosa número trece* (Barcelona: Seix Barral).

Loureiro, Ángel G. (2008), 'Pathetic Arguments', *Journal of Spanish Cultural Studies*, 9/2, 226–37.

Lyotard, Jean-François (2004), 'Anamnesis: Of the Visible', *Theory, Culture & Society*, 21/1, 107–19.

Mangini, Shirley (1995), *Memories of Resistance: Women's Voices from the Spanish Civil War* (New Haven: Yale University Press).

Marías, Miguel (2007), 'Las vacilaciones de Montxo Armendáriz', in *Montxo Armendáriz: Itinerarios* (Cáceres: Asociación Cinéfila Re Bross), 223–8.

Mayo, Lola (2007), 'La historia más sencilla: Una conversación con Montxo Armendáriz', in *Montxo Armendáriz: Itinerarios* (Cáceres: Asociación Cinéfila Re Bross), 65–97.

Mendoza, Eduardo (1992), *El año del diluvio* (Barcelona: Seix Barral).

Molina Foix, Vicente (2003), *Manuel Gutiérrez Aragón* (Madrid: Cátedra).

Mookherjee, Nayanika (2007), 'The "Dead and Their Double Duties": Mourning, Melancholia, and the Martyred Intellectual Memorials in Bangladesh', *Space and Culture*, 10/2, 271–91.

Mount, Ferdinand (2009), 'The Power of Now', *The Guardian*, sec. Review. http://www.guardian.co.uk/books/2009/jul/04/politics-in-literature.

Mulvey, Laura (1992), 'Pandora: Topographies of the Mask and Curiosity', in Beatriz Colomina (ed.), *Sexuality and Space* (New York: Princeton Architectural Press), 53–72.

Nash, Mary (1995), *Defying Male Civilization: Women in the Spanish Civil War* (Denver: Arden).

Nichols, Bill (1976), *Movies and Methods* (Berkeley: University of California Press, 1976).
—— (1983), 'The Voice of Documentary', *Film Quarterly*, 36/3 (Spring), 17–30.
—— (1991), *Representing Reality: Issues and Concepts in Documentary* (Bloomington: Indiana University Press).
—— (2008), 'The Question of Evidence, the Power of Rhetoric and Documentary Film', in Thomas Austin and Wilma de Jong (eds), *Rethinking Documentary: New Perspectives, New Practices* (Maidenhead and New York: Open University Press/McGraw-Hill), 29–38.
Nora, Pierre (1989), 'Between Memory and History: Les Lieux de Mémoire' *Representations*, 26, 7–24.
Oliver, Kelly (2001), 'Witnessing Otherness in History', in Howard Marchitello (ed.), *What Happens to History: The Renewal of Ethics in Contemporary Thought* (New York and London: Routledge), 41–66.
Passerini, Luisa (1979), 'Work in Progress: Work Ideology under Italian Fascism', *History Workshop*, 8, 82–108.
Payán, Javier Juan (2006), *Las cien mejores películas sobre la guerra civil española* (Madrid: Cacitel).
Paz, María Antonia (2003), 'The Spanish Remember: Movie Attendance during the Franco Dictatorship, 1943–1975', *Historical Journal of Film, Radio and Television*, 23/4, 357–74.
Pena, Jaime (2004), *El espíritu de la colmena. Víctor Erice* (Barcelona: Paidós Pelìculas).
Portelli, Alessandro (1991), *The Death of Luigi Trastulli and Other Stories: Form and Meaning in Oral History* (Albany: State University of New York Press).
Pressburger, Emeric (1961), *Killing a Mouse on Sunday* (London: Collins).
Preston, Paul (1990), *The Politics of Revenge in 20th Century Spain* (London: Unwin Hyman).
—— (2003), *Las tres Españas del 36* (Barcelona: Debolsillo).
Ramblado Minero, M. Cinta (2009), 'Re-imaginando al Maquis: La guerrilla antifranquista en el cine español contemporáneo', in Alison Ribeiro de Menezes, Roberta Ann Quance and Anne L. Walsh (eds), *Guerra y memoria en la España contemporánea/War and Memory in Contemporary Spain* (Madrid: Verbum), 181–97.
Ramos, Manuel (2002), 'Carles Balagué utiliza La Casita Blanca para revisar en un documental la Barcelona de posguerra', *El País. Cataluña*, 27 November. http://www.elpais.com/articulo/cataluna/Carles/Balague/utiliza/Casita/Blanca/revisar/documental/Barcelona/posguerra/elpepiespcat/20021127elpcat_25/Tes.
Reigosa, Carlos (1989), *Fuxidos de sona* (Vigo: Serais De Galicia).
Renan, Ernest (1990), 'What is a Nation?', in Homi K. Bhabha (ed.), *Nation and Narration* (London and New York: Routledge), 8–22.
Renov, Michael (2008), 'First-person Films: Some Theses on Self-inscription', in Thomas Austin and Wilma de Jong (eds), *Rethinking Documentary: New Perspectives, New Practices* (Maidenhead and New York: Open University Press/McGraw-Hill), 39–50.

Richards, Michael (1998), *A Time of Silence: Civil War and the Culture of Repression in Franco's Spain 1936–1945* (Cambridge University Press).
—— (2006), 'Between Memory and History: Social Relationships and Ways of Remembering the Spanish Civil War', *International Journal of Iberian Studies*, 19/1, 85–93.
Ricoeur, Paul (2004), *Memory, History, Forgetting*, trans. Kathleen Blamey and David Pellaver (University of Chicago Press).
Romero, Emilio (1979), *La paz empieza nunca* (Barcelona: Planeta).
Romeu Alfaro, Fernanda (2002), *El silencio roto: Mujeres contra el franquismo* (Barcelona: El viejo topo).
Sánchez Agustí, Ferran (2006), *El maquis anarquista: De Toulouse a Barcelona por los Pirineos* (Lleida: Milenio).
Sánchez Barba, Francesc (2007), *Brumas del franquismo: El auge del cine negro español (1950–1965)* (Barcelona: Universitat de Barcelona).
Sánchez-Biosca, Vicente (2006), *Cine y Guerra civil: del mito a la memoria* (Madrid: Alianza).
—— (2008), '*Silencio roto* (Montxo Armendáriz): Imperativos del relato y política de la memoria', in Pietsie Feenstra and Hub Hermans (eds), *Miradas sobre pasado y presente en el cine español (1990–2005)* (Amsterdam: Rodopi), 39–47.
Sánchez Noriega, José Luis (1998), *Mario Camus* (Madrid: Cátedra).
Savat, José V. (2009), 'La function de la naturaleza en *Luna de lobos* de Julio Llamazares, *Galceran, l'heroi de la Guerra negra* de Jaume Cabré y *Una questione private* de Beppe Fenoglio', in Alison Ribeiro de Menezes, Roberta Ann Quance and Anne L. Walsh (eds), *Guerra y memoria en la España contemporánea/War and Memory in Contemporary Spain* (Madrid: Verbum), 166–79.
Sayer, Derek (2004), *Going Down For Air: A Memory in Search of a Subject* (Boulder: Paradigm).
Scanlon, Geraldine (1976), *La polémica feminista en la España contemporánea 1868–1974* (Madrid: AKAL).
Serrano, Secundino (2002), *Maquis: Historia de la guerrilla antifranquista* (Madrid: Temas de Hoy).
Shohat, Ella and Robert Stam (1994), *Unthinking Eurocentrism: Multiculturalism and the Media* (New York and London: Routledge).
Singer, Ben (2001), *Melodrama and Modernity* (New York: Columbia University Press).
Stallybrass, Peter (1986), 'Patriarchal Territories: The Body Enclosed', in Margaret Ferguson, Maureen Quilligan and Nancy Vickers (eds), *Rewriting the Renaissance* (University of Chicago Press), 123–44.
Teitel, Ruti G. (2000), *Transitional Justice* (Oxford University Press).
Todorov, Tzvetan (2001), 'The Uses and Abuses of Memory', in Howard Marchitello (ed.), *What Happens to History: The Renewal of Ethics in Contemporary Thought* (New York and London: Routledge), 11–22.
Torreiro, Casimiro (2000a), '¿Una dictadura liberal? (1962–1969)', in José Enrique Monterde, Román Gubern, Julio Pérez Perucha, Esteve Riambau and Casimiro Torreiro (eds), *Historia del cine español* (Madrid: Cátedra), 295–340.

—— (2000b), 'Del tardofranquismo a la democracia (1969–1972)', in José Enrique Monterde, Román Gubern, Julio Pérez Perucha, Esteve Riambau and Casimiro Torreiro (eds), *Historia del cine español* (Madrid: Cátedra), 341–97.

Trapiello, Andrés (2001), *La noche de los cuatro caminos: Una historia del Maquis, Madrid, 1945* (Madrid: Aguilar).

Triana Toribio, Nuria (2003), *Spanish National Cinema* (London: Routledge).

Vázquez Montalbán, Manuel (2000), *Cancionero general del franquismo, 1939–75* (Barcelona: Crítica).

Velasco, Andrés and Pedro Gil Paradela (1974), *'Una muerte llamada destino'* (typescript: Madrid, National Library: BNE [Biblioteca Nacional de España] T/48435).

Vidal Castaño, José Antonio (2004), *La memoria reprimida: Historias orales del maquis* (Valencia: Universitat de València).

Vidal Sales, José Antonio (2006), *Maquis: La verdad histórica de la 'otra guerra'* (Madrid: Espasa-Calpe).

Wayne, Mike (2008), 'Documentary as Critical and Creative Research', in Thomas Austin and Wilma de Jong (eds), *Rethinking Documentary: New Perspectives, New Practices* (Maidenhead and New York: Open University Press/McGraw-Hill), 82–94.

Williams, Linda (1998), 'Mirrors without Memories: Truth, History, and *The Thin Blue Line*', in Barry Keith Grant and Jeannette Sloniowski (eds), *Documenting the Documentary: Close Readings of Documentary Film and Video* (Detroit: Wayne State University), 379–96.

Williams, Raymond (1980), 'The Writer: Commitment and Alignment', *Marxism Today*, 24/6, 24–6.

Index

Agrupación Guerrillera de Levante y Aragón (AGLA), see maquis
Agudo, Sixto, 152
Aguilar, Carlos, 169
Aguilar, Paloma, 4, 178
Alcalá Zamora, Niceto (President), 3
Alexandre, Margarita, 47, 54–5, 68–9, 178
Allies, 27, 29, 31, 99, 122, 170, 172
Almodóvar, Pedro, 94
Álvarez, Daniel, 23, 139, 153
Amnesty Law (1977), see laws
anarchists, 22, 26, 64–5, 67, 75, 82, 84, 132, 155, 179, 181, 186; see also unions
anarcho-syndicalists, see unions: Confederación National de Trabajadores (CNT)
apoyo, puntos de, see enlaces
armed forces
  Blue Division, 46, 70–1
  Nationalist, 4, 10, 30–1, 49, 61, 95, 111, 113, 154, 187–8, 190–1
  Republican, 26, 29, 72, 112, 121, 147, 151, 168, 172
  see also Aviazione Legionaria; Condor Legion; International Brigades
Armendáriz, Montxo, 9, 27–8, 32, 110, **115–20**, 170–1, 187, 189, 190, 191
Asociación por la Recuperación de la Memoria Histórica, see memory
Asturiano (Manuel Zapico), 146
Audiencias Provinciales, 166
Austin, Thomas, 145
autarky (1939–59), see Francoism; governments: dictatorship
Aviazione Legionaria, 2

Axis powers, 10, 46, 71, 117, 195
Ayala, Juan Francisco (Juanín), 78–9, 179, 181
Aznar, José María, 2, see also political parties: Popular Party

Balagué, Carles, 139, 155–6, 195
Balfour, Sebastian, 27
Bardem, Juan Antonio, 47–8
Barroso, Eulalio (Carrete), 151–2
Basques, 166
  Basque separatists, see ETA
Bazin, André, 142, 193
Bedoya, Francisco (and Juanín, Cantabrian maquis), 78–9, 173, 181
Berlanga, Luis García, 47, 128
Beverley, John, 143, 153, 156–7, 192, 194
black market (estraperlo), 20, 33, 48, 89–90, 156, 172, 182
Blakeley, Georgina, 38
blood, see symbolism
Blue Division, 46, 70–1; see also armed forces
Bodnar, John, 190
Bosch, Juan, 64
Bourbon Restoration, 166
Brasino, Floreado (Eduardo Pons Prades), 138, 146, 151, 152
Brecht, Bertolt, 120
Brevers, Antonio, 181
Brewer, John, 159, 164
Buñuel, Luis, 141

Camino, Jaime, 94
Camus, Mario, 9, 20–1, 31, 76, 77–8, 86, 87, 90, 97, 100, 102, 177, 182, 185
Canudo, Ricciotto, 141

208

Caracremada/Caraquemada (Ramón Vila Capdevila), 22, 110, 132, 179
Carlists, 167, 175
Carlist wars (1833 and 1876), 180
Caruth, Cathy, 174, 196
Casín Alonso, Juan, 30
Catalan collaboration with Franco, 156
Catalan resistance, 114–15
Catholicism, 3, 11, 18–19, 45, 51, 52, 74, 187, 190–1
  National Catholicism, **11–13**, 18, 21, 44, 46, 52, 54, 60–1, 69, 71, 76–7, 175, 176
Caudillo, El, *see* Franco
CEDA, *see* political parties
Celia (Remedios Montero), 138, 146, 192
censorship, 9, 40, 47–8, 55, 62, 65, 67, 75, 80, 87–8, 91, 160, 173, 178, 180, 192
Cercas, Javier, 24, 107, 192
Chávarri, Jaime, 22, 94, 110, 127, 130–1
Christian Democrats, *see* political parties
cinema, 175, 194
  anti-Francoist, 77, 95, **110–27**
  cine de cruzada (crusade cinema), 10, 16, 43, 45, 49, 167, 169, 175–6
  destape, 76, 78, 80 (Fig. 3.2), 82
  documentaries, **6–9**, 11, **22–4**, 27, 40–1, 77, 107–8, 135, **137–58**
  epochs in Spain, 168
  Francoist cinema, 10–11, **15–17**, **18–20**, 22, 167
  Italian neorealism, 47, 66
  melodrama, **10–16**, **44–6**, 48, 72, 107, 131, 144, **168–71**
  Nouvelle Vague, 76
  Nuevo Cine Español, 76, 94
  of opposition, 75, 95
  post-Transition cinema, 21, 40
  and social issues, 94
  Spanish *noir*, 10, 17, 63–4, 67, 76
  Transition cinema, 19
  war films, 13, 15
Citizen Kane, 142
Civil Guard, 20, 77, 86–7, 103, 128, **141–52**, 153
Contrapartidas, 20, 87, 103, 104
Cobo, Paco (Teodoro del Real Yáñez), 147, 151
Cold War, 4, 7, 33, 44
Comandante Ríos (José Murillo), 23, 138, 146, 153
Committee on Un-American Activities, 61
communism, 17, 21, 181, 183
  anti-communism, 4, 27, 44
  Communist Party, Spanish, *see* political parties
  Frente Revolucionario Antifascista y Patriótico (FRAP), 181
Condor Legion, 2, 26
Conesa, Julia, 24
Connerton, Paul, 38, 40, 174
Conrad, Joseph, 103
Constitution, Spanish (1978), 1–2, 37, 38
Corcuera, Javier, 139
Corner, John, 140, 192, 193, 194
coups, 3, 4, 77, 109
Cubitt, Geoffrey, 173

Day of the Guerrilla (*Día del Guerrillero*), 7
de la Loma, José Antonio, 63, 76
del Toro, Guillermo, 21, 110
democracy, 77, 96, **109–27**, 167
Derrida, Jacques, 39
Díaz, Benito, 147, 150, 152
dictatorship, *see* Francoism; governments: dictatorship
documentaries:
  España: Historia inmediata (1985), 139, 140, 153
  Girón, el hombre que murió dos veces (2000), 139, **153–5**
  La Casita Blanca: la ciudad oculta (2002), 139, **155–6**

documentaries – *continued*
　La guerra de Severo (2008), 9. 23, 139–40, **146–52**
　La guerrilla (1985), **139–40**, 153
　La guerrilla de la memoria (2002), 9, 23, 139, 146, 190
　Los del monte (2006), 23, 139
　see also cinema
Douglas, Mary, 51–2, 164, 177

Eisenhower, Dwight D., 175
Eisenstein, Sergei, 141
elections, general, 1, 2, 5; *see also* governments
Elsaesser, Thomas, 13–14, 168
Erice, Victor, 20, 21, **86–90**, 181, 182, 186, 188
Erikson, Kai, 161, 196
estraperlo (black market), 89, 156
ETA (*Euzkadi Ta Askatasuna*), 4, 153, 167, 181
Eucharistic Congress (1952), 114, 156
European Union, 109

Facerías, Josep Lluís i, 64, 67, 84, 155, 156
Falange, *see* fascism; political parties
fascism, 1, 4, 6, 9, 10, 12, 17, 19, **26–8**, 30, 33, 38, 41, 45–6, 49, 54, **57–60**, 61, 62, 71, 81, 123, 166, 167, 168, 175, 176, 178,
　anti-fascism, 75, 104, 105, 113, 115, 117, 121, 134, 145, 181
　neo-fascists (ultras), 9
　see also political parties: Falange
Fernán Gómez, Fernando, 49, 183
Fernández, César, 9, 23, 139, 146, 150
Fernández, Suso, 147, 149
FET y de las JONS (*Falange Española Tradicionalista y de las Juntas de Ofensiva Nacional Sindicalista*), *see* political parties: Falange
films
　Alba de América (1951), 48

Asignatura pendiente (1977), 94, 95, 183
A tiro limpio (1963), 63, 67–8
Balarrasa (1951), 49, 176, 178
Behold a Pale Horse (1963), 18, 47, **61–3**, 84
Bienvenido Mister Marshall (1953), 48
Calle Mayor (1956), 47
Canciones para después de una guerra (1971/76), 91
Caracremada (2010), 21, 22, 31, 110, **132–3**
Carta a una mujer (1963), 18, 22, 47, 63–4, **68–70**
Casa Manchada (1977), 19, 77–8, **81–4**, 107
Dos caminos (1954), **49–52**, 67, 176
El año del diluvio (2004), 22, 110, **130–1**
El cerco (1955), 47, 63–4
El corazón del bosque (1979), 21, 76, **102–6**, 171
El crimen de Cuenca (1979/81), 77, 90
El desencanto (1976), 94–5
El espíritu de la colmena (1973), 20, **86–90**, 98, 188
El frente infinito (1956), 79, 176
El laberinto del fauno (2006), 9, 110, 113, **120–7**, 163–4
El ladrido (1976), 20, **78–81**
El portero (2000), 22, 110, **128–30**, 134
El santuario no se rinde (1949), 50, 176
El verdugo (1963), 48
For Whom the Bell Tolls (1943), 61–3
Huidos (1993), 21, **113–14**
La ciudad perdida (1955), 54–6
La fiel infantería (1959), 79, 176
La paz empieza nunca (1960), 47, **56–62**, 71, 78
La vieja memoria (1979), 94
Las 13 rosas (2007), 24

Los atracadores (1962), 47, **63–7**, 178, 179
Los días del pasado (1978), 20, 76, 86–7, 90, **96–102**, 106, 164, 177, 184
Los jueves milagro (1957), 48
Los santos inocentes (1984), 185
Luna de lobos (1987), 21, 106, **110–13**, 171, 186
Metralleta Stein (1975), 20, 63, 76, 84
Muerte de un ciclista (1955), 47
Pim, pam, pum … ¡Fuego! (1975), 20, 76, **88–94**, 98, 106–7, 164, 172, 177
Raza (1941), 48, 175, 177
Silencio roto (2001), 9, 21, 27, 31–2, 110, **115–20**, 122, 126, 164, 171, 187, 189, 190, 191
Soldados de Salamina (2003), 24, 107
Surcos (1951), 48, 175
Terra de canons (1999), 21–2, 110, **114–15**
Torrepartida (1956), 47, **52–3**, 79
You Are the One (Una historia de entonces) (2000), 110
see also cinema; documentaries
Flores, Pepa (Marisol), 20, 78, 97
Fonseca, Carlos, 24
Fórmica, Mercedes, 54
Fortunoff Video Archive for Holocaust Testimonies, 173
Fraga Iribarne, Manuel, 62
Franco y Bahamonde, Francisco (*El Generalísimo, El Caudillo*), 4, 114, 176
  as Jaime de Andrade, 48
  receives 'Order of Christ', 50
Francoism, **3–29**, 37, 41, **44–53**, 58, 70, 71, 74, **75–7**, 88–9, 94–5, 107, **111–13**, 127, 138, 144, 160, **162–4**, 167, 176, 177, 178, 184, 187
  tardofranquismo (1970–75), 19, 74, 76, 94

see also fascism; governments; political parties; rebels (anti-Republican)
Fundación Trece Rosas, 21

Gades, Antonio, 78, 184
Gallego, Ferran, 95, 184
Galter, Lluís, 22, 110
Garci, José Luis, 22, 94, 110, 127
García, Alonso, 150
García, Donato (*Arruza*), 152
García, Florián (*Grande*), 138, 146, 170–1
García Granda, Cristino, 29–30
Garzón, Baltasar, 5, 157, 167
Gentile, Emilio, 13
Gil, Rafael, 47, 177
Gil Robles, José María, 3
Girard, René, 11, 52, 60
Girón, Emilia, 146, 154
Glazer, Peter, 153–4
Golob, Stephanie, 96, 187
Gómez Escudero, José María, 48
Gómez, María, 148
González, Alida, 155
González, Felipe (leader, PSOE), 167
governments
  CEDA (1933–36), 3
  dictatorship (1939–75), 3, 4, 6, 7, 27, 47, 51, 70–1, 75, 78, 84, 95, 104, 127, 145, 167
  Popular Front (1936), 3, 5, 141, 166
  Popular Party, 2, 109
  Republic (Second), 1, 2, 3, 5, 11, 17
  Socialist Party (PSOE) (1982–96), 2, 6, 109
Gracia, Sancho, 21, 110
Grande (Florián García), 138, 146, 170–1
graves, mass, 8
Grierson, John, 141, 193
Gubern, Román, 49, 61, 167, 175, 176, 177, 178, 179, 181
Guernica, 2, 170

guerrillas/*guerrilleros*
  Agrupación de Guerrilleros Españoles (AGE), 30, 32
  Agrupación Guerrillera de Levante y Aragón (AGLA), 146
  definition of, 29
  Federación de Guerrilleros de León y Galicia, 155
  see also maquis
Gutiérrez Aragón, Manuel, 21, 23, 31, 76, 77, 87, 102–3, 106, 139, 171, 186, 187

Halbwachs, Maurice, 34–5, 157, 165, 174
Hemingway, Ernest, 18, 47, 61
Heredero, Carlos, 48
Hierro (Gregorio Sierra), 152
Hirsch, Marianne, 39
historical memory, see memory
Hobsbawm, Eric, 158, 193
Holocaust, 161
Huyssen, Andreas, 35, 173

Ibárruri, Dolores (La Pasionaria), 2
Iglesias, Eulàlia, 189
Iglesias, Miguel, 47, 63
Instituto de Investigaciones y Experiencias Cinematográficas (Spanish Film Institute), 175
International Brigades, 26, 170
International Monetary Fund, Spain's integration into, 51
isolation, international 33

Jaspe, Álvaro, 172
Jordanova, Ludmilla, 193, 197
Juanín (and Bedoya, Cantabrian *maquis*), see Ayala; Bedoya
Junta Española de Liberación, 31

Kallis, Aristotle, 13, 60
Kinder, Marsha, 12, 45–6, 64, 87, 168, 176, 181
Klimovsky, León, 47, 56, 78, 175
Kritzman, Laurence, 37

Labanyi, Jo, 88
LaCapra, Dominick, 39
La Gavilla Verde (The Green Sheaf), 7–8; see also Santa Cruz de Moya
Landsberg, Alison, 39
Laub, Dori, 157, 160–1, 173, 195, 196, 197
law courts
  Audiencias Provinciales, 166
  Consejo de Guerra, 30
  Tribunales Regionales, 166
laws
  Amnesty Law (1977), 2, 4, 5, 37, 95, 106, 157, 167
  international law, 5
  Ley de memoria histórica (Law of Historical Memory), 7, 157, 167
  Ley de responsibilidades políticas (Law of Political Responsibilities), 3, 60, 166
Lazaga, Pedro, 20, 21, **43–4**, 47, 52, 54, **76–9**, 94, 97, 177, 180, 181
League of Nations, 170
Lerner, Gerda, 160
Lezana, Sara, 180
lieux de mémoire, 8, 35, 139, 164, 173; see also memory; narrative
Llamazares, Julio, 110–11, 171
Losada, Ángela, 146
Loureiro, Angel, 140, 144, 183, 192
Luftwaffe, see Condor Legion
Lyotard, Jean-François, 40

Macías, Santiago, 161, 195
Mangini, Shirley, 11, 168
Manichaeism, 20, 28, 75, 109–10, 127, 131–2, 140, 175, 187–8
maquis, 4, **5–10**, 13, **16–24**, **26–41**, **43–72**, **74–8**, **86–8**, 99, 109–10, **113–16**, 119–20, 121, 126–7, **132–4**, 137–8, 147, 172, 179, 188, 195
  Agrupación de Guerrilleros Españoles (AGE), 30, 32, 172
  Asociación Guerrillera de Levante y Aragón (AGLA), 146

association with the mountains, 31, 53
Cazadores de la Ciudad, 30
enlaces (*puntos de apoyo*), 10, 17, 27, 86, 107, 134, 135, 138, 139, 146, 154, 191
Federación de Guerrilleros de León y Galicia, 155
Junta Española de Liberación, 31
portrayed as bandits, 4, 7, 8, 17, 21, 27, 30, 40, 44, 47, 57, **60–2**, 63, 65, **76–81**, 87, 103, 107, 127, 175
Soviet support for, 33
see also guerrillas
Marañón, Gregorio, 152, 194–5
Martín Patino, Basilio, 91, 175
Martínez, Esperanza (*Sole*), 138, 146
Martínez Francisco (*Quico*), 146, 179
Martínez Lázaro, Emilio, 24
Martínez Soria, Paco, 76
Masana, Antonio, 156
Mecía, Javier, 148–9
memory, 173–4, 190, 196, 197
Association for the Recovery of Historical Memory, 7, 161
historical memory, 1, **6–7**, 17, 23, 27, **35–42**, 111, **133–4**, 166
memory associations, 7, 25, 139, 161, 165
memory boom, 6, 7, 22, 25, **33–5**, 121, 125, 127, 132, 138, 161
Memory Studies, 17, 27
pact of silence, 4, 38, 109, 127, 164
see also Derrida; Halbwachs; Hirsch; Huyssen; *lieux de mémoire*; narrative; Nora; Ricoeur
militias, 10, 26
Miró, Pilar, 77
Monesma, Eugenio, **139–41**
Montero, Remedios (*Celia*), 138, 146, 192
Mora, Jesús, 64, 67
Mount, Ferdinand, 160

movida, La (*c*. 1976–85), 5
Mulvey, Laura, 15, 168, 169
Murillo, José (*Comandante Ríos*), 23, 138, 146, 153

narrative, 6, 8, 15
testimonial narrative (*testimonio*), 7–8, 23, 27, 33, 40, 42, **137–41**, 143, 145, 149, **152–4**, **156–8**, 160–1, 164, 168, 170, 173, 191, 192, 194, 196. 197; *see also* memory
Nash, Mary, 245
National Catholicism, *see* Catholicism
National Socialism (Nazism), 10, 12, 13, 33, 58, 176; *see also* fascism; Francoism
Nationalists, *see* Francoism
Negrín, Juan, 170
Nichols, Bill, 147, 192, 193
Nieves Conde, José Antonio, 19, 21, 47–9, 77, 78, 94, 178
Non-Intervention Committee (1936), 170
Non-Intervention Pact, 26, 170
Nora, Pierre, 8, 35, 173

Olea, Pedro, 20, 21, 76
Oliver, Kelly, 196
Opus Dei, 177

Panero, Leopoldo, 94
Pasionaria, La (Dolores Ibárruri), 2
Passerini, Luisa, 142–3
Patino, Martín, 182
Payán, Javier Juan, 16
PCE, *see* political parties
Pérez-Dolz, Francisco, 63, 67
Perón, Eva, 156
Picasso, Pablo, 2, 170
Piñar, Blas, 183
Pinedo, Iñaki, 23, 139, 153
Pinochet, Augusto, 167
Plan de Estabilización (Stabilization Plan, 1959), 51, 70, 184

political parties, 106
  Basque, 166
  Christian Democrats, 75
  Communist Party, Spanish (PCE), 4, 21, 26, 30, 75, 102, 106, 110, 132, 152, 183
  Confederación Española de Derechas Autónomas (Confederation of the Autonomous Right) (CEDA), 3, 167
  Falange (*Movimiento Nacional* after 1945), 4, 12, 19, 30, 46, 58, 82, 130, 148, 166, 167, 175; *Sección femenina*, 19; *see also* fascism; Francoism
  Junta Democrática, 106
  National Front (*Frente Nacional*), 166
  Popular Front (*Frente Popular*), 3, 5, 141, 166
  Popular Party (*Partido Popular*), 2, 109
  Spanish Socialist Party (*Partido Socialista Obrero Español*, PSOE), 2, 4, 6, 106, 167
Pons Prades, Eduardo (Floreado Brasino), 138, 146, 150, 152
Portelli, Alessandro, 142, 193, 194
posguerra, 4, 46, 86, 90–2, 116–17, 182
Preston, Paul, 58, 128, 158, 170
Prime Ministers, *see* Aznar, José María; González, Felipe; Suárez, Adolfo
Primo de Rivera, José Antonio, 167
prisoners, political, 1, 4–5, 106, 127
PSOE, *see* political parties
Puig Antich, Salvador, 66, 181

Quico (Francisco Martínez), 146
Quinn, Anthony, 115

rebels (anti-Republican), 3, 26, 50, 52, 58, 96, 111, 176, 181; *see also* Franco; Francoism
reconciliation, 49
Reguilón, Tinita, 152

Reguilón García, Adolfo Lucas (*Severo*), 9, 23, 139, **146–54**, 189, 195
Renan, Ernest, 8, 167
repression, 2, 5–7, 9, 17, 19–20, 26–7, 44, 86, 87, 89, 91, 94, 96–7, 103, 106, 107, **111–13**, 115, 117, 128, 131, 134, 138, 144, 153, 159, 160, 163, 164–5, 191
  pact of hunger, 5
Republicans, 1, 2, 5, 26, 33, 44, 50, 62, 72, 89, 99, 110, 121, 147, 158, 166, 168, 170, 176, 180, 194
Republics
  First Republic (1873–74), 166
  Second Republic (1931–39), 1, 2, 3, 5, 11, 17, 20, 26–7, 28–32, 36, 45, 49, 50, 56, 58, 60–2, 74, 96, 99, 166, 170, 188, 195
  see also governments
Resistance, French, 29–30, 32, 132, 172
Ribas, Antoni, 21–2, 110, 114, 115, 187
Ribeiro de Menezes, Alison, 173
Richards, Michael, 5, 6, 11, 12, 36, 89, 167, 168, 173, 175, 178, 182, 190, 191, 197
Ricoeur, Paul, 39, 196
Romero, Emilio, 19, 47, 56–8, 71, 78, 84, 178, 181
Romeu Alfaro, Fernanda, 191
Rovira Beleta, José, 17, 47, **63–5**, 178
Rubio, Benjamín, 146
Ruiz-Castillo, Arturo, 47, 49

Sabaté, Quico (Francisco Sabaté Llopart), 62, 67, 179
Saenz de Heredia, José Luis, 47, 177
Salom, Jaime, 68
Salvador, Julio, 177
Salvador, Tomás, 65; *see also Los atracadores*
Sánchez Agustí, Ferran, 65–7, 178
Sánchez-Biosca, Vicente, 28, 166, 167, 171, 189

Sánchez Noriega, José Luis, 100, 184, 185, 186
Sánchez Valdés, Julio, 21, 110, 171, 186
Santa Cruz de Moya, 7, 8, 132
Saura, Carlos, 184
Serrano, Secundino, 32–3, 171, 191, 195
Severo (Adolfo Lucas Reguilón García), 9, 23, 139, **146–54**, 189, 195
Sierra, Gregorio (*Hierro*), 152
silence, *see* memory
Silva, Emilio, 161
Singer, Ben, 14
Socialist Party (PSOE, UGT), *see* political parties
Sole (Esperanza Martínez), 138, 146
Spanishness, 9, 52, 71, 74, 176, 186
Stallybrass, Peter, 52
Steer, George, 2
Suárez, Adolfo, 106, 156
Suárez, Gonzalo, 110
symbolism
  blood, 10–13, 56, 84, 190
  fascist, 12
  in Francoist film, 18
  political religion, 13, 66
  women as motherland, 51

tardofranquismo, *see* Francoism
Teitel, Ruti, 96, 187
television, 75, 107
testimonial narrative, *see* memory; narrative
testimonio, *see* memory; narrative
Todorov, Tzvetan, 36
Torrecilla, Rafael, 47, 54, 68–9
Torreiro, Casimiro, 94, 180, 181, 183
torture, 5, 77, 88, 111–12, 135
tourism, 7, 70, 96, 177, 181
Transición, La (The Transition), 1, 2, 4, 5, 19, 37, 38, 73–4, 95–7, 105–6, 108, 109, 140, 152, 160, **183–7**
  as model, 96, 108
Trapiello, Andrés, 171

Tribunales Regionales, 166
Trueba, David, 24, 94, 107, 108, 131

UGT, *see* unions
unions
  Confederación National de Trabajadores (CNT), 27, 132, 186
  SEU (Students' Union), 175
  Union General de Trabajadores (UGT), 27, 154
United Nations, Spain's membership of (1955), 50, 176
United States of America, pact with Spain (1953), 50
universities, 75

Vatican Concordat with Spain, 50
Vázquez Montalbán, Manuel, 91, 182
Velasco, Concha, 20
Vertov, Dziga, 141
Vidal Castaño, José Antonio, 135, 191, 192
Vidal Sales, José Antonio, 172
Vila Capdevila, Ramón (Caracremada/Caraquemada), 22, 110, 132, 179
Villalba, Isabel, 147, 151
Vitini, José, 29–31, 171
Vlock, Laurel, 173

war correspondents, 2
Welles, Orson, 142
Williams, Linda, 155
Williams, Raymond, 143
women, 168, 175, 191
  Catholic womanhood, 18, 19, 77–8
  enlaces, 17, 27, 115–16, 134–5
  in Francoist films, 10, 18, 48, 51–4, 76, **78–81**, 85–6
  in home front, 10
  in *maquis*, 27
  marianization of, 13

women – *continued*
  in militias, 10
  in post-Franco films, 19, 98, **110–34**
  in the Republic, 11, 168
  Trece rosas rojas, 24
  see also maquis: *enlaces*
Wood, Sam, 17, 18, 47, 61–3

Yánez, Teodoro del Real (*Paco Cobo*), 147, 151

Zapico, Manuel (*Asturiano*), 146
Zinnemann, Fred, 17, 18, 47, 61, 62–3, 84